Leadership in Energy and Environmental Design

LEED® PREP GA

What You Really Need to Know to Pass the LEED Green Associate Exam

Holly Williams Leppo, AIA, LEED AP

The Power to Pass™
www.ppi2pass.com

Professional Publications, Inc. • Belmont, California

Benefit by Registering this Book with PPI

- Get book updates and corrections
- Hear the latest exam news
- Obtain exclusive exam tips and strategies
- Receive special discounts

Register your book at **www.ppi2pass.com/register**.

Report Errors and View Corrections for this Book

PPI is grateful to every reader who notifies us of a possible error. Your feedback allows us to improve the quality and accuracy of our products. You can report errata and view corrections at **www.ppi2pass.com/errata**.

LEED PREP GA: WHAT YOU REALLY NEED TO KNOW TO PASS THE LEED GREEN ASSOCIATE EXAM

Current printing of this edition: 2

Printing History

edition number	printing number	update
1	1	New book.
1	2	Minor corrections.

Printed in the United States of America

PPI
1250 Fifth Avenue, Belmont, CA 94002
(650) 593-9119
www.ppi2pass.com

ISBN: 978-1-59126-178-0

Table of Contents

Preface and Acknowledgments

This book is designed to help you prepare to demonstrate your knowledge of LEED and of green building practices and principles on the LEED Green Associate exam. It will provide you with an introduction to LEED, to methods of sustainable project delivery, and to green building principles, and familiarize you with the myriad terms, referenced standards, and credits and prerequisites that make up the LEED rating systems. It will also introduce you to the reference materials (listed in the *LEED Green Associate Candidate Handbook*) that you need to be familiar with for the exam.

Many people have contributed to this book. Editorial director Sarah Hubbard and project editor Courtnee Crystal of PPI spearheaded the publication of this work on PPI's end, developing the original concept, keeping me informed of USGBC's and GBCI's announcements as they were released, helping to sort through the new ratings systems, and keeping the project organized as we raced to get this book into print in time for the first LEED Green Associate exam candidates to use it as a resource.

I was so pleased to have the opportunity to work with project editor Scott Marley again; this is our sixth collaboration, as he also edited all the PPI books for the ARE exam that I have written or contributed to. His clean style and attention to detail makes my job as author so much easier. Thanks as well to Amy Schwertman, who designed the cover and layout of the book, to Tom Bergstrom, who rendered the illustrations, and to production director Cathy Schrott, who kept everything moving ahead at top speed.

Much of this book's content has been adapted and updated from *LEED Prep: What You Really Need to Know to Pass the LEED NC v2.2 and CI v2.0 Exams*, originally developed by the same team at PPI. Brad Saeger, LEED AP, and I served as contributing editors for that book, and I am very appreciative of his work in strengthening and refining it. The U.S. Department of Energy's Energy Efficiency and Renewable Energy Building Technologies Program and online Building Toolbox were the basis for much of the material in a section of the earlier book, which in turn has been adapted in the Green Building Basics chapter in this book.

My thanks go to my colleagues at SMB&R, Inc., who afforded me the flexibility to work on this project and meet a highly accelerated production schedule, and to my husband Shawn and our boys for their support, patience, and encouragement.

Finally, despite the multiple stages of editing, proofreading, reading, and rereading, I recognize there always exists the chance that an error or two made it through. If you think you've found a mistake, I invite you to use PPI's errata submission form at **www.ppi2pass.com/errata**.

–Holly Williams Leppo, AIA, LEED AP

How to Use This Book

This book, *LEED Prep GA: What You Really Need to Know to Pass the LEED Green Associate Exam*, is written to be easy to read and easy to look things up in.

You can read and study it from the beginning, in chapter order, because each new subject builds on earlier subjects. And it is thoroughly indexed to help you locate specific subject areas and pieces of information quickly.

Here is a suggested four-week reading and study schedule for this book. After studying each chapter, see how well you can answer the corresponding review questions, which can be found in the back of this book. If you have difficulty answering a question, check the page number given for that question and review that part of the chapter.

week	book chapters	main subject areas (in specifications)	review questions
1	Introduction	—	1–5
	An Overview of LEED	I	6–37
	LEED in Practice: Credit Synergies and the Cost of Building Green	I	38–40
2	LEED Project and Team Coordination: Pre-Design	IV	41–56
	Green Building Basics: Design (pp. 67–75)	II	57–61
3	Green Building Basics: Design (pp. 75–76)	III	62–68
	Green Building Basics: Design (pp. 76–102)	IV	69–80
4	Green Building Basics: Design (pp. 102–105)	V	81–84
	Putting It All Together: Construction, Operations, and Maintenance	VII	85–89
	Referenced Standards	I	90–100

PPI's *LEED GA Flashcards: Green Associate* can help you speed up the process of absorbing and assimilating the material. Then, a week or two before the actual exam, prepare yourself for the experience of recalling the information under time pressure with PPI's *LEED GA Practice Exams: Green Associate*.

A list of subject areas covered by the LEED Green Associate exam is given in the "Specifications" section of the *LEED Green Associate Candidate Handbook*. The following is a guide to where in this book you can find each of the subjects listed in the specifications.

I. Synergistic Opportunities and LEED Application Process

Most of the subject areas in this category are covered in the chapters *An Overview of LEED 2009* and *LEED in Practice: Credit Synergies and the Cost of Building Green*.

Look for information about standards that are referenced in LEED credits in the chapter *Referenced Standards*. The difference between the property boundary and the LEED project boundary is described in the chapter on *LEED Project and Team Coordination: Pre-Design*.

II. Project Site Factors

The subject areas in this category are covered in the chapter *Green Building Basics: Design*, in the section on "Sustainable Sites: Issues and Approaches."

III. Water Management

The subject areas in this category are covered in the chapter *Green Building Basics: Design*, in the section on "Water Efficiency: Issues and Approaches."

IV. Project Systems and Energy Impacts

The subject areas in this category are covered in the chapter *Green Building Basics: Design*, in the section on "Energy and Atmosphere: Issues and Approaches."

V. Acquisition, Installation, and Management of Project Materials

Information on recycled and locally harvested and manufactured materials is covered in the chapter *Green Building Basics: Design*, in the section on "Materials and Resources: Issues and Approaches."

Information on construction waste management is covered in the chapter *Putting It All Together: Construction, Operations, and Maintenance*, in the section on "The Construction Phase."

VI. Stakeholder Involvement in Innovation

The subject areas in this category are covered in the chapter *LEED Project and Team Coordination: Pre-Design*.

VII. Project Surroundings and Public Outreach

Information on codes is covered in the chapters *LEED Project and Team Coordination: Pre-Design* and *Green Building Basics: Design*, organized according to the subject area of the codes.

Introduction

LEED Prep GA: What You Really Need to Know to Pass the LEED Green Associate Exam is designed to prepare you for the Leadership in Energy and Environmental Design (LEED®) Green Associate exam administered by the Green Building Certification Institute (GBCI). The LEED Green Associate exam is a broad-based exam that assesses your knowledge of general green building principles and your ability to implement the most recent versions of the LEED Green Building Rating System™ created and maintained by the U.S. Green Building Council (USGBC®).

This book is organized to help you understand the LEED rating systems and give you an overview of green building design that will help you prepare for the Green Associate exam.

- This *Introduction* contains information about the LEED Accredited Professional (AP) credentialing program, the relationship between USGBC and GBCI, how to register for the test, and how the test is administered, along with suggestions for exam preparation and materials. The references given in the Candidate Handbook that should be studied for the exam are introduced in this chapter. Also included is a short guide to the use of GBCI and USGBC logos and trademarks.

- *An Overview of LEED* describes the appropriate uses of the various rating systems, the changes introduced with LEED 2009, the nuts and bolts of the LEED registration and certification process, and the minimum requirements that all LEED-certified projects must meet.

- *LEED in Practice: Credit Synergies and the Cost of Building Green* discusses project cost analysis, a critical first step in deciding which credits are appropriate and economical to pursue.

- *LEED Project and Team Coordination: Pre-Design* suggests ways to organize a project team to facilitate interaction and cooperation and take advantage of the synergistic opportunities presented by LEED credits. This chapter also covers the steps that should be taken in the pre-design phase of a green building project.

- *Green Building Basics: Design* presents critical information about the design phase and provides information on common green building strategies.

- *Putting It All Together: Construction, Operations, and Maintenance* covers the construction phase and the operations and maintenance phase in a green building project.

- *Referenced Standards* lists and summarizes the principal standards, external documents, and other information referenced in the rating systems. This collection of information makes up the "tool kit" for technical analysis of the strategies applied to a LEED project and provides a benchmark against which the project can be evaluated.
- *Terminology* contains a glossary of terms and a list of acronyms with which you should be familiar.
- *Resources* contains pointers to additional online resources and a list of 100 open-ended and short-answer review questions to help you study the material.

USGBC and GBCI

The LEED Green Building Rating System is a product of the U.S. Green Building Council (USGBC), a nonprofit organization committed to encouraging sustainable building practices that lead to environmentally responsible, profitable, and healthy places to live and work. Since 1993, USGBC has encouraged such practices through the establishment, continued development, and promotion of the LEED Green Building Rating System and through education and training efforts. Members of USGBC include architects, engineers, developers, owners, contractors and subcontractors, product representatives and manufacturers, and public and private groups committed to sustainability.

In its document *Foundations of the Leadership in Energy and Environmental Design Environmental Rating System: A Tool for Market Transformation*, USGBC defines LEED as

- the most extensive, authoritative, and well-recognized certification standard that distinguishes green buildings by their design, construction, and operation
- a design guideline to move building construction and operation toward sustainability
- an integrated training program in green building design to encourage best practice and provide support to the entire real estate industry

Although other rating systems have been introduced into the marketplace to measure and evaluate green buildings, LEED is the most popular and well-established assessment tool in use in the United States, and is used by both public and private entities. In the U.S. government, LEED is used at the General Services Administration, the Environmental Protection Agency, and the Departments of State, Energy, Agriculture, Health and Human Services, and Interior to encourage and evaluate green building design and construction for all new and major renovation projects. LEED is also used in construction projects of the Navy, Army, and Air Force. Most states require new state-funded projects to achieve a minimum level of LEED certification, and increasing numbers of local governments, higher education institutions, and public schools are encouraging or requiring their new facilities and major renovations to be LEED certified. Many corporations are also choosing LEED certification for their facilities when construction of green buildings supports their corporate mission.

As LEED has grown in scope and popularity, the number of project applications and the number of people interested in attaining LEED professional credentials have increased tremendously. New ways of dealing with the demand have had to be found. Many project teams have experienced delays in review of their project applications, due in part to how much data was being submitted to substantiate compliance with credit requirements.

In addition, USGBC's system was not in accordance with International Organization for Standardization (ISO) recommendations for certification programs. ISO recommendations do not permit an accreditation or certification body to be subordinate to the organization that set the standards, which was the case at USGBC as long as the organization was both the author of the rating systems criteria and the arbiter for certification.

As part of the changes introduced with LEED 2009, USGBC addressed these issues by transferring accreditation and certification responsibilities to the Green Building Certification Institute (GBCI). GBCI is an independent, nonprofit organization now responsible for the administration of individuals' LEED credentials and the certification of LEED projects. To establish credibility in this new role, GBCI will be evaluated according to the American National Standards Institute (ANSI) accreditation process for personnel certification agencies complying with ISO Standard 17024.

This break between the two organizations allows USGBC to be responsible for developing and publishing the requirements for LEED certification, while GBCI evaluates projects based on the rating systems and criteria developed by USGBC. USGBC and GBCI also expect this new structure to shorten the review period and allow projects to be certified more quickly after the final application materials have been submitted.

Figure 1 Relationship between USGBC and GBCI

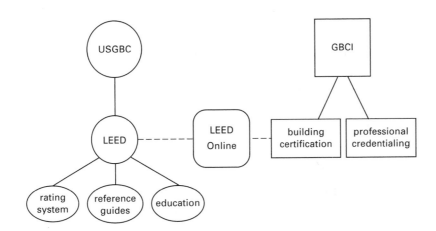

GBCI has two roles.

1. *Administering the LEED credentials.* GBCI writes and evaluates examinations, evaluates applications for the exams, and manages exam registration. Prometric, a provider of testing services worldwide, is contracted by GBCI to administer the examinations. In addition, GBCI maintains records of those who have earned the LEED Green Associate, LEED AP with specialty, and LEED AP Fellow credentials, and keeps track of those professionals who earned the LEED AP designation before the new system was introduced. GBCI also administers the Credentialing Maintenance Program.

2. *Overseeing evaluation of project applications and determinations of LEED certification.* GBCI coordinates the efforts of a team of certification bodies who are responsible for evaluating applications for LEED certification. GBCI contracts with these independent testing and certification agencies to manage the review of the data submitted. These agencies include

- ABS Quality Evaluations
- BSI Management Systems America
- Bureau Veritas North America
- DNV Certification
- DQS
- Intertek
- KEMA-Registered Quality
- Lloyd's Register Quality Assurance
- NSF–International Strategic Registrations
- SRI Quality System Registrar
- Underwriters Laboratories

Final project certification is awarded by GBCI, but the work of reviewing the applications and making recommendations to GBCI regarding compliance with requirements falls to the certification agencies.

USGBC retains responsibility for

- development of the LEED rating systems
- publication of the LEED reference guides
- educational programming

The educational programming developed and offered by USGBC plays a role in the Credentialing Maintenance Program. Before the 2009 changes to the LEED AP exams, no continuing education was required for maintaining the LEED AP credential. The rapid advances in green building technology and research make it essential to stay abreast of the newest developments; therefore, the LEED AP credentials now are linked to a credentialing maintenance program that is administered by GBCI.

LEED Credentialing Exams

LEED Accredited Professional credentials are the standard for verifying an individual's expertise in the principles of green building design, construction, and operation. The Green Associate and LEED AP exams, along with the professional experience requirements, are designed to allow you to demonstrate that you have the knowledge and skills necessary to participate in the design process, to support and encourage integrated design, and to streamline a project's LEED application and certification process. Exam questions test your understanding of green building practices and principles, and your familiarity with LEED requirements, resources, and processes. Questions are based on the LEED rating systems and their accompanying reference guides, the LEED implementation process, the references and standards identified by GBCI, and other related materials.

Before 2009, there was only one LEED credential: the LEED Accredited Professional, or LEED AP. Exam candidates could achieve this credential by one of three "tracks"—LEED for New Construction, LEED for Commercial Interiors, and LEED for Existing Buildings: Operations & Maintenance—each of which focused on the corresponding LEED rating system. No particular education or experience with green building was required; anyone who studied one of the LEED rating systems, paid the fee, and passed the test could earn the credential. Some argued that the lack of prerequisites lessened the value of the credential.

The LEED AP program was completely overhauled in 2009 to align with LEED 2009. The program now includes three "tiers" of credentials. Each tier indicates the level of knowledge, experience, and proficiency in green building design held by the credentialed individual. These three tiers are

- LEED Green Associate
- LEED AP with specialty
- LEED AP Fellow

LEED Green Associate

LEED Green Associate is the fundamental credential, and can be pursued by anyone who is employed in a field related to green building. There are no educational prerequisites for taking the LEED Green Associate exam, but you must either have professional experience related to green building or be a student enrolled in coursework related to sustainable design, in which case you may take the exam without professional work experience.

Knowledge of the LEED rating systems and other LEED resources is essential, and practical experience with the LEED documentation process and with multidisciplinary integrated design is beneficial. This credential is available not only to design professionals—such as architects or engineers—but also to marketing professionals, attorneys, developers, real estate agents, owners, maintenance staff, specialty consultants, product or manufacturers' representatives, lenders, contractors, and any others involved in the design, construction, or operation of green buildings.

The LEED Green Associate exam is designed to test broad knowledge of sustainable design principles and basic understanding of the LEED rating systems. You don't need in-depth knowledge of credits, specific requirements, or technologies. Rather, the exam will test your knowledge of what LEED is, the process through which a building becomes LEED certified, standard terminology, potential strategies for meeting sustainability goals, and how to be involved with and support other members of a LEED project team. Questions may be drawn from any of the rating systems, from USGBC's website (www.usgbc.org), and from the LEED reference guides, which are USGBC publications written to accompany and further explain the rating systems. The rating systems and the introductory chapters of recent versions of the reference guides are available online; current links to them can be found at **www.ppi2pass .com/LEEDreferences**.

To apply for this exam, you must pay the registration fee plus the examination fee. The application form requires verification of your employment in an appropriate field of work, your enrollment in a related educational program, or your involvement in support of LEED projects. You must agree to abide by GBCI's disciplinary policy, and agree to the requirements for maintaining your credential. You must also consent to an audit of your application; GBCI states on its website that 5% to 7% of applications will be selected for auditing.

You will have two hours to complete the exam, which is computer based and made up of 100 multiple-choice questions. These will be randomly chosen from a large stock of questions. Each question has four or more options to choose from. In some cases, more than one of the options is correct, and you must choose all the correct answers to receive credit for the question. The problem statement will give the number of correct options, and you will not be permitted to select more than that number.

When you have successfully completed the Green Associate exam, you will have earned your LEED Green Associate credential. To maintain the credential, every two years you will need to pay a maintenance fee of $50 as well as complete 15 hours of coursework, three hours of which must be LEED specific. Maintenance of the credential (collecting fees, verifying continuing education, and so on) will be administered by GBCI.

LEED AP with Specialty

LEED Accredited Professional (or LEED AP) is the second-level credential, and is described by GBCI as signifying "an extraordinary depth of knowledge in green building practices and specialization in a particular field." Candidates for the LEED AP credential must have professional experience on a LEED project within the three years before they apply, and this experience must be verified through LEED Online or with a statement from the candidate's employer. (If you are involved with a project registered with LEED Online, but your name is not included in the LEED Online documentation, verification from your employer may be required.) As with the Green Associate exam, you must also agree to abide by GBCI's disciplinary policy, agree to the requirements for maintaining your credential, and consent to an audit of your application.

There are two parts to the LEED AP exam. The first part is the same as the Green Associate exam and assesses general knowledge of the rating systems, the LEED certification process, and the approaches that can be used in sustainable design. If you have already passed the Green Associate exam and have kept your credential active, you can skip this part of the exam.

The second part of the LEED AP exam is a specialty exam that requires you to demonstrate in-depth knowledge of one or more of the following areas.

- *Building Design and Construction* (BD&C), which covers the LEED for New Construction and Major Renovations rating system, along with related commercial rating systems such as LEED for Healthcare, LEED for Schools, and LEED for Retail: New Construction
- *Interior Design and Construction* (ID&C), which focuses on the LEED for Commercial Interiors and LEED for Retail: Commercial Interiors rating systems
- *Operations and Maintenance* (O&M), which deals with the LEED for Existing Buildings: Operations & Maintenance rating system
- *Homes*, which tests knowledge of the LEED for Homes rating system
- *Neighborhood Development* (ND), which covers the LEED for Neighborhood Development rating system

(Those who earned their LEED AP credentials before the LEED 2009 exam changes retain their credentials. There is more about this later in this Introduction.)

Like the Green Associate exam, the LEED AP exam is multiple choice and administered by computer. Each part contains 100 questions and the testing time is about two hours.

When you have passed the LEED AP exam, you must take part in the Credentialing Maintenance Program (CMP) to maintain your LEED AP credential. Every two years you must pay a $50 maintenance fee and complete 30 hours of coursework, six hours of which must be LEED specific. Maintenance of the credential (collecting fees, verifying continuing education, and so on) will be administered by GBCI.

LEED AP Fellow

The third and highest level of credential is the LEED AP Fellow. The LEED AP Fellow designation will be reserved for professionals who have demonstrated the highest level of accomplishment and proficiency in green building design. According to GBCI, LEED AP Fellows will be recognized for "major contributions to the standards of practice and body of knowledge for achieving continuous improvement in the green building field." As of this printing, criteria for this credential are still under development, but are unlikely to include a new exam. It is expected that LEED AP Fellows will be nominated and approved through a peer review process.

What If I Am Already a LEED AP?

So what does all this mean for those who were LEED APs before the 2009 changes?

If you have tested under the former system and have already earned the LEED AP credential, you will remain a LEED AP under the new system, and will not be required to retest.

GBCI encourages current LEED APs to opt into the new credentialing system during the transition period, from June 30, 2009, through June 30, 2011. Opting in means signing the GBCI disciplinary policy and agreeing to participate in the Credentialing Maintenance Program (CMP). Transitioning LEED APs do not have to pay the $50 CMP fee for the first two years, but will be required to pay it after the transition period ends in June 2011.

If you are already a LEED AP before the transition, and you opt into the new tiered system, you may use the LEED AP title with one specialty designation as follows.

- If you passed the LEED for New Construction exam, you will automatically be designated a LEED AP in Building Design & Construction (BD&C). (If you passed the LEED AP exam before more than one track was offered, you took the LEED for New Construction exam, as that was the only exam offered then.)
- If you passed the LEED for Commercial Interiors exam, you will automatically be designated a LEED AP in Interior Design & Construction (ID&C).
- If you passed the LEED for Existing Buildings: Operations & Maintenance exam, you will automatically be designated a LEED AP in Operations & Maintenance (O&M).
- If the specialty designation you are automatically assigned is not the most appropriate to the types of projects with which you are involved, you may request a different designation (BD&C, ID&C, or O&M) from GBCI during the transition period.

To earn a LEED AP credential in a second specialty as well, you must take the corresponding specialty portion of the LEED AP exam. (If you are already a LEED Green Associate or AP, then you don't have to take the first part of the LEED AP exam.) For example, if you became a LEED AP under the former system by passing the LEED NC exam, then when you opted into the new system you would automatically be designated as a LEED AP BD&C. If you felt the ID&C credential was more appropriate, you could request it from GBCI during the transition period. But, if you wanted to hold the ID&C credential in addition to the BD&C credential, then you would need to take the specialty exam in that track.

A current LEED AP who chooses not to opt in will still be a LEED AP, but will not have a specialty designation.

It isn't possible for a current LEED AP to opt into one of the new designations, such as Homes or Neighborhood Development. LEED AP credentials in these areas can only be earned through testing.

Preparing for the LEED Green Associate Exam

To pass the LEED Green Associate exam, you must have a strong understanding of the integrated approach to green building design and construction, as well as a general knowledge of the principles of sustainable design. You will not need to memorize each prerequisite and credit's number, name, intent, requirements, strategies, exemplary performance possibilities, point value, submittal requirements, and decision makers. Likewise, in-depth knowledge of referenced standards or green technologies will not be required of you. The Green Associate exam tests your understanding of the LEED certification process, familiarity with the terminology used in the ratings systems, and ability to contribute to a LEED project team.

As an example of the differences in the level of knowledge needed for the exams, consider Water Efficiency Prerequisite 1: Water Use Reduction, which is common to the NC, CI, CS, and EBO&M rating systems. For the LEED Green Associate exam, you would probably need to know that the overall goal of the Water Efficiency prerequisite and credits is to reduce building water consumption, that the baseline levels of water use are determined by the requirements of the Energy Policy Act and other plumbing codes and standards, and that the project building needs to use 20% less water than the baseline to fulfill the requirements of this prerequisite. For the LEED AP exam, it would be advisable to know the baseline flow or use rates for each type of fixture included in the calculations, which fixtures or appliances are excluded from the calculations, and potential strategies—such as the use of composting toilets, waterless urinals, and graywater capture systems for nonpotable uses such as irrigation or flushing toilets—that can be employed to meet the requirements of the credit. The Green Associate exam tests familiarity; the LEED AP exams test implementation.

How much time you will need to prepare for the exam will depend on your experience with the rating systems and prior knowledge of how a LEED project works. Study schedules may range from two to twelve weeks or more depending on your previous roles in green building projects and how much time per day you have allotted for your review.

One way to assess your readiness and set an appropriate study schedule is to take a sample exam and use the results to determine what you need to study most. Estimate the time you would need to review the material until you can remember it without referring to your references, evaluate your commitments and available time, and set your study schedule accordingly. Only you can decide if it makes the most sense to schedule your exam and study until test day, or study until you are ready and then schedule your exam. In either case, it is useful to check your progress periodically by answering exam-like questions, such as the ones in PPI's print and online LEED sample exams. One hundred questions are provided at the end of this book to help you get started.

This book should be studied along with the LEED rating systems and the USGBC website. The LEED reference guides published by USGBC are also valuable; these are available for purchase from PPI at **www.ppi2pass.com/LEED** or from USGBC at www.usgbc.org.

It's also important to study the other references listed in GBCI's *LEED Green Associate Candidate Handbook*, which are listed here. All these documents are available online; a list of current links to them is in the Candidate Handbook. They can also be found, along with links to further resources, at PPI's website at **www.ppi2pass.com/LEEDreferences**.

Primary References

- *Cost of Green Revisited: Reexamining the Feasibility and Cost Impact of Sustainable Design in the Light of Increased Market Adoption* by Davis Langdon (2007)
- *Guidance on Innovation & Design (ID) Credits* (U.S. Green Building Council, 2004)
- *Guidelines for CIR Customers* (U.S. Green Building Council, 2007)
- *LEED for Homes Rating System* (U.S. Green Building Council, 2008)
- *LEED for Operations & Maintenance Reference Guide*: Introduction and Glossary (U.S. Green Building Council, 2008)
- *Sustainable Building Technical Manual: Part II* by Anthony Bernheim and William Reed (Public Technology, Inc. & U.S. Green Building Council, 1996). Although the rest of this book is not included in GBCI's list of primary references, the book as a whole is an excellent primer on green building approaches and technologies.
- *The Treatment by LEED of the Environmental Impact of HVAC Refrigerants* (U.S. Green Building Council, LEED Technical and Scientific Advisory Committee, 2004)

Ancillary References

- *AIA Integrated Project Delivery: A Guide* (American Institute of Architects Documents Committee & AIA California Council, 2007)
- *Americans with Disabilities Act (ADA): Standards for Accessible Design* (Department of Justice, 1994)
- *Best Practices of ISO 14021: Self-Declared Environmental Claims* by Kun-Mo Lee and Haruo Uehara (Asia-Pacific Economic Cooperation, Ministry of Commerce, Industry and Energy, Republic of Korea, 2003)
- Bureau of Labor Statistics website: Construction and Building Inspectors
- *Energy Performance of LEED for New Construction Buildings: Final Report* by Cathy Turner and Mark Frankel (New Buildings Institute, 2008)
- *Foundations of the Leadership in Energy and Environmental Design Environmental Rating System: A Tool for Market Transformation* (U.S. Green Building Council, LEED Steering Committee, 2006)
- *GSA 2003 Facilities Standards* (General Services Administration, 2003)
- *Guide to Purchasing Green Power: Renewable Electricity, Renewable Energy Certificates and On-Site Renewable Generation* (U.S. Department of Energy, U.S. Environmental Protection Agency, World Resources Institute, and Center for Resource Solutions, 2004)
- International Code Council website: Codes and Standards
- *Review of ANSI/ASHRAE Standard 62.1–2004: Ventilation for Acceptable Indoor Air Quality* by Brian Kareis (Workplace Group).

Applying for the LEED Green Associate Exam

The Candidate Handbook available from the GBCI website (www.gbci.org) explains the most current testing policies and procedures. Refer to this document for up-to-date information on policies, scheduling, and fees. Candidate Handbooks are valid for only one month and new handbooks will be released on the first business day of each month, so visit the GBCI website often to make sure that you are referring to the most current information.

To apply for the test, you must register at www.gbci.org. The log-in screen on this website requests a USGBC user name and password, so visit www.usgbc.org first to establish an account. Be sure to register with the exact name that appears on your identification (driver's license, passport, etc.). A nonrefundable $50 application fee must be paid with a credit or debit card. If your employer is a member of USGBC, you may be eligible for a discount; you will need your firm's Corporate Access ID number when you register to request the reduced rate. Students are eligible for special pricing as well, and must submit current transcripts to verify their enrollment status.

The application form requires documentation of eligibility and agreement by electronic signature to the disciplinary policy and credential maintenance requirements. Exam eligibility is documented with a letter from a supervisor, client, project manager, or teacher qualified to speak to your experience and involvement. This letter must be uploaded with the application.

Candidates requiring special provisions due to a documented disability, health impairment, or learning disability may make arrangements through GBCI for special accommodations, such as a reader, a scribe, or extended testing time. Plan to apply more than one month in advance of your desired test date if you need special accommodations. Check the appropriate box on the online exam application form and a GBCI representative will be in contact with you to assist you. Medical documentation is required; see the Candidate Handbook for a list of the required information and forms. All special arrangements must be confirmed with GBCI before scheduling the test with Prometric. (If the exam is scheduled first, alternative arrangements may be prohibited.)

You'll receive notice within seven days on whether your application is approved or not, or if more information is required. If it is denied, you must wait 90 days before reapplying. An approved application remains valid for one year; in that year, you have three chances to pass the test. If you allow your registration to expire, or do not pass the test in three attempts, you must wait 90 days to reapply.

If you are notified that your application is approved, you may then register for an exam through the GBCI website. You will receive an ID number that you can then use to schedule an exam appointment.

The exam is administered by computer at Prometric test sites. Prometric is a third-party testing agency with over 250 testing locations in the United States. Schedule your exam appointment, using your ID number, through the Prometric website at www.prometric.com/GBCI. You will need to provide payment information at this time, but if you take the exam within the United States you will not be charged until your exam appointment. (Outside the United States you will be charged when you schedule.) Take note of your confirmation number; you will need this information to make any changes to the exam date or time and to confirm your appointment.

All cancellations and rescheduling must be arranged directly with Prometric. See the Candidate Handbook for more information about rescheduling and cancellation policies, deadlines, and fees, for information on testing center hours of operation, test-day emergencies and other last-minute cancellations, and all other GBCI and Prometric policies.

Tips for Taking the LEED Green Associate Exam

Dress comfortably and allow plenty of time to get to the exam site to avoid transportation problems and delays. Candidates should plan to arrive at least 30 minutes before the exam is scheduled to begin to allow adequate time to find the testing center, check in with the proctors, and prepare to take the test. If you arrive after your appointment time, you will be considered absent and will forfeit the test fee.

Prior to entering the testing center, spend some time reviewing the information that was most difficult for you to remember. You will not be permitted to take anything into the testing room, so leave notes and books in the car. Small lockers are generally provided for personal belongings like keys or a cell phone. Use the restroom, get a drink of water, take a walk around the building—whatever will help you to relax and be comfortable—before you check in.

When you are ready to begin, register with the attendant. Remember to bring along multiple forms of photo ID and any paperwork you may have received from GBCI or Prometric. See the Candidate Handbook for a list of acceptable forms of identification; ID must include a photograph and a signature. You will be given scratch paper and pencils to use during the exam; you must surrender these when you exit the testing room. Calculators are not permitted.

After you are shown to your computer testing station and before the exam begins, a short tutorial will introduce you to the exam format and software. Completing the tutorial is a good way to warm up, and it may answer any questions you have about administrative procedures. If you have a moment before starting the tutorial, use it to take a sheet of scratch paper and write down some of the information you want to remember during the exam, while it is fresh in your mind.

You will have two hours to complete the 100 multiple-choice questions on the exam. Questions and answer choices are shown on the computer screen, and the computer keeps track of which answers you choose. You can freely skip or revisit questions, mark questions for later review, and change your answers until the time limit is up. Problem statements will identify when you must select more than one option to correctly answer the question, and you will not be allowed to select more options than are required.

There are many possible strategies for taking timed multiple-choice exams, but the following approach proves successful for many examinees.

- Take the time to read each question carefully, making sure you understand it.
- Answer every question, because an unanswered question is counted as a wrong answer. If you are unsure of an answer, take a guess anyway and then mark the question so that you can review your answer if you have time later.
- You can mark any question—that is, flag it so you can find it again quickly—and this will not affect the question or exam in any other way. A summary screen will allow you to review which questions you have completed, which questions are unanswered, and which questions you have marked.
- Some questions may give insight into the answers of others, so you may be able to identify a few more correct answers once you have read through all the questions.
- As long as time permits, you can look at any question again by double-clicking on it, and you may change your answer if you choose to. Spend the last minute or two confirming that no question has been left unanswered. Once you have reviewed and answered each question to your satisfaction, click "Finish" on the summary screen (or allow time to run out). Do not click "Finish" until you are sure you are ready to end the test; it cannot be restarted.

There is a short (10 minute) exit survey that completes the exam experience. Remember to turn in any materials or scratch paper you may have used while taking the exam. Your exam results will be emailed to you.

When you pass, a LEED Green Associate certificate will be sent in the mail from GBCI in two to three months, along with information on Credentialing Maintenance Program fees and requirements and additional information about using your newly acquired LEED Green Associate credential on business cards and professional communications.

Examinees receiving failing scores may retake the exam. Candidates have three chances to pass within one year from the time that their application is approved, but the full examination fee must be paid each time. Candidates who do not pass will receive a score report that will identify performance on each section. If you do not pass, write down all the information that you can remember about the exam questions; this will be an excellent resource when you study for your next attempt. (Remember, however, that it is in violation of the GBCI disciplinary policy to share information about examination material with others.) It is best to retake the exam within two to four weeks, which will give you enough time for further review, but not so much that you are likely to forget what you have learned.

Using GBCI and USGBC Logos and Trademarks

In order to present a consistent image and identity, GBCI and USGBC have created guidelines for the use of their logos and trademarks. The documents *GBCI Logo Guidelines* and *USGBC Logo Guidelines* contain detailed instructions, which should be followed by USGBC members and holders of LEED credentials. Current links to both of these documents can be found at **www.ppi2pass.com/LEEDreferences**. The following is a summary of the most important points.

Logos

The GBCI logos include

- the GBCI logo
- the LEED AP logo
- the LEED Green Associate logo
- the LEED AP specialty logos

The USGBC logos include

- the USGBC logo
- the USGBC member logo
- the LEED logo
- the LEED for Homes logo
- LEED certification marks (Certified, Silver, Gold, and Platinum)
- the USGBC chapter logo
- the USGBC Education Provider Program (EPP) logo
- the Greenbuild logo

Colors

With a few exceptions, a GBCI or USGBC logo may be printed in any of three ways.

- in its official color or combination of colors
    - gray: LEED AP, USGBC, USGBC chapter, USGBC member, LEED
    - gray and green: GBCI, LEED Green Associate, LEED for Homes
    - other: LEED AP specialty (color varies with specialty), EPP (two official colors: gray on a light background, or green on a dark background), Greenbuild (teal, green, and blue), LEED certification mark (any solid color)
- in black on a white or light background
- in white on a dark background

No other colors or combinations of colors may be used. The following cases are the exceptions.

- The LEED AP speciality logos may not be used in white on a dark background.
- The logo for LEED for Homes may be used in all gray but not in all black.
- The LEED certification mark may appear in any solid color and may be printed with certain effects to add the appearance of depth.

Acceptable Uses

The *GBCI logo* and the *USGBC logo* should be used to refer to GBCI or USGBC, respectively, or its products. Each logo may be used to indicate GBCI or USGBC sponsorship, or to accompany text about the corresponding organization. Each logo may be used on a webpage as a link to the home page of GBCI or USGBC, respectively.

The *LEED AP logo*, the *LEED Green Associate logo*, and the *LEED AP specialty logos* should be used to indicate that an individual has achieved the corresponding LEED credential. The appropriate logo may be used on the individual's business and marketing materials. The logo may also be used to accompany text about the corresponding credential.

The *USGBC member logo* may be used by any USGBC member in good standing. It may be used on the member's stationery, business cards, brochures, and other business materials. It may be used on the member's website, and may be used as a link to the USGBC home page. It may be used on product packaging, as long as the terms and conditions described in *USGBC Logo Guidelines* are followed.

The *LEED logo* may be used to accompany text about the LEED program. On a webpage, it may be used as a link to the LEED home page.

The *LEED for Homes logo* may be used by a project seeking LEED for Homes certification. The project must have already received a preliminary rating by a LEED for Homes provider. The logo may be used in the project's on-site signage and its marketing and other materials. On a webpage, the logo may be used as a link to the LEED for Homes webpage.

LEED certification marks may be used to promote LEED-certified projects.

The *USGBC chapter logo* should always be used with the name of a USGBC chapter.

The *EPP logo* may be used by chapters and USGBC member organizations participating in the Education Provider Program. If used on a webpage, it may link to the EPP home page.

The *Greenbuild logo* may be used to promote the Greenbuild International Conference and Expo. If used on a webpage, it may link to the Greenbuild home page.

Unacceptable Uses

Logos should only be taken directly from graphic files prepared by GBCI and USGBC, not copied from websites or publications. The entire logo must be used, not just part of it. The registration symbol ® or TM is part of each logo and should not be left off.

The appearance of the logos should be preserved. Logos should not

- be distorted, animated, or morphed
- be changed in color (other than the logo's authorized colors)
- be used as a watermark behind text
- have additional text wrapped around them

- be resized to less than 20% or more than 380% of their original print size
- be resized to less than 50 pixels high or more than 200 pixels high for web use (for the LEED AP logo, no less than 40 pixels or more than 100 pixels)

GBCI and USGBC logos and trademarks should only be used to refer to USGBC, GBCI, and their products. None should be used as a logo or as a part of a logo for a different organization or its products, or used on another organization's official documents except as described earlier under Acceptable Uses. Logos and trademarks should not be use to imply an endorsement of any product or service. USGBC members and LEED Accredited Professionals should not use any GBCI or USGBC logo or trademark with anything that disparages either organization or presents either organization negatively.

The *LEED logo* should not be used on product packaging or in advertising. It should not be used to accompany a claim about a product's suitability for use in a LEED project, or to imply an endorsement.

The *LEED for Homes logo* is not a symbol that a person or organization is officially certified or authorized to work on LEED for Homes projects, and it should not be used in a way that could imply that this is its meaning. Once a LEED for Homes project is certified, it should no longer use the logo; the appropriate certification mark should be used instead.

No logo should be used on a website as a link to any page or website other than those described earlier under Acceptable Uses.

Authorization

The use of all GBCI and USGBC logos must be authorized by the appropriate department, as indicated in *GBCI Logo Guidelines* and *USGBC Logo Guidelines*.

A notice of GBCI or USGBC ownership should appear with the logo. The text to be used depends on the particular logo and is given in the corresponding set of guidelines. For example, if the USGBC logo is used in a document, the notice should read "'USGBC' and related logo is a trademark owned by the U.S. Green Building Council and is used by permission." This notice should appear at the bottom of a webpage or on the copyright page or at the end of a printed document.

Trademarks

Refer to "the Green Building Certification Institute" the first time you refer to it in a piece of writing, and to "GBCI" on later references. Similarly, refer to "the U.S. Green Building Council" the first time you use it in a piece of writing, and to "USGBC" on later references. Don't use "the" before either abbreviation (except when using the abbreviation as an adjective, as in "the GBCI logo" or "the USGBC website").

You don't need to refer to LEED by its full name, "Leadership in Energy and Environmental Design," when you use it in a piece of writing for the first time. But you should follow it with the registered trademark symbol—"LEED®"—the first time you use it. In a long document with several sections, you should use the ® symbol after the first use of "LEED" within each section.

On passing the LEED Green Associate exam, you may use the phrase "LEED Green Associate" (not "LEED GA") on your business cards and signatures. You need not use the ® symbol after "LEED" in this context. In all other contexts, follow the guidelines in the previous paragraph.

See *GBCI Logo Guidelines* and *USGBC Logo Guidelines* for more detailed examples of acceptable and unacceptable usage of trademarks.

An Overview of LEED

In 1998, USGBC developed the first version of the LEED Green Building Rating System. Since that time, the LEED rating systems have continually evolved to keep up with changing technologies and to encourage sustainable building practices in a growing variety of market segments. The LEED rating systems are nationally accepted benchmarks for evaluating the design, construction, and operation of high-performance green buildings and interiors, and may be applied to buildings of all types and sizes. Each rating system establishes performance criteria for green building and describes acceptable building and development strategies. Projects that register, submit the required documentation, meet the prerequisites, and earn the specified numbers of points as defined in the most applicable rating system can become LEED certified at the Certified, Silver, Gold, or Platinum level.

Different Rating Systems for Different Project Types

To allow a variety of different types of projects to participate in LEED, USGBC has developed LEED rating systems for several market segments. Each rating system contains the intents, requirements, and potential technologies and strategies for the prerequisites and for all possible credits. The rating system for each market segment is available for download (free of charge) on the USGBC website, www.usgbc.org.

LEED comprises the following rating systems.

Green Building Design & Construction

- *LEED for New Construction and Major Renovations* (LEED NC) applies to entire commercial buildings such as offices, retail stores, hotels, institutional facilities such as libraries and churches, and residential buildings with four or more habitable stories. The owner should intend to occupy more than 50% of the building; otherwise, the project should use LEED CS. LEED NC also may be used for major renovations to existing buildings that are beyond the scope of the LEED for Existing Buildings: Operations & Maintenance rating system, which focuses on the life of the building after construction.

design and construction	operations and maintenance
buildings • LEED for New Construction • LEED for Core & Shell Development • LEED for Schools • LEED for Healthcare • LEED for Retail: New Construction interiors • LEED for Commercial Interiors • LEED for Retail: Commercial Interiors residential • LEED for Homes communities • LEED for Neighborhood Development	• LEED for Existing Buildings

- *LEED for Core & Shell Development* (LEED CS) is designed to complement the LEED for Commercial Interiors rating system. LEED CS covers core building elements such as structure, building envelope, and HVAC systems, and can be applied to speculative development projects where the owner occupies less than half of the leasable area.

- *LEED for Schools* (LEED S) is used for certification of K-12 educational facilities, and can also be used for prekindergarten or post-secondary buildings.

- Under development in 2009: *LEED for Healthcare* (LEED HC) is used for inpatient, outpatient, and long-term care facilities.

- *LEED for Retail: New Construction* (LEED R-NC) is adapted to the needs of the retail environment.

Green Interior Design & Construction

- *LEED for Commercial Interiors* (LEED CI) is used for certification of tenant spaces in commercial and institutional buildings. This rating system allows occupants who do not own the building, and who therefore do not have control over whole-building systems or management, to participate in the LEED program. The tenant spaces may be office, retail, hospitality, healthcare, or educational facilities within a privately or publicly owned structure.

- *LEED for Retail: Commercial Interiors* (LEED R-CI) is used for interior retail spaces.

Green Building Operations & Maintenance

- *LEED for Existing Buildings: Operations & Maintenance* (LEED EBO&M) is designed to encourage sustainable maintenance, cleaning, and operation of existing commercial structures. It must be applied to the building as a whole; individual tenants may not seek certification for their portions of the building. This rating system can be applied to buildings that have already been LEED certified under the New Construction, Core & Shell, or Schools rating systems, or it can be used for a building that has not been previously certified.

Green Home Design & Construction

- *LEED for Homes* (LEED H) applies to single-family homes and low-rise residential construction (fewer than four stories). All properties must meet the definition of "dwelling unit" as stated in local building codes, which generally means that the building must have a cooking area and a bathroom. The LEED for Homes certification process may be initiated either by a homeowner or by a residential developer, but every LEED for Homes project team must work with a USGBC-certified LEED for Homes provider. *LEED for Homes has not been changed under LEED 2009; the January 2008 version remains in effect.*

Green Neighborhood Planning & Development

- *LEED for Neighborhood Development* (LEED ND) emphasizes the elements of site selection, design, and construction that create vibrant, walkable, mixed-use neighborhoods.

The LEED Reference Guides

USGBC publishes reference guides to accompany the rating systems. Each reference guide includes information on the rating systems and referenced standards, credit approaches and implementation, technologies, calculations, documentation, resources, and other considerations. The reference guides correspond to the rating systems as shown in the following table.

reference guide	rating systems
Green Building Design & Construction Reference Guide	LEED for New Construction and Major Renovations
	LEED for Core & Shell Development
	LEED for Schools
Green Interior Design & Construction Reference Guide	LEED for Commercial Interiors
Green Building Operations & Maintenance Reference Guide	LEED for Existing Buildings: Operations & Maintenance
LEED for Homes Reference Guide	LEED for Homes

The reference guides can be purchased from USGBC, or from PPI at **www.ppi2pass.com/ LEED**.

The LEED rating systems continue to evolve. USGBC has announced plans to update the rating systems on a biannual schedule, similar to the way that the International Code Council's family of building codes is revised every three years.

How are the Rating Systems Developed?

LEED rating systems are developed by USGBC staff and volunteer committees. The volunteers are all members of USGBC and represent a variety of professional classifications.

- contractors and builders
- corporate and retail
- educational institutions
- federal government

- insurance companies and financial institutions
- nonprofit and environmental organizations
- professional firms, including accountants, architects, attorneys, commissioning providers, consultants, engineers, interior designers, landscape designers, and planners
- professional societies and trade associations
- real estate and real estate service providers, including building owners, facility managers, developers, brokers, property managers, and appraisers
- state and local governments
- utility and energy service companies

Membership in USGBC is open to anyone who is part of one of these groups. (Membership is corporate, and all employees of the member organization can take advantage of the benefits. Membership benefits include discounts on exam fees and publications, so if your company is a member of USGBC, you'll need the corporate ID number to take advantage of these discounted rates.)

Figure 2 Relationship between LEED Steering Committee and
Technical Advisory Groups (TAGs)

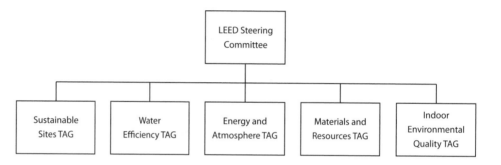

The LEED Steering Committee oversees the development of the rating systems and coordinates the efforts of the technical advisory groups (TAGs) that focus on specific practice areas. This same group of TAG volunteers is involved with all credits in their field in all rating systems. This helps ensure continuity throughout the LEED family of products. Committees are used to ensure that the rating systems are fair. The following excerpt from USGBC's LEED Policy Manual explains the importance of consensus-based development.

> The committee structure, with its balanced representation of stakeholders and conflict of interest policies, ensures that development of LEED versions is consensus based and even-handed. The Technical Advisory Groups ensure consistency and rigor in the development, interpretation, and enforcement of the standards between LEED versions helping to assure the quality and integrity of the LEED brand. The balloting of new versions with the USGBC membership reinforces the open consensus process. The appeal processes and procedures implements by the Council assure the fair treatment of individual LEED applicants. All of these measures are essential to protecting and enhancing the integrity, authority, and value of the LEED brand.

After the TAGs write their sections for a new version of a rating system, the information is compiled into a draft version of the proposed document. The Steering Committee releases the draft for public comment, and the review process begins.

The draft documents are published on the USGBC website and current members of USGBC are invited to review the draft and submit comments. Generally the comment and review period ranges from thirty to sixty days. When the comment period has ended, USGBC compiles the comments and refers them back to the Steering Committee, which directs the comments to the TAGs as needed for revision or further analysis.

The second draft of the document is posted online for another fifteen-day comment period, and further changes are made as necessary. After two comment periods are completed, the rating system is "balloted," which means that the revisions to the rating system are put to a vote. All USGBC members are notified of the ballot and encouraged to submit a vote for or against approval. A two-thirds affirmative vote is required to approve the revisions.

If approved, the rating system is published and implemented. If it fails, it may go back to the Steering Committee and TAGs for further revision and could be considered again later.

What's New in LEED?

USGBC's announcement of LEED 2009 identified major changes to the building review and certification process.

- Revised rating systems were released for LEED for New Construction, LEED for Commercial Interiors, LEED for Core & Shell, LEED for Existing Buildings: Operations & Maintenance, and LEED for Schools.
- Upgrades were made to LEED Online to improve and streamline the application process and help resolve technical problems.
- Responsibilities for building certification were assigned to GBCI.
- The LEED AP credentialing program was comprehensively revised, including the launch of the tiered credentialing system administered by GBCI and discussed in the Introduction to this book.
- New rating systems were announced for health care, retail, existing schools, and neighborhood development.

In revising the LEED rating systems, a number of technical changes were incorporated, including

- aligning and harmonizing of prerequisites and credits
- transparent weighting of credits by environmental/human impact
- regionalization
- minimum program requirements

The following changes are common to all the LEED 2009 rating systems. Each rating system is described in greater detail later in this chapter.

Aligning and Harmonizing Prerequisites and Credits

In the eleven years between LEED's initial introduction and the unveiling of LEED 2009, the organization has introduced a variety of rating systems for specific building types. In the past, each system was developed independently, so although many of the strategies and technologies referenced in one rating system could be applied to another, there was little correlation among rating systems as to how prerequisites and credits were named and numbered.

The new organizational structure better coordinates rating systems so that prerequisites and credits have what USGBC calls a "most effective common denominator." For example, all rating systems now require the control of environmental tobacco smoke and fundamental building commissioning, and the requirements use similar language. LEED 2009 is the first version of the rating systems to align prerequisites and credits throughout all market segments. Differences exist only where necessary to address specific market needs, and all LEED-certified buildings now display common characteristics.

The revised rating systems generally refer to the same standards to set the requirements for credit achievement and required performance levels. For more information, see the chapter Referenced Standards. Each standard summary includes a list of related prerequisites and credits; this is often the same credit or prerequisite section and number in each rating system. This approach makes it easier for a design team to switch from one rating system to another for different project types without needing to become familiar with a whole new set of requirements.

Transparent Weighting of Credits by Environmental/Human Impact

The number of points assigned to each LEED credit has been adjusted to reflect the potential environmental impact of achieving the credit requirements. Each rating system in LEED 2009 is based on a hundred-point scale, with ten bonus points available for innovative design approaches and meeting regionally established goals. The credits that have the most positive impact on the environment earn the most points.

The impact of each credit was evaluated using a complex credit-weighting tool developed by USGBC. The analysis combines information about each credit and its corresponding activity group (as defined by USGBC) with information about the credit's impact categories (as established by the National Institute of Standards and Technology's Tool for the Reduction and Assessment of Chemical and other Environmental Impacts, or TRACI). Detailed information about how the points were allocated is available through USGBC. Prerequisites and credits that address what USGBC has determined to be the most pressing environmental concerns or those that have the greatest potential for positively impacting the environment are worth the most points.

Figure 3 Relative Importance of Environmental Concerns
(as assessed by the National Institute of Standards and Technology)

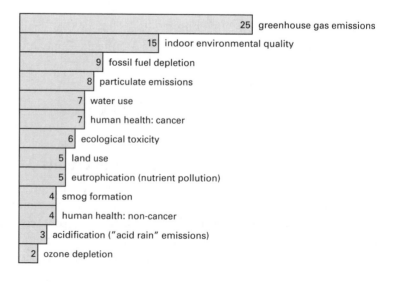

LEED credits address a range of issues, including

- carbon footprint
- fossil fuel depletion
- water use
- land use
- acidification (decrease in the pH levels of bodies of water)
- eutrophication (high levels of nutrient discharge in waters encouraging invasive plant and algae growth)
- ozone depletion
- smog formation
- ecotoxicity (toxic effects of biological, chemical, and physical stressors on ecosystems)
- particulate emissions
- human health: cancer (generation of cancer-causing particulates)
- human health: non-cancer (generation of other particulates harmful to human health)
- indoor air quality

In LEED 2009, more points are awarded for credits in the Energy and Atmosphere, Water Efficiency, and Sustainable Sites categories than given in LEED NC 2.2, and fewer points are distributed to the Materials and Resources and Indoor Environmental Quality categories.

Figure 4 Greater Emphasis on Reducing Carbon Footprint

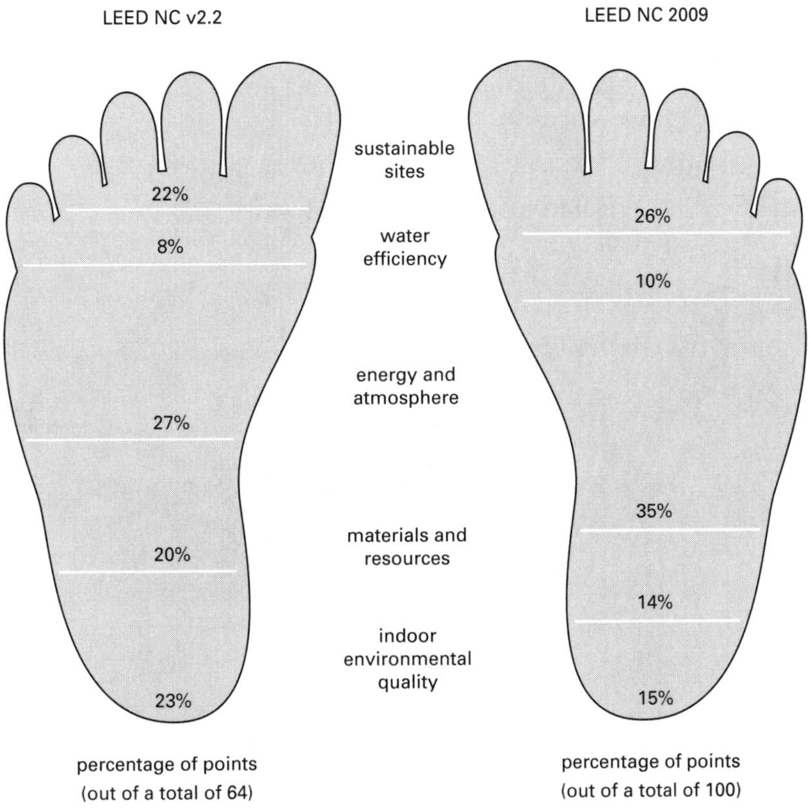

LEED NC v2.2

LEED NC 2009

sustainable sites

water efficiency

energy and atmosphere

materials and resources

indoor environmental quality

22%

8%

27%

20%

23%

26%

10%

35%

14%

15%

percentage of points
(out of a total of 64)

percentage of points
(out of a total of 100)

Regionalization

Another important change to the rating systems is the introduction of Regional Priority credits. USGBC recognizes that the importance of achieving a given credit may be relative to the project's specific environment or region. Each area of the country has opportunities and challenges which must be addressed in the design of buildings in that locale; for example, the use of solar collectors may be desirable for a building in Florida, but not appropriate for a project in Alaska.

USGBC sponsors eight regional councils, which are made up of representatives from the local USGBC chapters within their boundaries. Each regional council elects or appoints a representative to the USGBC Board of Directors. States and portions of states are included in a specific regional council because they share common environmental concerns. The boundaries of the regional councils do not necessarily follow state lines because different parts of a state may have very different concerns; for example, environmental conditions in Manhattan are more similar to those in Philadelphia or Washington, D.C., than to those in upstate New York, so New York City and its suburbs are a part of the Northeast Corridor Regional Council, while upstate New York belongs to the Upper Northeast Regional Council.

The regional council for each environmental zone is responsible for identifying the six credits most important for that zone. Projects within a given zone may earn up to four additional points for meeting the requirements of that zone's Regional Priority credits. Each regional council determines the best way to break its area into environmental zones and to prioritize credits. Some regional councils have selected credits that are important to the region as a whole. Others, like the Upper Northeast Regional Council, have divided the region into zones such as "small towns," "urban," and "coastal," each with its own Regional Priority credits. Still others, like the Northeast Corridor Regional Council, have designated Regional Priority credits by county. When a building project registers in LEED Online, the database will use the ZIP code of the project location to identify applicable Regional Priority credits. (A current link to lists of Regional Priority credits arranged by state and ZIP code can be found at **www.ppi2pass.com/LEEDreferences**.)

Figure 5 USGBC Regional Councils

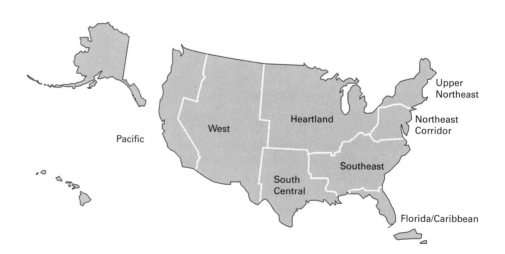

The regional councils are

- *Pacific Regional Council*, comprising Hawaii, Alaska, California, Oregon, Washington, and British Columbia
- *Northeast Corridor Regional Council*, comprising Pennsylvania, New Jersey, Maryland, Washington, D.C., Delaware, eastern, southeastern, and central Virginia, West Virginia, and southeastern New York (including New York City and Long Island)
- *Upper Northeast Regional Council*, comprising Maine, New Hampshire, Vermont, Massachusetts, Rhode Island, Connecticut, and most of New York (excluding New York City and Long Island)
- *West Regional Council*, comprising Arizona, Colorado, Idaho, Nevada, New Mexico, Utah, and western Texas
- *South Central Regional Council*, comprising Oklahoma, Louisiana, and all but the western part of Texas
- *Florida/Caribbean Regional Council*, comprising Florida, Puerto Rico, and other islands in the Caribbean
- *Heartland Regional Council,* comprising North Dakota, South Dakota, Minnesota, Nebraska, Iowa, Kansas, Missouri, Wisconsin, Illinois, Indiana, Michigan, and Ohio
- *Southeast Regional Council*, comprising Kentucky, Tennessee, Mississippi, Alabama, Georgia, South Carolina, North Carolina, and western Virginia

Minimum Program Requirements

LEED 2009 introduced *minimum program requirements*. MPRs are the eight basic characteristics all projects must possess in order to be eligible for LEED certification. Failure to meet these requirements will prohibit a project from becoming certified or may result in revocation of an existing certification by GBCI.

At minimum, all or part of at least one building in the project area must meet the requirements of the selected rating system. Specific minimum program requirements for New Construction, Commercial Interiors, Core & Shell, and Existing Buildings: Operations & Maintenance projects are detailed in the rating systems; the following is a general overview of common requirements.

In addition to completing all the prerequisites of the selected rating system and earning the proper number of points to meet certification requirements, all projects seeking LEED certification must do the following.

Comply with environmental laws. Environmental laws include building codes, zoning ordinances, and local, state, and federal regulations in effect at the project site and applicable to all work performed on the project during the design and construction phases. LEED for Existing Buildings: Operations & Maintenance projects must comply with all applicable laws from the start of the performance period through the expiration of LEED certification, including any new laws passed within that time period.

Be a building. Any project seeking LEED certification must be permanently located on a specific site. The project must include either new construction or comprehensive renovations to at least one building "in its entirety," which is defined by a supplemental guidance document.

Use a reasonable site boundary. The LEED project area is defined as everything within the LEED project boundary; however, the LEED project boundary may differ from the legal boundary of the project site. The LEED project area includes all buildings, other structures, and land (both green space and parking areas, as well as certain water features, if applicable) within the designated area.

The maximum project area is all contiguous land owned by the building owner (it is acceptable to exclude easements, large waterbodies, road or railroad right-of-ways, and so on). The minimum project area is all land disturbed by construction or renovations to the building. All portions of the site associated with the building's operation, including parking, retention areas, and so on, must be included. Noncontiguous sites are permitted if they meet the requirements outlined in the rating systems.

Comply with minimum FTE and floor area requirements. The project must serve at least one full-time equivalent (FTE) occupancy to use a LEED rating system in its entirety. If the project serves less than one FTE, it may use a rating system, but cannot earn any credits in the Indoor Environmental Quality category.

All LEED for New Construction, Core & Shell, and Existing Buildings: Operations & Maintenance projects must include 1000 gross square feet (93 gross square meters) of indoor, enclosed building floor area. LEED for Commercial Interiors projects must include 250 gross square feet (22 gross square meters) of indoor, enclosed building floor area.

Comply with minimum occupancy rates. This MPR is required only for projects evaluated under the LEED for Existing Buildings: Operations & Maintenance rating system. The project must be fully occupied for at least one year (12 months) preceding submission of the certification application and at least 75% of spaces within the building must be physically occupied at normal capacity during that time. Spaces that are leased but unoccupied do not count toward fulfilling this requirement. This requirement is designed to ensure that people inhabit the building and the building systems are functioning at normal capacity for at least one year to generate appropriate operations data.

Comply with reasonable timetables and rating system sunset dates for registration and certification activity. A sunset date is the last date that certification will be permitted after an old version of a rating system has been superseded by release of a new version. Introduction of a new rating system will coincide with the close of registrations for the previous rating system. From the date that registration is closed, a project team has six years to complete the certification application under the then-current rating system. If more than six years is needed, the project will be required to meet the requirements of the version of the rating system in effect when the certification application is completed.

Project teams must demonstrate a "substantial level of application activity" within four years of establishing the project's registration. After four years of inactivity, the registration may be cancelled by GBCI.

The project team must complete the application for LEED certification within two years of the project's completion. A project is determined to be complete when it receives a certificate of occupancy or a similar milestone is reached and the building is ready for its intended use.

Allow USGBC access to whole-building energy and water usage data. For research and development purposes, USGBC must be permitted access in perpetuity to all available energy and water consumption statistics for the building, even if the property changes ownership.

Meet a minimum building area to site area ratio. The gross area of the project building may not be less than 2% of the LEED project site area.

The LEED Rating Systems

The existing LEED rating systems, with the exception of LEED for Homes, were reorganized in 2009 with the intention of maintaining each rating system as an independent set of criteria tailored for specific project types, while making those prerequisites and credits thought to be valuable to all sustainable projects more uniform among all the rating systems. This section will cover the updated LEED 2009 rating systems. LEED for Homes, which was not updated for 2009, and LEED for Neighborhood Development, which is new for 2009, have many differences and will be covered later in this chapter.

The project team is responsible for determining which rating system best applies to the project. This is typically an easy choice, but occasionally more than one rating system may be appropriate. In such a case, the team should use the rating system checklists and the descriptions of the eligibility requirements (available at www.usgbc.org) to review the prerequisites and credits for each rating system. If questions still exist, the project team should consult USGBC for guidance.

In the updated LEED 2009 rating systems, prerequisites and credits have been expanded into seven categories, as follows.

- Sustainable Sites (SS)
- Water Efficiency (WE)
- Energy and Atmosphere (EA)
- Materials and Resources (MR)
- Indoor Environmental Quality (IEQ)
- Innovation in Design/Operations (ID or IO)
- Regional Priority (RP)

Innovation Credits

A total of up to six points may be awarded for Innovation credits. (This category is called Innovation in Design everywhere except in LEED for Existing Buildings, where it is called Innovation in Operations, and LEED for Homes, where it is called Innovation and Design Process.)

There are two credits in the Innovation in Design category, and a total of six possible points. A project may earn up to five points for ID Credit 1: Innovation in Design, by demonstrating exemplary performance in surpassing credit requirements and/or by making use of innovative approaches to sustainability.

- Up to three of these points may be earned for "exemplary performance" by exceeding the requirements of up to three other credits. The level of performance that must be achieved to earn an exemplary performance point for a credit is specified in the reference guide for the rating system. One point may be awarded for each credit in which the requirements are exceeded.
- Additional points for ID Credit 1 (up to a total of five points) may also be awarded for "comprehensive strategies which demonstrate quantifiable environmental benefits." Typically, these are unique approaches not addressed in existing credit requirements.

One point is awarded for ID Credit 2: LEED Accredited Professional to a project that includes at least one LEED Accredited Professional as a principal participant of its design team.

The Innovation in Operations category in LEED for Existing Buildings is slightly different, and there is one additional credit, but a total of six points is still possible. A project may earn up to four points for IO Credit 1: Innovation in Operations, and up to three of these four points may be for exemplary performance. One point may be earned for IO Credit 2: LEED Accredited Professional. One additional point may be earned for IO Credit 3: Documenting Sustainable Building Cost Impacts, by documenting operating costs as described in the Operations & Maintenance reference guide.

The Innovation and Design Process category in LEED for Homes is described later in this chapter in the section on the LEED for Homes rating system.

LEED for New Construction and Major Renovations

LEED NC Prerequisites

SSp1	Construction Activity Pollution Prevention
WEp1	Water Use Reduction
EAp1	Fundamental Commissioning of Building Energy Systems
EAp2	Minimum Energy Performance
EAp3	Fundamental Refrigerant Management
MRp1	Storage and Collection of Recyclables
IEQp1	Minimum Indoor Air Quality Performance
IEQp2	Environmental Tobacco Smoke (ETS) Control

The LEED for New Construction and Major Renovations rating system was originally developed for use in certification of commercial office buildings. But since then, LEED NC has proven to be the rating system most adaptable to a variety of building types, such as churches, museums, libraries, hotels, and high-rise residential buildings with four or more habitable stories. (Low-rise residential buildings are evaluated under LEED for Homes.) As long as the project can be classified as a commercial building according to local building codes, and it fits other USGBC criteria, LEED NC may be applied.

Major renovations are defined by the rating system as "major HVAC renovation, significant building envelope modifications, and major interior rehabilitation." Typically, this type of work requires significant design and construction effort. This criterion is what distinguishes a LEED NC project from a project that should make use of the LEED for Existing Buildings: Operations & Maintenance rating system.

To distinguish between a LEED NC project and a project that should use the LEED for Core & Shell Development rating system, look at how much of the leasable area of the building will be occupied by the owner. If the owner will occupy more than half, the project should be evaluated using LEED NC. If half or less, or if the owner will not occupy the building at all, then using LEED CS is more appropriate.

LEED for Commercial Interiors

LEED CI Prerequisites

WEp1	Water Use Reduction
EAp1	Fundamental Commissioning of Building Energy Systems
EAp2	Minimum Energy Performance
EAp3	Fundamental Refrigerant Management
MRp1	Storage and Collection of Recyclables
IEQp1	Minimum Indoor Air Quality Performance
IEQp2	Environmental Tobacco Smoke (ETS) Control

LEED for Commercial Interiors can be used to certify leased spaces in office, retail, and institutional buildings. Typically, a tenant does not have the ability to make decisions about or control whole-building systems and operations. LEED CI was developed to allow an organization that does not own the building where its offices or businesses are located the opportunity to participate in the LEED certification program.

LEED CI works in conjunction with LEED for Core & Shell Development. Developers can use LEED CS to certify the building envelope and major building systems. Individual tenants can apply the requirements of LEED CI to the spaces they lease within a LEED CS-certified building. However, the shell building need not have been LEED CS certified for a tenant to participate in LEED CI.

LEED for Core & Shell Development

LEED CS Prerequisites

SSp1	Construction Activity Pollution Prevention
WEp1	Water Use Reduction
EAp1	Fundamental Commissioning of Building Energy Systems
EAp2	Minimum Energy Performance
EAp3	Fundamental Refrigerant Management
MRp1	Storage and Collection of Recyclables
IEQp1	Minimum Indoor Air Quality Performance
IEQp2	Environmental Tobacco Smoke (ETS) Control

LEED for Core & Shell Development is designed for use on speculative development projects such as office buildings, retail centers, laboratories, and warehouses. This rating system evaluates the design and construction of the building envelope, systems, and core. It recognizes that the developer will not have control over the fit-out of individual tenant spaces.

LEED CS can be used for buildings where the property owner will occupy 50% or less of the leasable square footage. (If the owner will occupy more than half of the leasable area, LEED NC should be used.) The fit-out of the owner's space only is considered in the evaluation of compliance with the requirements for LEED CS. Tenants may opt to pursue certification of their leased spaces under the LEED CI rating system.

The appendices to the LEED CS rating system address some of the unique issues encountered in a LEED CS project.

CS Appendix 1: Default Occupancy Counts. The developer of a speculative building may not know what types of tenants will move in when the building is complete, which makes it difficult to determine a final occupant count. Appendix 1 allows the use of a default occupancy table to estimate occupancy where actual occupant counts are unknown. All calculations are based on gross square footage. If local codes require a occupancy count less than that given in the table, the code requirements may be used instead. Where occupant counts are known, those numbers must be used rather than estimates derived from the table. Appendix 1 also explains how to calculate full-time equivalent occupancy with occupant counts taken from the table. **Related Credits:** *SSc4.2, SSc4.4, WEp1, WEc2, WEc3, EAp2, EAc1, IEQp1, IEQc1, IEQc2, IEQc6, IEQc7, IEQc8*

CS Appendix 2: Core & Shell Energy Modeling Guidelines. Appendix 2 details the procedure that should be used to conduct energy modeling, based on the building performance rating method from ANSI/ASHRAE/IESNA Standard 90.1. This procedure requires any constraints affecting the tenant's fit-out plan, such as lighting levels or occupancy restrictions, to be spelled out in the lease agreement.

CS Appendix 3: Core & Shell Project Scope Checklist. The sample table provided in Appendix 3 establishes responsibility for and defines the use of the spaces within the building. It also charts who maintains control of specifying finishes, choosing and maintaining HVAC equipment and plumbing fixtures, and selecting lighting fixtures and controls.

LEED certification can be a critical marketing tool, so LEED CS allows the optional submission of a "precertification application." In the application, the project team outlines the proposed strategies that will be used to pursue certification. When a successful preliminary review of the project's goals has been made by GBCI, the project may advertise that it has been "precertified." Precertification is not required, and it does not equal certification. To achieve LEED certification, the project team still must compile documentation of credit achievement and submit its project data for final review.

LEED for Existing Buildings: Operations & Maintenance

LEED EBO&M Prerequisites

WEp1	Minimum Indoor Plumbing Fixture and Fitting Efficiency
EAp1	Energy Efficiency Best Management Practices: Planning, Documentation, and Opportunity Assessment
EAp2	Minimum Energy Efficiency Performance
EAp3	Refrigerant Management: Ozone Protection
MRp1	Sustainable Purchasing Policy
MRp2	Solid Waste Management Policy
EQp1	Minimum IAQ Performance
EQp2	Environmental Tobacco Smoke (ETS) Control
EQp3	Green Cleaning Policy

LEED for Existing Buildings: Operations & Maintenance differs from LEED for New Construction, Commercial Interiors, and Core & Shell, because no design or construction is required to participate. LEED EBO&M evaluates the performance, operation, and maintenance of existing buildings. A single, whole building must be considered under this rating system; tenant spaces are ineligible. The entire floor area of the building must be considered in the analysis, unless a portion of the building is controlled by separate management. In that case, up to 10% of the floor area may be excluded. (See the section on Exemptions for Multitenant Buildings later in this chapter.) LEED EBO&M may be applied to existing office buildings, retail and service establishments, institutions such as libraries, schools, museums, and churches, and high-rise residential buildings. LEED EBO&M may also be applied to educational institutions until LEED for Existing Schools is released.

LEED EBO&M projects are the only ones required to comply with requirements for minimum occupancy rates as defined in the LEED 2009 Minimum Program Requirements. The project must be fully occupied for at least one year (12 months) before the certification application is submitted, and at least 75% of spaces within the building must be physically occupied at normal capacity during that time. Spaces that are leased but unoccupied do not count toward fulfilling this requirement. This requirement ensures that the building is inhabited and the building systems are functioning at normal capacity for at least one year so that appropriate operations data is generated.

LEED EBO&M can be used to evaluate additions and alterations that affect the usable space in an existing building. This excludes upgrades to building systems that do not alter usable area; these are considered maintenance. In addition, to remain within the purview of LEED EBO&M, the work must comply with the following.

- Alterations can affect no more than 50% of the total floor area and cause relocation of no more than 50% of regular building occupants. Additions can increase total floor area by no more than 50%. (Projects that exceed these thresholds must be evaluated using LEED NC.)
- Minimum requirements defined in the LEED EBO&M reference guide include the following.

  –More than one trade specialty must be included.

  –Substantial changes must be made to at least one entire room in the building.

  –The work site must be isolated from regular building occupants for the duration of construction.

  –Additions must increase total floor area by at least 5%. (Below 5%, the modifications are considered to be repairs, routine replacements, or minor upgrades, and are ineligible to earn points under LEED EBO&M.)

Participating buildings may be LEED certified under the New Construction, Schools, or Core & Shell programs, but are not required to be previously certified to participate.

Design & Construction Streamlined Credits

Projects seeking certification under the LEED EBO&M rating system that have already earned certain credits under another rating system may submit documentation for those same credits using a streamlined submittal template. If the project achieved any of the following credits under a Green Building Design & Construction rating system (LEED NC, LEED for Schools, or LEED CS), the LEED EBO&M project team may use a streamlined path by uploading the BD&C project scorecard, including any changes to the relevant elements of the credit, and including relevant LEED O&M practices where applicable.

SSc5	Site Disturbance: Protect or Restore Open Habitat
SSc6	Stormwater Quality Control
SSc7.1	Heat Island Reduction: Non-Roof
SSc7.2	Heat Island Reduction: Roof
SSc8	Light Pollution Reduction
WEp1	Minimum Indoor Plumbing Fixture and Fitting Efficiency
WEc2	Additional Indoor Plumbing Fixture and Fitting Efficiency
WEc3	Water Efficient Landscaping
EAp3	Fundamental Refrigerant Management
EAc5	Enhanced Refrigerant Management
IEQp2	Environmental Tobacco Smoke (ETS) Control
IEQc2.2	Controllability of Systems: Lighting
IEQc2.4	Daylight and Views
IEQc3.5	Green Cleaning: Indoor Chemical and Pollutant Source Control

Licensed Professional Exemption Form

LEED EBO&M offers the option of waiving certain submittal requirements through use of the licensed professional exemption form. This gives a project team's registered architect, professional engineer, or landscape architect the option to submit streamlined documentation for certain credits. See the LEED EBO&M reference guide for information on required submittal materials. This waiver may be applied to the following credits.

SSc5, Options 2 and 3	Reduced Site Disturbance: Protect or Restore Open Space
SSc6, Option 2	Stormwater Management
SSc7.1, Option 2	Heat Island Reduction: Non-Roof
SSc7.2, Option 2	Heat Island Reduction: Roof
EAc3.1	Performance Measurement: Building Automation System
EAc5, Option 2	Refrigerant Management
IEQc1.2, Options 1 and 2	IAQ Best Management Practices: Outdoor Air Delivery Monitoring
IEQc1.3, Option 3	IAQ Best Management Practices: Increased Ventilation
IEQc2.3	Occupant Comfort: Thermal Comfort Monitoring

Performance Periods

Because LEED for Existing Buildings focuses on the life of a building rather than on its conception and birth, the requirements for certification differ significantly from those of other rating systems. The LEED EBO&M rating system is the only one that includes provisions for recertification, and the only one that requires evaluation and documentation of the building's operation through a performance period. LEED EBO&M is designed to recognize sustainability in the operation and management of a building after the construction period is complete. As such, recertification ensures that the practices that earned the project LEED certification in the first place continue to be implemented.

For LEED EBO&M projects, the performance period begins after the project is registered and strategies have been implemented, and ends within 60 days of the certification application submittal. It is preferred that a project team apply consistent performance periods across credits, but the required performance period varies for some of the credits.

The following general conditions apply.

- The performance period for any individual credit may not have any gaps longer than seven contiguous days.
- All performance periods must overlap, and all must end within one week of each other.
- The certification application must be submitted no later than 60 days after the last day of the latest performance period.
- For initial certification of a project, the performance period for EA Prerequisite 1 must be between three and 36 months, for EA Credit 1 it must be 12 months, and for all other credits it must be at least three months, but may be up to 24 months.
- For recertification of credits previously achieved under a LEED EBO&M rating system, the performance period is the time between the previous certification and the current recertification application. For new credits, the initial certification performance period guidelines apply.

Recertification

LEED EBO&M-certified projects can be *recertified* under LEED EBO&M as often as every year, and must submit for recertification at least every five years to maintain their status. The first time a project registers for and achieves LEED EBO&M certification is considered the initial certification, and any subsequent registration is considered recertification.

This is true even for projects that have already been certified under a different LEED rating system. For example, a project that has been certified under LEED NC now applies for LEED EBO&M certification. This will be the building's initial certification under LEED EBO&M, and subsequent applications under LEED EBO&M would be considered recertification. (LEED NC-certified projects need not be recertified under LEED NC; the LEED NC certification is good for the life of the building.)

To be recertified, a project must complete the registration process, adding "recertification" to the original project title, and provide all recertification application submittals. The project team must also submit the required performance data for all previously achieved credits for the entire period from the most recent LEED EBO&M certification through the current certification application.

There is no fee for registering a recertification project, and recertification application costs half as much as initial certification.

Exemptions for Multitenant Buildings

Multitenant buildings are defined by the LEED EBO&M reference guide as "single buildings that contain floor area under the ownership or tenancy of more than one entity." To meet the minimum program requirements for participation in the LEED EBO&M rating system, at least 90% of the total gross floor space must be included in the building analysis. The project team must try to obtain data from all tenants; however, if it is not possible to gather data from all tenants in a multitenant building, the project team may choose to exclude up to 10% of the gross floor area for all prerequisites and credits except IEQp2, Environmental Tobacco Smoke (ETS) Control.

LEED for Schools

LEED for Schools Prerequisites

SSp1	Construction Activity Pollution Prevention
SSp2	Environmental Site Assessment
WEp1	Water Use Reduction
EAp1	Fundamental Commissioning of Building Energy Systems
EAp2	Minimum Energy Performance
EAp3	Fundamental Refrigerant Management
MRp1	Storage and Collection of Recyclables
IEQp1	Minimum Indoor Air Quality Performance
IEQp2	Environmental Tobacco Smoke (ETS) Control
IEQp3	Minimum Acoustical Performance

LEED for Schools applies to educational projects. Though it was originally designed for use on K-12 academic buildings it is now appropriate for any educational project, including college projects. It is similar in structure to LEED for New Construction, but contains two additional prerequisites dealing with acoustical performance and site assessment. The site assessment prerequisite includes a determination of any contaminants that may exist on the proposed site; buildings constructed on sites that were previously used as landfill are ineligible for certification under LEED for Schools.

The rating system can be applied to either new construction or renovation projects. All K-12 projects must use LEED for Schools. Nonacademic buildings on a school's campus, such as administration buildings, dormitories, and maintenance facilities, may choose to use either LEED for Schools or LEED NC. Likewise, prekindergarten and post-secondary academic buildings may also choose between those two rating systems.

LEED Application and Certification Process

The following process applies to all the LEED rating systems except LEED for Homes. Because the requirements and process are different in many ways, LEED for Homes will be covered separately later in this chapter.

Step 1: Registration

Projects pursuing LEED certification must first be registered. One member of the project team should take responsibility for registering the project, which is done by submitting an online registration form. The registrant indicates the chosen rating system and gives general account, contact, and project information, including project owner, primary contact, site conditions, occupant type, square footage, budget, and current project phase.

Fees for registration and certification vary depending on the project type, size, and whether the applicant is a member of USGBC. The current fee schedule is available on the USGBC website at www.usgbc.org.

As an incentive to strive for the highest level of certification, projects that are awarded LEED Platinum certification under the LEED for New Construction, Existing Buildings, Commercial Interiors, Core & Shell, or Schools program will receive a full refund of all certification fees, not including the application fee and any costs for Credit Interpretation Requests, appeals, or expedited review.

Once a project is registered, a project number is assigned and sent to the applicant, along with the information needed to access LEED Online. LEED Online is a protected website where project team members can download submittal templates, submit completed templates, review rulings of Credit Interpretation Requests, and manage project details. Only members of registered project teams can access LEED Online.

One project administrator should be designated to oversee the entire project certification process. The project administrator can then share log-in information with team members. Team members are only permitted to access information about credits assigned to them.

Step 2: Use Project Checklists to Develop a Preliminary List of Credits to Pursue

The rating systems' project checklists available on USGBC's website are a valuable tool for assessing which LEED credits a project should try to attain. The project team can use the checklist to analyze which credits may be possible given the parameters of the project, which credits are "maybes," and which are not attainable. This preliminary analysis can help the project team determine a "preliminary rating," or a target level of certification to pursue. It also helps the team identify the appropriate consultants whose input will be needed to earn the points during the project.

Step 3: Identify Design Phase and Construction Phase Credits

The LEED for New Construction, Commercial Interiors, Core & Shell, and Schools rating systems offer the option of splitting the review process into two phases: the design phase and the construction phase. If the team wishes to take advantage of this "split review" option, it should identify which credits will be included in the design phase submission and which will be part of the construction phase submission. No points are awarded at the design review stage, but submission of this material at this point in the project can help the team foresee which credits will be achieved.

Step 4: Design Process

Between kicking off the project with registration on LEED Online and providing the certification application (all submittal templates) to USGBC, the project team works on the design and implementation of strategies to comply with the prerequisite and credit requirements, while documenting their performance and technical analysis. The design information and technical analysis data are used to complete the submittal templates for all prerequisites and for all credits that the project team intends to achieve.

LEED Online is a repository for information and documentation gathered during the design and construction phases. The online tools can assist in performing calculations, organizing the efforts of project team members, and summarizing the approaches that have been taken to earn points. Each possible credit is listed in LEED Online, along with submittal templates designed to prompt the user to enter appropriate documentation. The project administrator can activate credits (allowing information to be entered into the templates), invite team members and share project information with them, and coordinate completion of the application through this web-based tool. It is also possible to upload supplemental information, such as drawings or photographs, where applicable.

LEED Online Scorecard

LEED Online's Scorecard is the primary tool used to track progress on a LEED project. The project administrator is responsible for using the Scorecard to activate and assign credits and track their status. When project team members log in to LEED Online, the Scorecard will indicate which credits have been assigned to them and let them enter information. Only team members assigned to a specific credit can add or change information relevant to that credit.

The Scorecard also indicates which credits are eligible for design phase submission and which are eligible for construction phase submission. This can help a design team plan its submission strategy.

On the USGBC website, the terms "Checklist" and "Scorecard" are used somewhat arbitrarily. Both terms refer to a list of available credits, with space for a project team to track its progress. A Scorecard is generally an interactive document that is a part of LEED Online, while a Checklist is generally a Microsoft Excel spreadsheet or an editable PDF file that can be downloaded from the website.

Declarants/Decision Makers

For each prerequisite and credit, one or more declarants, or decision makers, are specified. A declarant is the professional responsible for submitting and signing off on the LEED submittal template and documentation for a specific prerequisite or credit. This may be the owner, contractor, architect, engineering specialist, facility or other manager, or LEED AP. Generally, this person represents the discipline that has the most control over or responsibility for the design and/or implementation of that particular credit. For example, the civil engineer would be responsible for verifying that the design of erosion and sedimentation control measures meets LEED credit requirements, while the mechanical engineer would be responsible for documenting the design of mechanical systems that meet minimum energy performance standards. Similarly, the contractor would be responsible for verifying that proper indoor air quality control techniques were used during the construction phase. For many prerequisites and credits, there is more than one possible declarant.

Credit Interpretation Requests

LEED Online also features a searchable database of rulings on Credit Interpretation Requests (CIRs). A project team may submit a CIR at any time during the analysis and documentation stage. CIRs are used when a project team encounters an issue with a credit or an unusual project circumstance that doesn't fit the credits as written. USGBC established this mechanism to provide technical and administrative guidance to project teams. Originally, each CIR was submitted to clarify an issue on a specific project, but the decisions of the technical advisory group (TAG) regarding the credit in question may also be applied to similar situations encountered on other projects. Therefore, a search of the database of CIRs published on the USGBC website may provide insight into the position the TAG has taken on similar issues in the past (and may save the project team the expense and delay of submitting a new CIR).

A project team should try to answer its own question before deciding to go through the CIR process. Before submitting a CIR, the team should review the intent of the credit or prerequisite and evaluate whether the approach taken on this project meets this intent. The online CIR library mentioned above, as well as the information provided in the appropriate LEED reference guide, may provide the solution. If the library of precedent CIRs does not address the project team's situation, the team's next contact should be LEED customer service to confirm that the concern warrants a new CIR. Typically, CIRs address highly technical and/or unique applications or cutting-edge technologies. Generally, the customer service staff can assist with administrative inquiries, and these sorts of questions rarely require submission of a CIR.

If this preliminary research and investigation does not lead to a satisfactory solution, the project team may submit a CIR. CIRs can be submitted through LEED Online; there is a charge for each CIR submitted. Consult www.usgbc.com for current fees.

Each CIR can address one credit only. A separate CIR must be submitted for each credit that needs an interpretation, and the Credit Interpretation Request fee applies to each request. It is unnecessary to state the credit name or project team contact information; the database will automatically track this data when the request is submitted online.

Confidential project details should be omitted. Remember that all submitted text will be posted on the USGBC website.

Keep the question brief. Do not format the CIR as a letter. Submit only the inquiry and essential background information. CIR submission text is limited to 600 words (4000 characters including spaces). It is helpful to discuss the problem within the context of the credit in question. Attachments (cut sheets, plans, drawings, etc.) are not permitted. Proofread all submissions.

Rulings on Credit Interpretation Requests

CIRs are gathered twice a month for review. First, CIRs are researched by USGBC and a draft ruling is prepared. Then the CIRs and draft rulings are referred to the relevant technical advisory groups for consideration. The TAGs determine whether an action proposed by a project team fulfills the intent of the LEED credit requirements. Finally, the TAG chairs meet to debate the CIRs and finalize the rulings.

The rulings are posted to LEED Online and project teams are advised of the outcome. This information becomes part of the library of CIRs that can be referenced by all project teams. As new LEED products are developed, relevant information from this library of CIRs may be incorporated to clarify credit requirements.

A successful ruling on a CIR does not guarantee that a credit will be awarded; the project team must still demonstrate and document the achievement of each credit requirement during the LEED application process.

Credit Interpretation Appeals

If the project team is unsatisfied with the TAG's ruling on a CIR, it may choose to appeal. Appeals are filed using the LEED Online CIR submission process, giving the original ruling date as well as additional reasoning and backup information. The statement of additional information must not exceed 600 words. CIRs that fail to include additional relevant information will not be reviewed again.

In addition to the written information, the CIR submitter may request a ten- to fifteen-minute conference call with a second TAG or product committee. No ruling will be made or response given during the call, but panel members will have the opportunity to ask questions or provide additional commentary.

When the appeal is received, the TAG's original ruling and the project team's additional documentation are sent to a CIR review consultant. If the supplemental information provided by the project team convinces the TAG to reverse the earlier ruling, USGBC staff will facilitate the revision with the TAG and CIR review consultant. If the additional information does not convince the TAG to reverse the original ruling, the TAG will draft an appeal ruling and forward all information to the relevant product committee.

If the product committee agrees that the original TAG ruling should not be reversed, the CIR is final and no further recourse is available through the CIR process. If the product committee feels the TAG ruling should be reversed, the product committee will draft an alternate appeal ruling and forward all materials to the LEED Steering Committee (LSC). The LSC will review the information and make a final ruling. If the project team disagrees with the LSC's appeal ruling, no further recourse remains.

Design Phase Review

If the project team has chosen to split its application into a design phase submission and a construction phase submission (see Step 3), it may submit credits achieved during the design phase for review in advance of substantial completion. Documentation is submitted to LEED Online, and is reviewed for completeness. If further clarification is asked for, the team has up to 25 business days to prepare and submit a response.

When all the needed information has been submitted, it is reviewed and each credit is designated as "anticipated" or "denied." The team may choose to accept the review or appeal. Even if a credit is marked as "anticipated," points are not awarded until the final review. Any credits denied in the design phase review may be appealed at the end of the construction phase review.

Step 5: Construction Phase

During the construction phase, the project is built. The team continues gathering documentation that the project has complied with credit requirements, using the tools in LEED Online. The construction effort may involve many new team members, so it is important that the project administrator makes sure all appropriate parties have access.

Step 6: Complete the Certification Application

The final certification application is made after substantial completion. The project team submits the required documentation for all prerequisites and for the credits the project hopes to achieve. For projects choosing a split review (see Step 3), this submission should include all construction phase credits as well as any new design phase credits being tried for. Other projects should submit all credits at this time.

USGBC provides a submittal template (also called *letter template*) for each prerequisite and credit in each rating system. Sample templates are available to all USGBC members on the USGBC website, but official templates are available through LEED Online only to those with registered projects. Each submittal template identifies what information is required, which could include project drawings or plans, site and building areas, test and procedure results, lists of materials or products used, project data (local temperatures, energy usage, water usage, etc.), descriptions of processes or special circumstances, and/or supporting documentation. The declarant, or decision maker, responsible for signing off on the submittal template is also indicated.

The design team will be prompted by LEED Online to provide the following information as a part of its certification application.

- the selected rating system
- LEED registration information, including
  - project contact
  - project type
  - project size
  - number of occupants
  - usage
  - date of substantial completion
- a project narrative, including descriptions of three project highlights
- the LEED project checklist, including project prerequisites and credits and total projected score
- copies of the most recent LEED submittal templates and supporting documentation
- a complete list of all CIRs requested for this project, including dates of applied rulings
- drawings and photos illustrating the project, including
  - site plan
  - typical floor plan
  - typical building section

    –typical or primary elevation

    –photo or rendering of project

- payment of appropriate certification fees

All applications for LEED certification must be documented in English with U.S. customary units of measurement (not metric units). A project team should not include more documentation than is requested, as this slows the application review process.

Step 7: Review and Appeals Process

When the project team has submitted its documentation on LEED Online, its application is reviewed for completeness. Credits may be marked as "earned," "clarify," or "denied." If any credits are marked "clarify," the team has up to 25 business days to prepare and submit a response.

When any supplemental information needed has been submitted, the information is reviewed, each credit is indicated as "earned" or "denied," and the team is notified of the LEED certification decision. The team may choose to accept the review or appeal within 30 days of notification. Projects earning certification may appeal denied credits if they wish to try to achieve a higher level of certification.

If the project team chooses to appeal the decision on a particular credit, they must prepare and submit all previously submitted documentation, including the initial filing and any further information submitted in response to reviewer comments, as well as additional documentation supporting the appeal. If new documentation is not submitted, the credit will be denied.

If the appeal is successful, the credit is awarded and no further action is required on the part of the project team. If the appeal is denied, there is one last chance: the final appeal. Final appeal applications must include all the information required in the initial appeal documentation, plus further final appeal documentation. If new information is not included, the appeal will be denied. There is also an additional fee for final appeals.

The final appeal package is referred to the LEED Steering Committee's Management Subcommittee (MSC), who refer review of the data to the appropriate TAG or product committee, or to the Technical and Scientific Advisory Committee. The assigned committee prepares a ruling recommendation and submits it to the MSC. The MSC makes the final decision on the appeal, and all MSC rulings are final. No further appeals are permitted.

Step 8: Certification

Projects that fulfill all Minimum Program Requirements, complete all prerequisites, and achieve the prescribed number of points become LEED certified. The point system is based on 100 base points, with six possible Innovation points and four possible Regional Priority points also available.

The total number of points the project earns determines the level of LEED certification it receives. LEED 2009 certification is available in four levels.

Certified	40–49 points
Silver	50–59 points
Gold	60–79 points
Platinum	80+ points

LEED for Homes

LEED H Prerequisites

IDp1.1	Preliminary Rating
IDp2.1	Durability Planning
IDp2.2	Durability Management
SSp1.1	Erosion
SSp2.1	No Invasive Plants
EAp1.1	Performance of Energy Star for Homes
EAp11.1	Refrigerant Charge Test
MRp1.1	Framing Order Waste Factor Limit
MRp2.1	FSC Certified Tropical Wood
MRp3.1	Construction Waste Management Planning
EQp2.1	Basic Combustion Venting Measures
EQp4.1	Basic Outdoor Air Ventilation
EQp5.1	Basic Local Exhaust
EQp6.1	Room-by-Room Load Calculations
EQp7.1	Good Filters
EQp9.1	Radon-Resistant Construction in High-Risk Areas
EQp10.1	No HVAC in Garage
AEp1.1	Basic Operations Training

The LEED for Homes rating system is different in many ways from the LEED 2009 rating systems discussed earlier. LEED for Homes is applied to single family detached and low-rise multifamily residential properties that fall under the residential project definitions established by local residential codes. The structure must have "permanent provisions for living, sleeping, eating, cooking, and sanitation," which means that all projects must have a cooking area and a bathroom. The credit categories and the structure, eligibility, and participation requirements are very different for LEED for Homes from those of the other rating systems.

One of the most significant differences between LEED for Homes and the 2009 rating systems is that an owner or builder must work in cooperation with a LEED for Homes provider—a company under contract with USGBC—to enter the program. The relationship with a provider must be established at the beginning of the project; if drywall is installed before the provider is contacted, the project cannot be certified.

One criticism of the current system is that LEED for Homes providers are few and far between; in March 2009, there were only 31 providers in the United States. Each provider manages a team of "green raters," who may be their own employees; these individuals perform inspections and field testing and verify that the requirements of the rating system have been met. In addition to registration and certification fees assessed by USGBC, providers and green raters must be compensated as well.

LEED for Homes has a lot of competition in the marketplace. Many state and local agencies provide programs to assist homeowners in building green, and a number of national programs offer rating systems with the same goals—often with fewer administrative requirements and at a lower cost. The following are some of the competing systems in the United States.

National Green Building Standard was developed jointly by the National Association of Home Builders and the International Code Council. This is the first residential green rating system to be approved by ANSI.

Green Point Rated is a California initiative sponsored by Build It Green. A major difference between this program and LEED for Homes is that it allows certification of existing buildings. LEED for Homes can only be used for new construction or major ("substantial gut/rehab") renovations.

Energy Star Homes focuses primarily on energy efficiency and recognizes new homes that are at least 15% more energy efficient than those built according to the standards of the 2003 International Residential Code. This program is sponsored by the U.S. Department of Energy. LEED for Homes incorporates the requirements of this program into the rating system.

Residential rating programs are available in other countries as well, such as the BRE Environmental Assessment Method used in the United Kingdom; BuiltGreen, used in Canada (as well as LEED Canada for Homes); and Green Star, used in Australia.

Credit Categories and Certification Levels

There is some overlap in credit categories between the other LEED rating systems and LEED for Homes, as the SS, WE, EA, MR, and IEQ credits are also a part of this rating system. In addition to those credits, the residential program introduces credits in three other categories.

Innovation and Design Process mandates an integrated design approach and compliance with the requirement for the participation of a provider and green rater. This category also requires a durability inspection, and offers incentives for incorporating innovative design concepts. Similar to the ID credits in the other rating systems, these credits for innovative design must undergo individual review.

Locations and Linkages credits are awarded to projects located in LEED for Neighborhood Development-certified communities, located within specified distances to public transportation and community resources, and with access to open space. The category also addresses environmentally sensitive sites and the importance of building within existing communities.

Awareness and Education requires basic operations training for the homeowner and awards points for additional training of building managers of multifamily properties.

Like the LEED 2009 rating systems, LEED for Homes requires that a number of prerequisites be completed and that a minimum number of points be achieved to reach the various levels of certification. A minimum number of points must also be earned in some categories.

category	prerequisites	minimum points
ID	3	0
LL	0	0
SS	2	5
WE	0	3
EA	2	0
MR	3	2
EQ	7	6
AE	1	0

LEED for Homes is not based on a 100-point certification scale as the LEED 2009 rating systems are; instead, 136 possible points are available. The Home Size Adjustment provision allows the number of points required for certification to be adjusted based on the size of the home and the number of bedrooms. Larger homes with more bedrooms must earn a greater number of points to achieve certification, while smaller homes with fewer bedrooms require fewer points. For example, a two-bedroom home with 950 ft² of living space would have to earn at least 35 points to become certified, an average ("neutral") two-bedroom home with 1400 ft² would have to earn 45 points, and a two-bedroom home with 2060 ft² would have to earn 55 points. See the Threshold Adjustment table and equations in the front matter of the LEED for Homes rating system to calculate the number of points required for certification of a specific project.

Point requirements are based on the size of the home relative to a baseline, or "neutral," home, which has the following characteristics and maximum square footage.

0 or 1 bedroom	900 ft²
2 bedrooms	1400 ft²
3 bedrooms	1900 ft²
4 bedrooms	2600 ft²
5 bedrooms	2850 ft²

The minimum number of points for each level of certification for a "neutral" home are as follows.

Certified	45 points
Silver	60 points
Gold	75 points
Platinum	90 points

A home that is larger or smaller than a "neutral" home may require up to ten points more or ten points fewer, respectively, to achieve a particular level of certification.

The Certification Process

Homeowners or builders must complete the following steps to certify a project under LEED for Homes.

- Contact a LEED for Homes provider and join the program.
- Identify a project team, including an architect, engineers, specialty consultants, and so forth. This step includes review of the home's design by a green rater and determination of a preliminary score. If the preliminary score is not high enough to achieve the homeowner's or builder's desired rating, redesign and another score assessment and report may be required.
- Build the home according to the final design. If significant changes are made during construction, the project may need to be rescored.
- Certify the project as a LEED home. All documentation must be completed and submitted, which requires the participation of and verification by the green rater. This is a hard-copy documentation process; LEED for Homes projects do not use LEED Online. The information is submitted to the provider, who is the official certifier of LEED homes on behalf of USGBC.

- Market and sell the home, if applicable. USGBC must approve all marketing materials released by the builder or developer.

LEED for Neighborhood Development

LEED ND Prerequisites

SLLp1	Smart Location
SLLp2	Proximity to Water and Wastewater Infrastructure
SLLp3	Imperiled Species and Ecological Communities
SLLp4	Wetland and Water Body Conservation
SLLp5	Agricultural Land Conservation
SLLp6	Floodplain Avoidance
NPDp1	Walkable Streets
NPDp2	Compact Development
NPDp3	Connected and Open Community
GIBp1	Certified Green Building
GIBp2	Minimum Building Energy Efficiency
GIBp3	Minimum Building Water Efficiency
GIBp4	Construction Activity Pollution Prevention

LEED for Neighborhood Development was introduced in 2009, after a process of public review, comment, and balloting. This rating system is used to certify new developments that focus on sustainability and community connectivity. The rating system is a joint effort of USGBC, the Congress for the New Urbanism (CNU), and the Natural Resources Defense Council (NRDC).

USGBC describes LEED ND as "encouraging smart growth and new urbanist best practices, promoting the location and design of neighborhoods that reduce vehicle miles traveled and communities where jobs are accessible by foot or public transit." The rating system also "promotes more efficient energy and water use—especially important in urban areas where infrastructure is often overtaxed."

LEED for Neighborhood Development includes four credit categories.

Smart Location and Linkage credits address issues of land conservation (including avoiding or properly addressing wetlands, habitats for endangered species, floodplains, agricultural land, and steep slopes); brownfield redevelopment; proximity to housing, jobs, existing community infrastructure, and public transportation; and provision of bicycle paths and storage.

Neighborhood Pattern and Design credits emphasize walkable, compact development that is connected both internally and to surrounding communities through a logical and accessible network of paths for pedestrians, bicyclists, and automobiles. Parking should be minimized. Communities should be diverse and universally accessible, providing residential properties at a variety of price points that can accommodate people of different abilities. The credits encourage construction of a network of transit stations and neighborhood schools, and reward initiatives to encourage community involvement in design, community gardens, community-supported agriculture, and farmers' markets.

Green Infrastructure and Buildings includes many of the priorities of the other LEED rating systems. It requires at least one green building (LEED certified or certified through another third-party agency) and awards credits for additional green buildings. The credits encourage energy efficiency (commercial buildings must meet ANSI/ASHRAE/IESNA Standard 90.1, and residential properties must meet Energy Star requirements); reduced water use (20% less than baseline); erosion and sediment control measures for all construction projects; waste management and recycling; reuse of existing structures and preservation of historic structures; minimal site disturbance; heat island reduction; stormwater management measures; light pollution controls; and on-site renewable energy. It encourages city planners to orient streets east-west, and awards neighborhood infrastructure that is energy efficient and contains recycled content.

Innovation and Design Process points are awarded for exemplary performance; for including the involvement of a LEED AP (and later, a LEED AP with a specialty in Neighborhood Development) or a professional credentialed by CNU or NRDC on the project team; and for Regional Priority credits.

LEED in Practice: Credit Synergies and the Cost of Building Green

One of the first questions that arises in discussions of LEED certification is one of the most important: "How much is all this going to cost?"

Fortunately, the answer is not much more than construction of a conventional building. When long-term utility savings are factored in, the price of a green building may actually be less over the long run than that of a comparable traditionally designed building. As building codes become more restrictive in their regulation of energy consumption, water use, insulation requirements, and the like, the premium for green construction relative to conventional construction will be further reduced.

A 2003 study of 33 LEED-certified office and school buildings found that a green building cost on average less than 2% more than it would have cost using conventional methods. Figure 6 summarizes the study's results.

Figure 6 Average Cost Increase by Certification Level

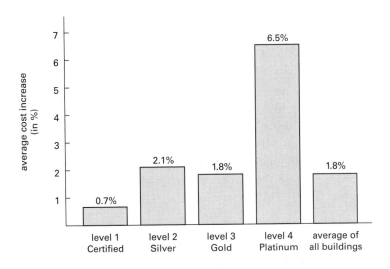

Adapted from *The Costs and Financial Benefits of Green Buildings: A Report to California's Sustainable Building Task Force*, by Greg Kats et al., p. 15, 2003, by California Integrated Waste Management Board.

In its 2006 study and report, *Cost of Green Revisited: Reexamining the Feasibility and Cost Impact of Sustainable Design in the Light of Increased Market Adoption*, the consulting firm Davis Langdon found that "there is no significant difference in average cost for green buildings as compared to non-green buildings." The report, available online (see **www.ppi2pass.com/ LEEDreferences** for a current link), lists the credits in LEED NC v2.2 and rates their impact on construction and soft costs, among other factors. (Costs for specific credits vary widely from project to project, however, and depend on existing conditions, local availability of specific technologies and materials, and the sustainability goals of the project.)

Credit Synergies and Trade-Offs

Two ways of helping to keep green building costs under control are to look for opportunities for credit synergies and to weigh the impact of credit trade-offs.

Credits can interact in both helpful and unhelpful ways. *Credit synergies* are groups of credits that work together in such a way that achieving one of them makes earning the others easier as well. For example, meeting the requirements of IEQ Credit 8.1: Daylight and Views through the use of daylighting will have the additional effect of reducing energy use for daytime lighting, which will help toward the requirements of EA Credit 1: Optimize Energy Performance.

On the other hand, some groups of credits present trade-offs: Earning one credit may make it more difficult to earn another. Achieving the requirements of IEQ Credit 2: Increased Ventilation, for example, could make it harder, not easier, to meet the requirements of EA Credit 1: Optimize Energy Performance.

For a LEED project to capitalize on credit synergies, the project team must use an integrated building design process in which multiple disciplines and seemingly unrelated aspects of a design are integrated in a manner that brings about synergistic benefits. (A variety of types of collaborative project structures are addressed in the chapter on project coordination.) The goal is to achieve high performance and multiple benefits at a total cost that is less than what those components would cost if implemented individually. This process often includes integrating green design strategies into conventional design criteria for building form, function, performance, and cost.

Using Integrated Building Design

A key to successful integrated building design is the participation of people from different specialties of design: architecture, HVAC and electrical engineering, lighting design, interior design, and landscape design. By working together at key points in the design process, these participants can often identify highly attractive solutions to design needs that would otherwise not be found. For example, in an integrated design approach, the mechanical engineer will calculate energy use and cost very early in the design, informing designers of the energy-use implications of building orientation, configuration, fenestration, mechanical systems, and lighting options early enough in the project that it is still possible to modify the design for greater efficiency.

Consider integrated building design strategies for all aspects of green design: improving energy efficiency, planning a sustainable site, safeguarding water, creating healthy indoor environments, and using environmentally preferable materials. Major design issues should be considered by all members of the design team—from civil engineers to interior designers—with each bearing in mind the common goals set in the pre-design phase. The procurement of architecture/engineering/construction (A/E/C) services should emphasize a team-building approach, and provisions for integrated design should be clearly presented in each professional's scope of work. For example, the scope of work should stipulate frequent meetings and a significant level of effort from all design professionals to evaluate and compare a variety of design options.

The design and analysis process for developing integrated building designs includes

- establishing a base case performance profile showing energy use and costs for a typical facility that complies with building codes and other measures for the project type, location, size, and so on
- identifying a range of solutions—including all that appear to have potential for the specific project
- evaluating the performance of individual strategies—considering each separately and in comparison to the others generated for the project
- grouping high-performing strategies into different combinations to evaluate performance
- selecting strategies, refining the design, and updating the analysis throughout the process

Whenever a green design strategy can provide more than one benefit, there is a potential for design integration. For example, windows can be highly cost effective when they are designed and placed to provide the multiple benefits of daylight, passive solar heating, summer heat gain avoidance, natural ventilation, and an attractive view. A double-loaded central corridor, a common feature of historic buildings, provides daylight and natural ventilation to each room, and transom windows above doors provide some natural light and ventilation to corridors. Building envelope and lighting design strategies that significantly reduce HVAC system requirements can have remarkable results.

Sometimes the most effective solutions have the lowest construction costs, especially when they are part of an integrated design. Some basic green strategies that can contribute to achievement of LEED points without significant additional cost are some of the simplest. The following list is adapted from "Low-Cost Green Design and Construction Practices" in the May 1999 issue of *Environmental Building News* magazine.

- renovate an existing building
- integrate the planning and design process
- design smaller buildings with more efficient floor plans
- look for opportunities in regulatory requirements
- orient buildings to take advantage of sun, wind, and light
- locate windows on the north and south faces of buildings rather than east and west facades
- skip the carpet and other floor finishes—leave the floor slab exposed
- eliminate suspended ceilings
- use open-plan layouts to reduce HVAC and lighting costs
- design with standard material dimensions to reduce waste
- specify water-efficient fixtures—the added cost is generally negligible
- cluster buildings to reduce infrastructure and parking requirements
- build on sites with existing connections to infrastructure
- avoid cut-and-fill

- protect existing trees and work them into the final landscape plan
- consider alternative landscaping strategies such as xeriscaping and native plantings
- use energy modeling to size HVAC systems appropriately
- specify appropriate windows for each elevation
- include operable windows
- move ductwork away from exterior walls
- use salvaged materials where appropriate
- make the structural materials and finish materials one and the same
- recycle construction waste

Finding the right building design recipe through an integrated design process can be challenging. Often, design teams first make incremental changes that result in high-performance buildings at affordable costs. But further exploring the opportunities for design integration can sometimes result in extraordinary cost savings.

Cost issues must play into every decision about which credits to pursue, which strategies to employ, and how much selected technologies will add to the bottom line. The team must constantly ask itself if there is a better or more economical way to achieve a credit. For example, NC SS Credit 7.1: Heat Island Effect: Non-Roof is intended to reduce temperature differences between developed and undeveloped areas on a site. This can be accomplished by planting trees in the parking lot and specifying white cement in the concrete mix for the sidewalks, or by constructing undercover parking areas with a vegetated roof. Obviously, the difference in cost between these two approaches is huge. However, the cost differential must be weighed against the project goals and opportunities before the best decision can be reached.

Even in the earliest phases of the project, a project team should look at the financing and cost issues, begin developing some rough cost estimates, and consider available financing options. After completing more detailed analyses later in the process, these initial cost estimates are refined and the best way to finance the project is selected. Following are some methods that can be employed to analyze the cost impact of the design team's decisions.

Cost/Benefit Analysis

There will usually be a number of acceptable design alternatives for any project. Cost/benefit analyses can help a team identify the alternatives that have the best potential for savings, and evaluate the impact these alternatives will have on LEED certification. There are three primary analysis methods.

- simple payback analysis
- standardized payback equations
- life-cycle cost analysis

The latest research indicates that, on average, it costs about 2% more to build green than to build in a conventional manner. Sometimes the additional upfront construction costs can be justified because the investment in sustainable technologies will reduce operating costs through the life of the building. The added cost, if any, of system investment each year is compared to the cost of fuel saved each year. Total energy costs for LEED-certified buildings are, on average, about 50% less than those for conventionally designed buildings. In many cases, correctly sizing the mechanical systems and making use of alternative strategies such as passive solar design can offset the costs for additional windows or controls. When an energy efficiency improvement, conversion, or purchase is considered, a cost/benefit analysis is made to determine if and when the expenditure will be repaid through energy savings. This helps the team set priorities among alternative improvement projects. A cost/benefit analysis may be a simple payback analysis or a more sophisticated analysis of total life-cycle costs and savings. Because most electric utility rate schedules are based on both consumption and peak demand, the project analyst should be skilled at assessing the effects of both.

Project costs are often divided into hard costs and soft costs. *Hard costs* are labor and materials. *Soft costs* include design fees, taxes, permit fees, office and project management expenses directly related to the project, insurance, legal fees, closing costs and finance charges, and contingency monies.

Before beginning any cost/benefit analysis, it is necessary to determine what acceptable design alternatives can meet the heating, cooling, lighting, and control requirements of the building being evaluated. The criteria for determining whether a design alternative or alternative fuel is acceptable should include reliability, safety, conformance to building codes, occupant comfort, noise levels, refueling issues, and even space limitations.

Simple Payback Analysis

An elementary form of cost/benefit analysis is called *simple payback analysis*. In this method, the total initial cost of the improvement is divided by the first-year energy cost savings that would result. This method gives an estimate of the number of years needed for the improvement to pay for itself. For new construction, this calculation can be used to compare the life-cycle cost of conventional construction against more energy efficient design alternatives.

In a simple payback analysis, it is assumed that the service life of the energy efficiency measure will equal or exceed the simple payback time. Simple payback analysis provides a relatively easy way to examine the overall costs and savings potentials for a variety of project alternatives. However, it does not consider a number of factors that are difficult to predict but can have a significant impact on cost savings. The more sophisticated life-cycle cost analysis method takes these factors into consideration.

As an example of the simple payback analysis method, consider the lighting retrofit of a 10,000 sq ft commercial office building. The owner decides to relamp all the existing light fixtures with T-8 lamps and high-efficiency electronic ballasts. These upgrades are estimated to cost approximately $13,300 ($50 each for 266 fixtures) and produce annual electricity savings of around $4800 per year (80,000 kWh at $0.06/kWh). The simple payback time for this improvement would be the initial cost divided by the annual savings, or $13,300 ÷ $4,800/year = 2.8 years. This means that the improvement would pay for itself in 2.8 years, which is a 36% simple return on the investment.

Standardized Payback Equations

The U.S. Department of Energy's International Performance Measurement & Verification Protocol (IPMVP) provides standard measurement and verification (M&V) terminology and defines four M&V options for measuring and verifying the energy and water savings that result from energy-conservation measures. It is a savings-verification tool with principles that are applicable to commercial and industrial energy efficiency projects.

IPMVP M&V options	description	typical applications
partially measured retrofit isolation	Savings are determined by partial field measurements of the energy use of the system(s) to which an ECM (energy conserving measure) was applied, separate from the energy use of the rest of the facility. Measurements may be either short term or continuous. Some, but not all, parameters may be stipulated.	Lighting retrofit where power draw is measured periodically. Operating hours of the lights are assumed to be one half hour per day longer than facility occupancy hours.
retrofit isolation	Savings are determined by field measurement of the energy use of the systems to which the ECM was applied, separate from the energy use of the rest of the facility. Short-term or continuous measurements are taken throughout the post-retrofit period.	Application of controls to vary the load on a constant speed pump using variable-speed drive. Electricity use is measured by a kilowatt-hour meter installed on the electrical supply to the pump motor.
whole facility	Savings are determined by measuring energy use at the whole-facility level. Short-term or continuous measurements are taken throughout the post-retrofit period.	Multifaceted energy management program affecting many systems in a building. Energy use is measured by the gas and electric utility meters for a 12-month base-year period and throughout the post-retrofit period.
calibrated simulation	Savings are determined through simulation of the energy use of components or the whole facility. Simulation routines must be demonstrated to adequately model actual energy performance measured in the facility. This option usually requires considerable skill in calibrated simulation.	Multifaceted energy management program affecting many systems in a building but where no base-year data are available. Base-year energy use is determined by simulation using a model calibrated by the post-retrofit period data.

Life-Cycle Cost Analysis

A life-cycle cost (LCC) analysis looks at the total cost of a system, device, building, or other capital equipment or facility over its expected useful life. This makes possible a comprehensive assessment of the expected costs associated with a design alternative. Factors commonly considered in LCC analyses are initial capital cost, operating costs, maintenance costs, financing costs, the expected useful life of equipment, and future equipment salvage values. The result of the LCC analysis is generally expressed as the value of initial and future costs in today's dollars as modified by an appropriate discount rate.

The first step in making an LCC analysis is to establish general study parameters. These parameters include the base date (the date to which all future costs are discounted), the service date (the date when the new system will be put into service), the study period (the life of the project or the number of years over which the investor has a financial interest in the project), and the discount rate. When two or more design alternatives are compared or when a single alternative is compared against an existing design, the parameters used must be the same or the comparison will not be valid. It is meaningless to compare the LCCs of two or more alternatives if they are computed using different study periods or different discount rates.

Selecting the "Best" Alternatives

Generally, all project alternatives should be screened initially with simple payback analyses. A more detailed and costly LCC analysis should be reserved for large projects or for improvements that require a large investment, since a detailed cost analysis would then be a proportionally small part of the overall cost. Both simple payback and LCC analyses will help the designer set priorities based on the measures that will bring the greatest return on investment. In addition, these analyses provide a preliminary indication of appropriate financing options.

- Energy efficiency measures that have a short payback period of one to two years are the most attractive economically and should be considered for immediate implementation using operating reserves or other readily available internal funds.
- Energy efficiency measures that have payback periods of three to five years may be considered for funding from available internal capital investment moneys, or may be attractive candidates for third-party financing through energy service companies or equipment leasing arrangements.
- Frequently, short payback measures can be combined with longer payback measures of 10 or more years to increase the number of approaches that can be cost-effectively included in a project. Projects that combine short- and long-term paybacks are recommended to avoid "cream-skimming"—implementing only those measures that are the most cost effective and have the quickest paybacks at the expense of other worthwhile measures. A selected set of measures with a combination of payback periods can be financed either from available internal funds or through third-party alternatives.

If the simple payback time of an upgrade is expected to be 10 years or more, economic factors are very significant and LCC analysis is recommended. On the other hand, if simple payback occurs within three to five years, a more detailed LCC analysis may not be necessary. This is particularly true when price and inflation changes can be assumed to be moderate; in cases such as these, the results of a simple payback analysis and a more detailed LCC analysis will often differ by only about 15% to 20%. In general, the expense of conducting LCC analyses may not be justified if the payback of the improvement is less than five years.

When calculating the benefits of any alternative, it is important to include avoided costs. When analyzing the cost of replacing building equipment, for example, the avoided cost of maintaining the existing equipment should be counted as a savings.

Weighing Societal Impacts

Some factors related to building system design are not considered in either simple payback or LCC analyses. Many of these are factors that are difficult to predict or quantify, such as the level of thermal comfort and the adequacy of task lighting, and the impact these may have on the productivity of building occupants.

Conventional cost/benefit analyses also do not normally consider the societal benefits from reduced energy use (for example, reduced carbon emissions, improved indoor air quality). In some cases, these ancillary benefits are assigned an agreed-on monetary value, but the values used depend strongly on local factors. In general, if societal benefits have been assigned appropriate monetary values by a local utility, they are considered in savings calculations. However, each team should discuss this issue with the local utility or consultants working with such values in the project area.

LEED Project and Team Coordination: Pre-Design

What Is Green Building?

Green building is the implementation of design, construction, and operational strategies that reduce a building's environmental impact during both construction and operation and improve occupants' health, comfort, and productivity throughout the building's life cycle.

Green building is part of the larger trend of *sustainable design*. The principles of sustainable design have a wide range of applications; everything from the design of small objects for everyday use to the planning and design of cities can be developed, constructed, and operated in ways that make better use of natural resources. The objective of sustainable design is to create places, products, and services in ways that reduce the use of nonrenewable resources, minimize environmental impact, and relate people to the natural environment.

Green buildings come in all shapes and sizes. Some look "green"; they proudly display their vegetated roofs and solar panels and other features that allow them to control energy and water consumption and the like. These sustainable approaches are visible elements of the design.

Just as many green buildings, however, are indistinguishable to the eye from other buildings that are designed and constructed in more traditional ways. There is no "typical" green building; each building's mix of sustainability techniques and technologies must be chosen given the opportunities and challenges presented by the project and the site.

The construction and operation of buildings has a significant impact on the environment. In the United States, the construction industry is a primary contributor of solid waste to landfills, generating nearly 2.5 pounds of waste per square foot of new commercial floor space during the course of construction. According to USGBC, typical building operations after construction is complete account for

> 30% to 40% of total U.S. energy use
> over 70% of total U.S. electricity consumption
> 10% to 20% of total U.S. water consumption
> 30% to 40% of total U.S. carbon dioxide emissions

The strategies outlined in the LEED rating systems can help reduce consumption of energy, electricity, and water, and decrease the amount of pollutants and other harmful substances in the atmosphere. Beyond the benefits to the environment and society, green building strategies can also have a positive economic impact for building owners and the economy as a whole. Green building design and construction may cost a bit more than conventional methods at first, but reduced operating expenses (such as lower costs for energy and water) and higher levels of productivity from employees enjoying a pleasant, sustainable environment can lead to greater profitability. This benefit to people, planet, and profit is called the "triple bottom line," and is part of the true cost and value of the project.

Throughout design, construction, and operation, effective green building projects require a collaborative, integrated approach between the design and construction professionals and the owners and end users of the building. Only by using a "whole building" approach—viewing the site, structure, systems, and anticipated use interdependently—can the project team effectively implement sustainable design strategies. Green building design teams work toward common goals.

- minimizing life-cycle costs
- reducing resource consumption
- reducing resource waste
- increasing equipment and system efficiency
- emphasizing source and waste reduction
- creating healthy environments

Green Projects and Teams

The LEED Green Associate exam focuses on a candidate's understanding of the green building design and construction process and how to coordinate projects and their teams. Such coordination may involve setting project goals, coordinating multiple job functions, evaluating the benefits and drawbacks of a number of project delivery approaches, reviewing codes and standards, understanding the interdependencies of building components, conducting a cost/benefit analysis, identifying opportunities for LEED credit synergies, and scheduling critical decisions and activities to meet project goals.

The process of designing and constructing a high-performance building is quite different than either the traditional design-bid-build or design-build methods of project delivery.

Design-Bid-Build

In traditional *design-bid-build* projects, an owner hires a design professional (architect or engineer) to prepare documentation of the scope and requirements of a project through a set of drawings and specifications. These documents are then released to the public, and contractors are invited to prepare a price proposal, or bid, and submit it for review. Depending on the owner and the type of project, he or she may be required to accept the lowest bid, or may have the option of choosing the firm that offers the best combination of qualifications and price. In design-bid-build projects, the design professional and the contractor are completely separate entities. The contractor would have no involvement in the design process, and the architect or engineer would play a limited role (that of contract administrator) in construction or may not be involved in this phase at all depending on the terms of the design professional's contract with the owner.

Figure 7 Traditional (Design-Bid-Build) Project Delivery Relationships

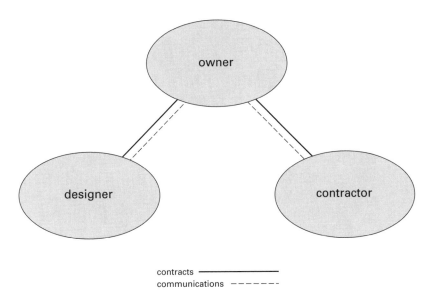

contracts ──────
communications ── ── ── ──

Design-Build

In a *design-build* project, an owner contracts with a single entity for both design and construction services. This entity can be a single firm, or it can be two or more firms structured as a joint venture or in a prime-consultant arrangement.

Design-build projects can be either contractor-led or design-led. In contractor-led design-build projects, the owner's agreement is with the contractor, and the contractor subcontracts design work to an architecture or engineering firm. In design-led design-build projects, the owner contracts with an architecture or engineering firm who subcontracts the construction responsibilities to a builder. Alternatively, a single company may be structured in a way that allows it to offer both types of services with in-house staff.

The advantages of the design-build approach include a shortened delivery schedule, availability of cost information at earlier phases of design (allowing adjustments to be made as necessary), more cooperation between the architect and contractor, greater accountability, and single-source provision of all of the resources necessary for completion of the project. On the other hand, a design-build approach may lead to a loss of owner control and a lower quality product, depending on the nature of the project team.

According to the Design-Build Institute of America, the construction industry is at a crossroads. Around the year 2010, for the first time more projects will be making use of a design-build approach than a traditional design-bid-build structure.

Integrated Project Delivery

Integrated Project Delivery (IPD) incorporates some features of the design-build model of project delivery and some of the attributes of the traditional project delivery approach. The structure of IPD is well-suited for a green building project because it encourages interdisciplinary collaboration from the start. The American Institute of Architects (AIA) defines IPD as an approach that "leverages early contributions of knowledge and expertise through the utilization of new technologies, allowing all team members to better realize their highest potentials while expanding the value they provide throughout the project lifecycle."

Figure 8 Design-Build Project Delivery Relationships

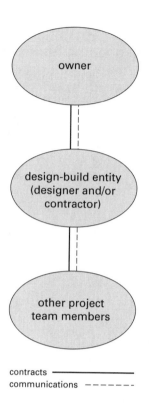

Figure 9 Rise of Design-Build Project Delivery

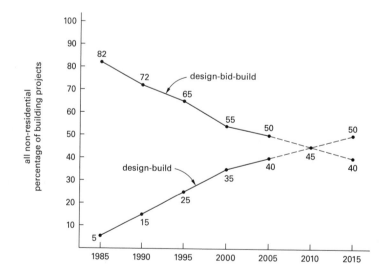

In IPD, the architect and contractor are not contractually bound to one another (as they are in design-build); each has a separate contract with the owner. The architect is responsible for coordinating the team of design professionals and consultants best suited for the project, while the contractor maintains responsibility for hiring and coordinating the efforts of subcontractors and those involved with construction of the building.

However, both parties agree to work cooperatively throughout design and construction. Inherent in this agreement is a willingness to look freshly at the roles each party traditionally plays and the structure of the relationships that bind team members.

One way to form IPD relationships is to use the model contracts offered by the AIA that are written specifically for IPD projects. These documents define the responsibilities of each party and offer guidance for specifying requirements for confidentiality agreements, compensation, dispute resolution, insurance, and the like.

- AIA Document A295: *General Conditions of the Contract for Integrated Project Delivery*
- AIA Document B195: *Standard Form of Agreement Between Owner and Architect for Integrated Project Delivery*
- AIA Document A195: *Standard Form of Agreement Between Owner and Contractor for Integrated Project Delivery*
- AIA Document C196: *Standard Form of Agreement Between Single Purpose Entity and Owner Member for Integrated Project Delivery*
- AIA Document C197: *Standard Form of Agreement Between Single Purpose Entity and Non-Owner Member for Integrated Project Delivery*

The AIA publication *Integrated Project Delivery: A Guide* is an excellent resource for understanding this new approach to design and construction phase services. The document is available for download from the AIA website at www.aia.org (search for it by title). It should be reviewed in preparation for the LEED Green Associate exam.

The IPD Guide addresses the following subjects.

Principles of Integrated Project Delivery

Mutual respect and trust. All team members are committed to the best interests of the project and are willing to work with colleagues to achieve project goals.

Mutual benefit and reward. Everyone benefits from the project. This may include incentives (financial or otherwise) for meeting project goals.

Collaborative innovation and decision making. Input from every member is considered. Decisions are made by the team, not by individuals.

Early involvement of key participants. To the greatest extent possible, owner representatives and primary and key supporting participants are all involved from the start.

Early goal definition. Owner representatives and primary and key supporting participants state the project goals at the beginning of the process. Progress is constantly checked against these desired outcomes.

Intensified planning. Better design and planning leads to more efficient, more economical construction.

Open communication. A "no-blame" culture. An attitude of "we're all in this together" that requires discussion, sharing of ideas and information, and working as a team to resolve problems.

Appropriate technology. There is a commitment to using technology and design standards to streamline interaction among members of the team.

Organization and leadership. Member roles are clearly defined. Leadership responsibilities are generally assigned based on the professionals' areas of expertise.

Figure 10 Integrated Project Delivery Relationships

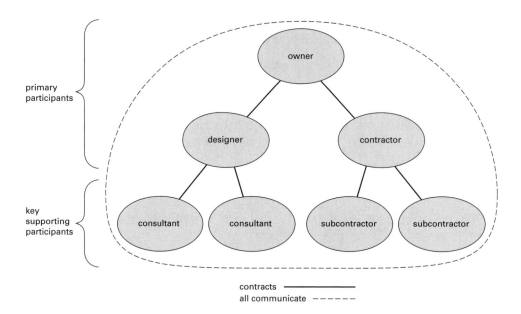

Setting Up an Integrated Project

IPD team building and functioning. A successful IPD project team must embrace the concept of "huddling versus hunkering": an understanding that individual goals are secondary to the best interests of the team. This approach is counterintuitive to many in the design and construction industry and can only be achieved with the full cooperation of the primary and key supporting participants.

- *Primary participants* are involved throughout the duration of the project and are charged with a range of responsibilities from start to finish. In addition to the owner, this may include the prime design professional and general contractor.
- *Key supporting participants* perform a distinct role relative to the project. This may include the commissioning agency, building systems or site engineers, specialty consultants, subcontractors, and the like.

Project team members consider options and make decisions together. This requires frequent meetings, an organized approach to gathering and sharing information, and a high level of collaboration that may be foreign to teams more familiar with traditional delivery methods. It is recommended that the team develop a protocol for communication early in the project to facilitate these interactions. A new tool in this effort is building information modeling (BIM): creating a three-dimensional computer model of a proposed building that links to a database of project data. (BIM is a relatively new technology and is not yet widely adopted.)

Primary participants are involved in every project decision, while key supporting team members' opinions are solicited for decisions relevant to their field of expertise. The challenge to the project leadership is to anticipate how the necessary decisions are interconnected and to include the appropriate team members in discussions. As touched on in earlier sections of this book, pursuit of LEED credits (really, any project decision) offers synergies and trade-offs. The project leadership must have the ability to anticipate these links and gather the right team of decision makers for each issue.

When problems arise, the team must deal with them quickly and openly. Retaining the original team is key to the continuity and success of the project. Every effort should be made to resolve conflicts in a way that keeps all players involved from beginning to end, without claims against the project or other team members, resignations or terminations, or lawsuits. This effort can include contract language that includes "no suit" provisions or requirements that all disputes are subject to mediation.

Adopting the IPD model can leave a lot to chance if things fall apart. Because the delivery system is new, there is not much legal precedent for resolving disputes. One way to minimize the potential for conflict is to develop a thorough, detailed assignment of responsibilities using documents such as the AIA contracts or similar; firms entering into these agreements must bear in mind, however, that this progressive approach to project delivery is not without risk.

Defining roles, responsibilities, and scope of services. Owners, design professionals, and builders take on specific roles as a part of their agreement to participate in an IPD project. Many of these roles differ from the parts they traditionally play in project delivery methods.

- Designers are charged with facilitating communication and synthesizing input from a variety of parties.
- Contractors are involved with the project much earlier than they would be in a traditional delivery system. Cost estimating, scheduling, and purchasing may become design phase tasks rather than bid or construction phase responsibilities.
- Owners set the project parameters and are responsible for keeping the project moving, which may include dispute resolution.

Defining and measuring project outcomes. The success of an IPD project can be determined by comparing the product to the parameters established at the start of the project. Successful projects are completed on time and within the budget and accomplish the goals defined at the start.

IPD offers the opportunity to eliminate value engineering. Value engineering, in a traditional project, is the process through which elements of the work are cut from the project in order to bring the total cost within the budget. Often, as portions of the project are cut in a value engineering effort, the interrelationships of those elements are not fully considered and the quality and coordination of the design suffers as a result. In IPD, costs can be analyzed throughout the design process and their cost implications and effects fully considered before cuts are made.

Thorough planning efforts in the design phase can reduce the amount of time necessary for construction of an IPD project. Eliminating the traditional bid phase saves significant time (generally a month or more). With contractor involvement during design, as decisions are finalized, materials can be ordered, construction schedules can be arranged, and preconstruction work can take place in parallel to design efforts.

Project goals may include benchmarks for sustainability measures and performance levels for building systems (often, congruent with the requirements of LEED credits) and satisfaction of owner design requirements, as well as positive financial returns.

Legal considerations. Parties entering into an IPD project must be aware of the risks and potential rewards of this project delivery system. At the beginning, participants should consider whether existing corporate structures are conducive to the structure of the project or if a separate joint venture or limited liability corporation should be formed specifically for this work. Licensed professionals must also consider the roles they are legally required to perform and establish their scope of work for the IPD project accordingly. Participants should consult their attorneys and insurance agents to ensure that their interests are protected—or alternatively, that they fully understand the risks they are choosing to incur—as a part of this venture.

Delivering an Integrated Project

Building an integrated project team. Building an integrated project team involves identifying the appropriate people for the job as early as possible. IPD depends on buy-in from all participants, such as the owner, architect, contractor, landscape architect, civil engineer, HVAC engineer, and facility manager, as well as the support of external organizations that are stakeholders in the project, such as local code officials, utility companies, lenders, and insurance companies. Everyone should be involved in drafting project goals and setting up the ground rules for the project. As mentioned previously, it may be advantageous to explore an alternative corporate structure specifically for this project. All parties' agreements should reflect their agreed-on roles and clearly state their responsibilities—both individual responsibilities and duty to work for the good of the project.

Project execution and redefining project phases. The desired outcome of each project phase is summarized in this section of the IPD Guide, as well as a listing of the responsibilities of team members during each period. Compare the project phases listed in the next section to the project phases prescribed in the IPD model, which include

- conceptualization (expanded programming)
- criteria design (expanded schematic design)
- detailed design (expended design development)
- implementation documents (construction documents)
- agency review
- buyout
- construction (construction/construction contract administration)
- closeout

Multiparty Agreements

A variety of legal structures and contracts may be used to establish the relationships among the project participants.

- *Project alliances* cover direct costs but tie additional compensation to performance. Participants waive their liability to each other.
- *Single purpose entities* are new, independent corporate structures formed specifically for a project. All implications of starting a new business (taxes, insurance, corporate structure, legal status, licensing, and so on) must be fully considered.
- *Relational contracts* are used to limit parties' liability, but liability is not waived. In the absence of team consensus, the owner is charged with making final decisions.

Delivery Model Commentary

This section of the IPD Guide summarizes the characteristics of the traditional methods of project delivery, including design-bid-build and design-build as discussed previously, as well as the following.

- *Multi-prime* is a form of design-bid-build in which the owner takes on much of the role of a general contractor and issues multiple construction contracts to independent subcontractors. The owner then bears the responsibility for coordination of the work.

- In *construction manager at risk*, a construction manager is responsible for total project delivery, including establishing an early price commitment and letting multiple construction contracts to accomplish the work of the project.

Whole-Building Design

The *whole-building design* approach reflected in the structure of IPD considers all building components and systems during the design phase and integrates them to work together. Whole-building design is not limited to projects that proceed using the IPD model; a variety of forms of project delivery can be adapted for this purpose. This holistic, interdisciplinary approach to design considers site, energy, materials, indoor air quality, acoustics, natural resources, and their interrelationships.

Because all building systems are interrelated, it is essential that the design team be fully integrated from the project's inception. The project team can include architects, engineers, building occupants and owners, construction professionals, and specialists in areas such as indoor air quality, materials, and energy use.

Whole-building design considers the building structure and systems simultaneously and examines how these systems can best work together to conserve resources and reduce environmental impact. For example, a strategy that extensively employs daylighting techniques will reduce the amount of heat given off by lighting fixtures, thus allowing for a smaller air conditioning system. In this scenario, the civil engineer should be involved in selecting an appropriate building site and placing the building on the site in a way that maximizes the opportunities for daylighting; the architect will be responsible for designing the building's fenestration and internal layout to locate spaces that need the most light in the appropriate locations; the lighting designer will coordinate the specification and placement of light fixtures so that desirable footcandle levels can be achieved with fewer fixtures; and the mechanical engineer will consider the impact of the daylighting strategy and modify the mechanical systems accordingly.

During the planning for design, construction of the project, and operation of the facility, many opportunities arise to reduce the project's impact on the environment. The *Sustainable Building Technical Manual*, developed through the cooperation of USGBC, Public Technology, Inc., the U.S. Department of Energy, and the U.S. Environmental Protection Agency, outlines the phases of the design process and advises that the groundwork for all collaborative efforts must be laid in the pre-design phase. (A current link to this document can be found at **www.ppi2pass.com/LEEDreferences**.) Like the AIA's IPD Guide, the *Technical Manual* is necessary reading when preparing for the LEED GA exam. GBCI's list of primary references requires only Part II, but at least a pass through the other chapters is recommended; this book is a comprehensive and valuable (and free!) tool for understanding how a green building project works.

Sections of the *Technical Manual* discuss the significance and activities of each project phase and suggest practices. A checklist is included for monitoring progress. Project phases include the following.

- *Pre-design.* Pre-design activities include setting project goals, reviewing the selected LEED rating system and the relevant building codes and standards, selecting the project team, planning for building commissioning, determining a project budget and analyzing projected costs, and possibly selecting the project site. This is also an opportunity to consider issues of durability, innovative design, and initiatives of regional importance. Once the team is assembled, members must collaboratively consider all building components (such as building siting, the building envelope, electrical and mechanical systems, lighting, and material selection) and their interrelationships.

- *Design.* During the design phase, team members are responsible for development of the building systems that fall under their purview and for coordination with the rest of the project team.

- *Construction.* When the design is complete and construction is under way, the team becomes responsible for ensuring that the project is built as designed. The construction sections address general energy and environmental guidelines, purchasing of materials that fulfill the requirements of the specifications, reducing site environmental impact, maintaining indoor air quality during construction, and construction waste management and recycling.

- *Operations and maintenance.* When a new building or an interior remodel is ready for occupancy, the operation and maintenance techniques employed within the building will impact energy use and occupant comfort. As much care should be paid to the operation of the building as was paid to the building planning, design, and component choices. For existing buildings, effective operation and maintenance procedures provide opportunities for energy savings. Existing, inefficient building components can be replaced with more energy-efficient models. Facilities staff can be trained to cut energy use. Further, the operation section addresses performance measurement.

The Pre-Design Phase

The following are agenda items in the pre-design phase.

- evaluate the building's purpose and set project goals
- set the project budget and schedule
- define the property boundary and LEED project boundary
- review applicable building codes and standards
- select the project team and assign responsibilities
- lay the foundation for building commissioning activities
- consider durability planning and management
- evaluate opportunities for innovative and regional design

Evaluate the Building's Purpose and Set Project Goals

The optimal time to set LEED credit goals is during the pre-design, or planning, phase of a project. At this time, the potential is greatest for realizing energy savings, making sustainable choices in building systems and material selections, and integrating all the building elements.

Though the target levels of energy and environmental performance should be set early in the project, specific measures to accomplish these goals need not be identified during the pre-design phase. The sustainability goals must also align with the project's goals for function, aesthetics, security, cost, and schedule. The challenge for all green building projects is to achieve environmental goals without compromising any of the project needs and objectives.

Set the Project Budget and Schedule

Determining the budget for the project as a whole is the owner's responsibility. However, the design team can play a role in advising the owner. When developing the overall project budget, the owner must be sure to include the cost of acquiring the property, the cost of design (including, perhaps, additional fees for research and coordination), the cost of construction, and LEED registration, documentation, and application fees.

The design team must also develop the project schedule. The team should establish a target completion date and intermediate milestone dates to keep the project on track.

Define the Property Boundary and LEED Project Boundary

A number of LEED credits refer to the project's site boundaries. It is important that all members of the team define these terms in the same way, and use the same measurements when developing calculations and documenting the design approach.

- *Property boundary* generally refers to a parcel of contiguous land owned by the owner and is defined in the property deed. The LEED project boundary may be smaller than the property boundary, or, in the case of "master plan" projects, the project boundary may exceed the owner's property boundary.
- *LEED project boundary* is defined in the Minimum Program Requirements as follows.

  > A LEED project boundary must include all relevant site features associated with the building's normal operation. The LEED project boundary must:

  > –At a maximum, include all the contiguous land owned by the building owner. Omitting surfaces not associated with the LEED construction contract that arise from natural features or infrastructure or owned by other parties (rivers, roads, train tracks, rights-of-way, and easements) is permitted.

  > –At a minimum, include all the land that was or will be disturbed for the purpose of constructing the building or performing alterations/additions to the project.

Review Applicable Building Codes and Standards

After setting overall project goals, the next step is to review the applicable LEED rating system and reference guide and the building codes and industry-related standards in force within the jurisdiction to determine the minimum levels of compliance for the building.

All new construction and renovation projects must comply with applicable building codes, so these requirements are not part of the LEED credit requirements. Although codes in effect vary by jurisdiction, many municipalities in the United States have adopted the codes published by the International Code Council (www.iccsafe.org). These codes include

- International Building Code (IBC)
- International Residential Code (IRC)
- International Fire Code (IFC)
- International Plumbing Code (IPC)
- International Mechanical Code (IMC)

- International Fuel Gas Code (IFGC)
- International Energy Conservation Code (IECC)
- International Wildland Urban Code (IWUC)
- International Existing Building Code (IEBC)
- International Property Maintenance Code (IPMC)
- International Private Sewage Code (IPSC)
- International Zoning Code (IZC)

A state or local jurisdiction may choose to adopt any or all of these codes as written or may amend the code as desired. Always confirm the codes in effect in a project area before beginning design and obtain copies of any local modifications.

United States projects are also required to comply with the provisions of the Americans with Disabilities Act (ADA), which are defined in 28 CFR Part 36: *ADA Standards for Accessible Design*. These regulations can be downloaded from the ADA website at www.ada.gov (a current link directly to the document can be found at **www.ppi2pass.com/LEEDreferences**.) The regulations are sometimes referred to as the Americans with Disabilities Act Accessibility Guidelines (ADAAG). ADAAG applies to public facilities and, where these regulations have been adopted by the local municipality, the standards included in this document are the minimum levels of accessibility acceptable for projects. Some municipalities choose to adopt ICC/ANSI A117.1, *Standard on Accessible and Usable Buildings and Facilities*, which the ICC codes adopt by reference.

Meeting credit requirements and complying with applicable building codes can often depend on meeting standards developed by independent agencies. These standards may be related to specific properties or ratings of building components or they may prescribe levels of performance. Many LEED credits refer to such standards; see the Referenced Standards chapter of this book for additional information on those included in LEED NC, CI, CS and EBO&M.

As an example of the scope of the standards and the topics they cover, consider these three published by the American Society of Heating, Refrigerating and Air-Conditioning Engineers (ASHRAE). The ASHRAE standards referenced most often in building design and operations of LEED buildings are Standards 90.1, 62.1, and 55:

- ASHRAE Standard 90.1 establishes minimum requirements for the energy-efficient design of buildings, including HVAC and lighting systems.
- ASHRAE Standard 62.1 establishes ventilation requirements for acceptable indoor air quality.
- ASHRAE Standard 55 establishes acceptable thermal environmental conditions for occupancy.

There are two methods for complying with the recommendations of ASHRAE Standard 90.1, a prescriptive method and a performance method. Other types of standards may offer similar alternatives for compliance.

The *prescriptive method* means that the designer strictly follows the guidelines laid out in the standard, such as providing a recommended constant level of ventilation air to a space.

The *performance method* means that overall building performance meets the intent of the standard. For example, a designer using the performance method may specify more or less ventilation air to a space at various times than what is recommended in the prescriptive portion of the standard. Complying with the intent of the standard using the performance method and adapting the requirements for the specific needs of a particular project often results in a building that consumes less energy and still maintains healthy and comfortable indoor conditions.

Select the Project Team and Assign Responsibilities

The members of a project team are critical to the success of the project. It is important for the owner or his or her representatives to select architecture/engineering/construction (A/E/C) professionals who have experience incorporating sustainable features into their building designs and who are willing to work collaboratively to achieve the project goals.

Before the design process begins, all members of the design team should be selected and have the opportunity to meet. All those who influence the building's design and construction should be represented on the design team, including architects, engineers, building owners and occupants, contractors, and specialists in areas such as indoor air quality, materials, and energy use. The size of the project, the aggressiveness of the design goals, and the types of sustainable strategies that may be employed will determine who should be on this team.

The project coordinator or owner, or other party responsible for the legal relationships among team members, should clearly state the goals of the building design and performance in the contracts for the design team, and make sure that all members have a solid understanding of these goals. It may be necessary to revise the standard contracts used for building projects to include the project goals and establish consequences if the design team does not meet these goals. (AIA Document B214, *Standard Form of Architect's Services: LEED Certification*, is an example of the type of contract that may be used to define the scope of a professional's responsibilities with reference to a LEED project.) At each stage throughout the design and construction processes, it should be verified that the design and performance goals of the building are being met before making payment for the design team services (similar to the way that an owner should verify the percentage of construction completion prior to releasing payment to a contractor).

Lay the Foundation for Building Commissioning Activities

Building commissioning is the process of ensuring that building systems and equipment are designed, installed, tested, and capable of being operated and maintained according to the owner's operational needs. Building commissioning is a key part of designing and constructing high-performance buildings because it ensures that the additional time and money spent on controls, sensors, and equipment will be paid back over time through energy efficient building operation. Commissioning plans should be established during the pre-design phase, and commissioning activities will continue throughout the design, construction, and operations phases. The investment in commissioning an energy efficient building is a small part of the overall project cost, yet the payback can be large.

Commissioning can ensure that a new building begins its functional life at optimal productivity. Commissioning can also make it likelier that the building will maintain this level of performance throughout its life cycle. Information gathered during commissioning studies can be used to restore an existing building to its designed productivity levels and can ensure that building renovations and equipment upgrades function as intended.

Fundamental commissioning is a prerequisite for LEED project certification. LEED requirements stipulate that there will be a designated experienced commissioning authority (CxA) assigned to the project. For projects over 50,000 sq ft, the CxA must be independent of the project's design or construction management team. Commissioned systems must include HVAC & R and associated controls, lighting controls, domestic hot water systems, and renewable energy systems (if all these are a part of the project's scope).

To meet the LEED commissioning prerequisite, the commissioning team must

- designate a commissioning authority
- document the owner's project requirements and the basis of design for the energy-related systems
- develop commissioning requirements and incorporate them into the construction documents
- develop and follow a commissioning plan
- verify the installation and performance of the commissioned systems
- complete a commissioning report

To earn credit for enhanced commissioning, the commissioning team must

- review the design before mid-construction documents are produced
- review contractor submittals for commissioned systems
- develop a systems manual for commissioned systems
- verify that training requirements are met
- review building operation within ten months of substantial completion

During the creation of the commissioning plan, it is important to identify the building systems that will be analyzed. (To fulfill the LEED prerequisite, HVAC & R, lighting and daylighting control, domestic hot water, and renewable energy systems must all be commissioned.) In large and sophisticated buildings, it may be desirable to expand commissioning activities to cover multiple, integrated systems. Additional systems that should be considered for commissioning include mechanical, plumbing, electrical, controls, fire management, sprinklers, elevators, and audiovisual systems. Often, commissioning activities and analysis compare building performance against the standards established by organizations such as ASHRAE, which has published guidelines for commissioning HVAC systems.

Next, develop a strategy to implement the building commissioning plan. (ASHRAE Guideline 0, *The Commissioning Process*, provides a good overall model.) Ensure that the commissioning strategy encompasses all the necessary activities in each stage of the process.

The commissioning process should be defined in the construction specifications so that the general contractor and subcontractors are aware of any additional requirements that commissioning activities may impose on their scope of work. Specify the *facility startup amount* in the commissioning specifications. The facility startup amount is the total dollar amount that the project sponsor will allocate to commissioning, and needs to be determined before construction begins. A percentage of this sum will be released to the general contractor for coordination and to specific subcontractors for their commissioning work as the work is completed.

Ensure that the commissioning process is addressed in contract documents and construction meetings. Contract documents should accurately reflect the process agreed on for building commissioning. The architect should be asked to describe the commissioning process at any pre-bid or pre-construction conferences and at pre-commissioning meetings, so that all parties are aware that commissioning activities will be a priority throughout the project.

Prepare the design documentation and design criteria for the commissioned systems, including the following information.

- system building commissioning design documentation form
- system design criteria
- system description

Use these system design documents to

- verify with the building owner or users the programmatic requirements for the building and the occupants' planned activities and equipment
- verify the fire and life safety code requirements for the expected number of occupants
- verify with the mechanical engineer the ventilation requirements for the occupants and their equipment, so that the HVAC system is designed with enough capacity to provide outside air for the expected building population and heat-producing equipment

The design team and building operators should review the documents to confirm that the building is properly designed for its intended uses. After completion, the owner must bear in mind that the building's population and equipment should not be increased beyond the design limits for the HVAC system.

Consider Durability Planning and Management

A well-built building can last for centuries, and a building with a long life span is one of the most sustainable types of buildings possible. The LEED rating systems include credits that reward reuse of existing buildings and salvage and reuse of building materials where such approaches make sense—for example, it is wise to reuse the exterior masonry shell of a 200-year-old brick warehouse, but not advisable to reuse the 200-year-old, single-pane, poorly insulated windows in those walls.

LEED for Homes is the only rating system that specifically requires durability planning. Innovation and Design Process Prerequisite 2: Durability Management Process requires the completion of a durability risk assessment form. This survey of the home identifies areas of potential concern, such as the presence of radon, common pests, location near a floodplain or bodies of water, likelihood of natural disasters such as hurricanes, tornados, earthquakes, floods, wildfires, and blizzards, climate zone and number of heating and cooling degree days, and issues relevant to exterior water, interior moisture, air infiltration, and interstitial condensation. The homeowner is then responsible for developing a plan to address any risk factors identified in this survey. The green rater must inspect and verify all the durability measures noted on the durability management plan.

The following are some durability approaches that can be considered for all green building projects.

- Design for flexibility. Will it be easy to upgrade this structure to accommodate building systems and technologies that have not yet been invented?
- Use materials with a long life. A brick wall lasts a lot longer than vinyl siding.
- Keep materials with short predicted life spans out of wall assemblies, where they can fail but cannot be accessed for replacement. They can subsequently cause the whole assembly to fail.
- Use materials that promise a long life without extensive or expensive maintenance.
- Don't be trendy. Choose neutral finishes that will not go out of style and "need" to be replaced in ten years.

- Control moisture in the building. For example, use water-resistant materials on walls and floors.
- Shield materials that are likely to degrade if exposed to the sun.
- Develop a pest management plan.
- Design to withstand natural disasters that are risk factors in the project area. Consider exceeding life safety code requirements if prudent.

Additional information on the predicted life span of building materials and other considerations relevant to durability of construction can be found in *Durability by Design: A Guide for Residential Builders and Designers*, published by the U.S. Department of Housing and Urban Development and the Partnership for Advancing Technology in Housing. Another report on the topic was prepared by the National Association of Home Builders in 2007, titled *Study of the Life Expectancy of Home Components*. This document includes predicted life spans for a variety of construction materials and common home appliances and furnishings. Current links to these documents can be found at **www.ppi2pass.com/LEEDreferences**.

Evaluate Opportunities for Innovative and Regional Design

The pre-design phase is the best opportunity to evaluate opportunities for unique approaches or region-specific activities that can improve a project's sustainability and increase its LEED point tally. The intent and specifications for Regional Priority credits and criteria for earning Innovation in Design credits are discussed in the previous chapter of this book.

Green Building Basics: Design

The Design Phase

During the design phase, project team members must gather and analyze data, develop and evaluate design alternatives, and make decisions regarding the project priorities relative to the opportunities and drawbacks each present. The design phase is led by the design professionals (usually architects or engineers) and considers and integrates the work of the project consultants, such as building systems engineers, specialty systems consultants, landscape architects, and the commissioning agency.

In a LEED project, the work of the design team will be guided by the combination of credits determined most appropriate for the project. A variety of issues, technologies, and approaches must be considered to develop a comprehensive building design. The discussion in this chapter of the issues under consideration during the design phase is structured to align with the five primary LEED NC, CI, CS and EBO&M credit categories. (Innovation in Design and Regional Priority credits are covered in the chapter An Overview of LEED 2009.)

- Sustainable Sites (SS)
- Water Efficiency (WE)
- Energy and Atmosphere (EA)
- Materials and Resources (MR)
- Indoor Environmental Quality (IEQ)

Sustainable Sites: Issues and Approaches

Site selection and site planning have a major impact on the relative "greenness" of any facility. Site selection takes into consideration issues such as transportation options and travel distances for building occupants to reach the site, impact on wildlife corridors, and impact on site and regional hydrology (stormwater flows, wetlands, and so on). Decisions made during site planning will affect the building's immediate natural community as well as its potential energy consumption and occupant comfort.

Good site planning keeps site clearing to a minimum (which can save money by requiring less site demolition), helps preserve existing vegetation, and provides a low-maintenance landscape that doesn't need supplemental irrigation and fertilizer. Mature stands of native vegetation often provide the desired energy-conserving shade and wind control that would otherwise require years to develop from expensive new plantings. Thoughtful placement of a building on a site can promote energy conservation by taking advantage of natural site features such as topography, sunlight, shade, and breezes.

Carefully planned building placement should

- minimize stormwater runoff
- reduce the risk of erosion
- minimize habitat disturbance
- protect open space
- conserve energy by providing opportunities for passive solar heating and cooling, natural ventilation, and daylighting

The natural characteristics of a site influence elements of both site design and building design, including shape, massing, materials, surface-to-volume ratio, structural systems, mechanical systems, access and service, solar orientation, and provisions for security and fire safety. An inventory of existing boundaries and features can be a useful tool when evaluating a potential project site, documenting the advantages and constraints of the site. Once the site inventory is complete, further analysis will contribute to finding the most appropriate ecological and physical fit between the building and its site.

Analyzing the Site's Relationship to Community Resources

Choose a site that is near existing infrastructure and community resources, keeping in mind the availability of

- transportation alternatives that can reduce dependence on automobiles
- pedestrian access
- zoning requirements

Sites that have been previously developed are more likely than greenfield sites to have access to existing community infrastructure, such as roads, water, sewers, and electricity. Choosing a site that already has paved areas for parking will reduce or eliminate the need to construct new parking areas. This not only reduces construction costs but has benefits for sustainable design.

The automobile has a tremendous impact on the environment. When cars are moving, they consume fossil fuels and produce noise and emissions. When they are not moving, cars must be parked, and a parking area can increase how much stormwater runs off a site, raise the level of emissions and pollutants in the site's air, water, and soil (introduced from exhaust fumes, drops of oil, leaking antifreeze, and so on), and heighten the heat island effect by increasing the amount of low-albedo material on the ground plane.

One way that a sustainable building project can mitigate the effects of cars is by reducing the need for them. Alternatives to automobile use include walking, bicycling, participating in a carpool, sharing vehicles through a program such as Zipcar, and using public transportation. A project site can earn LEED points if it is located within a half mile of commuter rail, light rail, or subway stations or within a quarter mile of bus stops served by at least two routes. Projects that provide bicycle storage and showers and changing facilities for bicyclists may also be recognized with credits. Other incentives to reduce vehicle use can include shuttle services to and from public transportation hubs, ride boards, and offering a share in a vehicle sharing program as an employee benefit.

When automobile use is necessary, encourage the use of the most efficient vehicles available. Use of low-emitting and fuel-efficient vehicles can be encouraged by providing preferred parking for these vehicles or by discounting the fee that drivers must pay for parking; these incentives can also be used to reward employees who choose to carpool. Facilities can make it more convenient to use newer, more efficient types of vehicles providing alternative-fuel refueling stations on site. An organization can provide fuel-efficient vehicles for employee use or organize a vehicle sharing program that makes these types of automobiles available to building occupants.

A network of pedestrian paths connecting the project site to residential areas, community services, and public transportation make it possible for more building users to leave their cars at home. LEED credits may be awarded to projects that are located on a previously developed site (to take advantage of existing infrastructure) and within a half mile of a residential neighborhood and basic community services, including

- banks
- places of worship
- retail and service businesses such as grocery stores, dry cleaners, beauty salons, hardware stores, laundromats, and pharmacies
- child care facilities
- fire stations
- community resources such as libraries and community centers
- medical and dental offices
- senior care facilities
- parks
- post offices
- restaurants
- schools
- cultural facilities such as theaters and museums
- fitness centers

Pedestrian paths should be safe, well lit, well defined, and accessible to people of all levels of ability, which includes compliance with accessibility codes in effect in the jurisdiction. Wherever possible, paths should avoid crossing vehicular traffic; this can be accomplished with underpasses, pedestrian bridges, and the like. Where pedestrian and vehicular traffic must intersect, safety measures can be provided such as raised crosswalks and speed bumps or signage in the path of vehicular travel to alert motorists to the presence of pedestrians. At crosswalks, provide WALK/DON'T WALK signage and ensure that the WALK period for pedestrians is long enough to allow them to cross the street safely before the light changes. All sidewalks, crosswalks, and ramps should comply with all requirements for accessibility.

Walkways should be provided in logical locations. Some universities have chosen not to install paved walkways until the worn areas in the grass show which paths students choose as they walk to and from buildings on campus. This strategy can be used to avoid installing and then removing pathways that will not be regularly used.

Considering Local Zoning Requirements

Almost all projects must comply with the zoning requirements in effect in the jurisdiction where the project is located. (Exceptions include some projects on university campuses and military bases, where local ordinances may not apply.) Zoning ordinances are enacted in municipalities to control what types of structures are built in certain locations, as well as to define requirements for parking and minimum amounts of open space on the site. They prohibit the construction of incongruent building types within a specific area, which helps stabilize property values; for example, zoning ordinances would likely separate residential neighborhoods from heavy industrial uses. Zoning also helps community governments plan for the future, by restricting the capacity of the land and helping predict the types and capacities of utility systems that will become necessary in a specific area.

Zoning requirements may reference the following.

- *density*: how much square footage can be constructed on a given site or how many units can be built within a given area
- *site area*: minimum and/or maximum sizes of lots
- *floor area ratio*: the total area of a building divided by the area of the site on which it is constructed
- *height limitations*: restrictions on the number of floors that can be constructed in a building, generally designed to preserve the character of a neighborhood, to preserve views, or for safety, such as for buildings near an airport
- *setback*: the distance from the property line beyond which all construction must be placed
- *construction limits*: restrictions on which parts of a site may be disturbed by construction activity
- *open space*: a portion of a site that may not be built on
- *building footprint*: the total area of the building that is in contact with the ground plane
- *development footprint*: the total area (generally in square feet or acres) occupied by a development, including structures, open space, and roads

There may be other restrictions than these as well, such as provisions to reduce light pollution or specific landscaping restrictions.

LEED credits may be awarded to projects that meet but do not exceed local regulations for parking. Zoning requirements such as setbacks, floor area ratios, and height limitations may also influence the form of the building that can be constructed on a site and consequently influence the appearance of a neighborhood, as well as the feasibility of attaining certain LEED credits.

Determining if the Project Involves Rehabilitation or In-Fill vs. Undeveloped Site

In the big picture of sustainable land use, it is preferable to renovate or build out an existing building than to construct a new building from scratch. Adaptive reuse projects—using an existing building's shell but changing its use—help preserve the character of an existing neighborhood and have less impact on the surrounding natural environment. Reusing existing building stock or building on formerly developed sites does not require the creation of new infrastructure. Existing transportation systems can be used. Adding parking spaces and altering the transportation paths to and through the site may be unnecessary.

However, existing buildings may limit a designer's ability to control certain aspects of the mechanical systems and building envelope design. Therefore, the designer's focus shifts to the parts of the design that can be controlled: the effectiveness of the plan layout, selection of materials, lighting efficiency, furniture and finish selection, views to the outside, and availability of natural light. If renovating an existing building, the difference between the cost of renovations and the cost of constructing a completely new facility can be put towards additional energy efficient features, and tax credits or incentive grants may be available to help fund the project.

It is far preferable to build on a previously developed site than to develop undisturbed land. Consider whether redevelopment of an existing site is feasible. When planning site design for a previously disturbed site, consider taking the funds that are saved by making use of an existing infrastructure and applying them to enhanced landscape restoration.

If the chosen site includes an existing building that will be demolished, consider deconstructing the building and reusing the materials instead of sending them to the landfill. *Deconstruction* is an innovative tool intended to contribute to a community's revitalization; this is the process of selectively dismantling or removing materials from buildings prior to or instead of demolition. Deconstruction isn't a new idea—builders through the centuries have created new structures from pieces of older structures that had served their useful purpose. Today, the industry is beginning to recognize the value in salvaging these old elements to reduce consumption of natural resources and introduce a "one of a kind" element into a new structure. In addition, the deconstruction process can potentially support and complement other community objectives. Deconstruction has the potential to create job training and job opportunities for unskilled and unemployed workers, foster the creation and expansion of small businesses to handle the salvaged material from deconstruction projects, and benefit the environment by diverting valuable resources from crowded landfills into profitable uses. These things in turn can enable deconstruction to pay for itself by generating revenues and reducing landfill and disposal costs.

If demolition is necessary during the project, it is important to establish a construction waste management program to recycle or reuse demolished materials such as gypsum board, metal framing, ceiling grids, wood, carpet, light fixtures, and doors.

Building Configuration and Placement

Solar accessibility should be a part of site analysis. Does the building receive unobstructed solar radiation and sunshine between the hours of 9 a.m. and 3 p.m.? Are there major sky obstructions such as hills, trees, or adjacent buildings? Does the site allow an elongated east-west configuration? Careful site selection and building placement will provide opportunities for optimal daylight and solar utilization.

Orienting the building on an east-west axis will increase the potential for using daylighting strategies. An elongated building that has its major axis running east-west will be better positioned to capture solar heat during the winter months and reduce heat gain in summer on the east- and west-facing surfaces. Exposed east- and west-facing glass should be avoided wherever possible because it will cause excessive summer cooling loads. South-facing glass should be used with properly sized overhangs that limit radiation in warmer months.

To minimize heat loss and gain through the skin of a building, a compact shape is desirable. This characteristic is measured in the "skin to volume" ratio of the building. The most compact building form is a cube. This configuration, however, may place much of the floor area far from perimeter daylighting. On the other hand, an elongated building shape can optimize daylighting and ventilation by placing more of the building area near the perimeter. This need not compromise the overall thermal performance of the building, however, because the electrical load and cooling load savings achieved by a well-designed daylighting system can more than compensate for the increased skin losses.

Designing to Minimize Impact to Site

After completing the site inventory and analysis, look at compatibility between the overall building footprint and the site. Identify alternative site design concepts to minimize resource costs and site disruption. As the schematic design is developed, consider the following guidelines.

Natural Site Features

- Preserve natural drainage systems. Locate buildings, roadways, and parking so that water flowing off the developed site during extreme storm events will not cause environmental damage. Also, consider how drainage systems will be affected during construction, and avoid sites where the impact will be excessive. Use of temporary barriers during construction can help maintain existing drainage systems by preventing sediment from overloading retention areas.

- Locate driveways, parking, entrances, and loading docks on the building's south side. Desirable locations for driveways and parking in snowy climates are generally on south-facing slopes or the south sides of buildings to help avoid snow and ice buildup. Balance these needs with other priorities for infrastructure and landscape.

- Mitigate summer solar heat gain and minimize the cooling load through optimal orientation of the building. Orient the building with its long side aligned east-west. This orientation allows for the greatest winter solar gains and minimizes summer solar gains. Orienting a building toward true south, as opposed to 45 degrees off true south, makes it easier to manage solar gains.

- Minimize ground level wind loads. Control wind at the ground level by using vegetation, walls, and fences as windbreaks. The ill effects of wind can also be minimized through berming and earth sheltering.

Vegetation

- Minimize the disruption of native vegetation. Choose the location and size of buildings to avoid cutting mature vegetation and to minimize disruption to or disassociation from other natural features. Balance this strategy with the fire risk reduction guidelines applicable to the project.

- Use natural vegetation and adjust the building plan to minimize the visual impact of buildings and their imposition on environmental context.

Hydrology

- Design erosion control measures such as seeding, mulching, and geotextiles. Locate and design buildings to minimize erosion and effects on natural hydrological systems.

- Avoid hydrological system contamination. Safeguard the hydrological system from contamination during construction activities and building operation by designing sediment control measures such as silt fences, sediment traps, and fiber rolls.

- Allow precipitation to recharge groundwater naturally by providing pervious surfaces wherever possible.

Geology and Soils

- Minimize excavation and disturbance to groundcover.
- Minimize erosion. Avoid large impervious surface areas and building footprints that collect rain and create concentrated runoff from the site.

Heat Island Effect

On warm summer days, the air temperature in urban areas can be 6°F to 8°F (3°C to 4°C) hotter than in surrounding areas. This *heat island effect* contributes to smog and higher energy use. Heat is captured by materials that have low *albedo* (ability to reflect visible, infrared, and ultraviolet light) and low *thermal emissivity* (ability to release heat, also called *thermal emittance*). Surfaces with low albedo absorb a high percentage of the solar energy that strikes them. An albedo of 0.0 indicates total absorption of solar radiation, and a 1.0 value represents total reflectivity.

Some absorbed energy is conducted into ground and buildings, some is convected to the air (leading to higher air temperatures), and some is re-radiated to the sky. Surfaces with low emissivity cannot effectively radiate to the sky and, therefore, get hot. The solar reflectance index (SRI) combines albedo and emittance into a single value, expressed either as a fraction (0.0 to 1.0) or as a percentage. ASTM Standard E1980, *Standard Practice for Calculating Solar Reflectance Index of Horizontal and Low-Sloped Opaque Surfaces*, can help in determining a material's SRI value, as can information from the manufacturer.

LEED credits distinguish between *roof* and *non-roof* surfaces. The non-roof surfaces that contribute most to the heat island effect are inanimate elements such as roads, sidewalks, parking lots, patios, and other paved areas; these are collectively known as *hardscape*.

Effective heat island reduction strategies include the following.

- Reduce the roof area by minimizing the building footprint.
- Plant trees for shade.
- Reduce or avoid the use of air conditioning.
- Use less pavement throughout the site. When pavement is needed, use paving that is at least 50% pervious.
- Use paving and roofing materials with a high SRI value. According to USGBC, new asphalt has an SRI of zero (all solar radiation is absorbed), while new white portland cement concrete has an SRI of 86. Other pavement types generally range between these extremes, with a 35 SRI for new gray concrete. Those LEED credits that address the heat island effect require an SRI of at least 29 for a minimum of 50% of the paved areas.
- Use a green roof, or vegetated roof. A green roof is a roofing system in which the outermost layer consists of plants growing in soil or other growing medium.

Parking and Pavement

Parking can be the single greatest use of land area at a facility. Choosing strategies that reduce the area devoted to parking results in

- less surface runoff (stormwater)
- fewer pollutants in surface runoff
- greater groundwater recharge
- more green space available for occupant use and enjoyment

•improved air quality from an abundance of oxygen-producing plants
•reduced heat island effect

Strive to increase the habitat for nature and decrease the "habitat" for cars. To reduce the demand for parking spaces, provide building occupants with alternative transportation options and incentives for using public transportation, carpooling, or bicycling. Another issue is the visual glare that often accompanies parking areas adjacent to buildings. Abate this glare by screening or shading the parking lot with vegetation.

LEED projects should strive to meet but not exceed local code requirements for parking. If significant parking areas must be included on the building site, design bioretention areas into the parking lot landscaping as part of the exterior water management strategy. Plantings within these areas have the added advantage of providing shade.

Exterior Water Management

Sustainable site development can help solve regional watershed problems at the source by minimizing runoff and treating water on site. Good site design and water management practices address water issues by

- increasing the permeability of constructed pavements
- capturing and treating excess runoff by means of natural soil and biological processes
- minimizing or eliminating potable water usage in the landscape (through xeriscaping and elimination of sprinkler systems)
- using natural landscape systems to maintain or restore the infiltrating, cleansing, and storing functions of soils, plants, and groundwater

Stormwater is precipitation that does not soak into the ground or evaporate but flows along the surface of the ground as runoff. Conventional practice for stormwater management—concentrating runoff and carrying it off a site as quickly as possible through storm sewers—contributes to various environmental problems, including erosion, downstream flooding, pollution of surface waters, and reduced groundwater recharge.

There are two basic challenges in sustainable stormwater management.

- *Quantity Control.* Drainage and flood control measures are designed to manage the quantity of stormwater runoff generated during a design-basis storm event (generally considered to be the most severe storm event likely to occur within a specified time period, such as 100 years). Impervious surfaces such as rooftops and parking lots increase the amount of water that leaves the site as runoff. Because these impervious surfaces make up most of a conventionally designed site, the water cannot seep into the ground and must be dealt with in other ways.
- *Quality Control.* Water quality control is based on management of on-site sources of pollutants found in the stormwater and, if necessary, treating these pollutants before they leave the site. Pollutants found in stormwater can include sediment, foreign substances such as motor oil or antifreeze that has leaked from vehicles, salts used on icy sidewalks, and fertilizers or pesticides that may be applied to landscape areas. In addition to pollutants at ground level, rooftop surfaces typically accumulate pollutants that are deposited from the atmosphere or carried by the air during adverse weather.

The primary goal of sustainable stormwater management is to allow no more runoff than was produced by the undeveloped site. Achievement of this design goal requires an integrated approach that minimizes runoff and by promoting infiltration of stormwater into the sub-surface. Other strategies include the use of pervious paving materials, reducing the amount of parking required on a site by locating the facility near alternative means of transportation, designing parking underneath the building to allow for more green space on the site, capturing rainwater for nonpotable uses inside the building or for irrigation, and integrating a vegetated roof into the design. These approaches all reduce the amount of runoff (and potential pollutants) that leave the site. An integrated design approach involves configuring the location and placement of impervious surfaces, specifying land-based structural practices (stormwater storage and treatment) for stormwater pollution control, and integrating native landscaping into the overall site development.

Investigate the feasibility of applying stormwater management strategies to treat and retain stormwater on the site. Each of these strategies requires specific maintenance practices for proper operation.

Water Efficiency: Issues and Approaches

Water efficiency is the planned management of potable (drinkable) water to prevent its waste, overuse, and exploitation. Effective water efficiency planning seeks to "do more with less," without sacrificing environmental performance.

Outdoor Water Efficiency

There are two approaches to using potable water more efficiently in the landscape.

- Reduce the amount of potable water used for irrigation and landscaping by preserving or reintroducing native or drought-tolerant vegetation that is already optimized for the area's natural levels of precipitation. This approach is sometimes referred to as *xeriscaping*. If plantings that need additional water are desired, group them by similar water and soil needs. Irrigate efficiently, using a surface drip or underground irrigation system rather than one that sprays water into the air.

- Recycle or use water collected by graywater or process recycling systems. Reclaimed wastewater, sometimes called irrigation quality (IQ) water, is another possible source for irrigation water. Reclaimed water is processed in a wastewater treatment plant, but is only minimally treated to make it suitable for nonpotable uses such as landscape irrigation, cooling towers, industrial process uses, toilet flushing, and fire protection. Reclaimed water must be scrupulously isolated from potable water distribution, and all IQ hose bibs must be clearly marked as "nonpotable."

Rainwater or stormwater can be *harvested* for nonpotable uses, such as by collecting runoff from a roof into a cistern and using it for irrigation.

Graywater is untreated wastewater that does not contain any organic matter. It is often generated from showers and baths, laundry machines, and bathroom sinks. Graywater can be used for below-ground irrigation, but it is not recommended for above-ground irrigation, and should never be used for watering edible plants, such as vegetable gardens, because of the risk of contamination. *Blackwater* is wastewater that is contaminated with organic matter and cannot be reused; this includes water from toilets, urinals, kitchen sinks, and dishwashers (and sometimes washing machines, if they are used for laundering cloth diapers). The most important distinction between graywater and blackwater is not its source, but what may be in it.

Indoor Water Efficiency

LEED prerequisites require a certified building to use at least 20% less water indoors than a baseline water use calculated for the building (irrigation is not included). The baseline water usage is calculated from several factors, including

- numbers of toilets and lavatory faucets
- number of urinals (for commercial buildings)
- number of pre-rinse spray valves (for food service uses)
- numbers of kitchen faucets and showerheads (for residential buildings)
- full-time equivalent (FTE) occupancy

The FTE occupancy is essentially the total number of occupant-hours spent in the building, divided by eight hours, which is regarded as the length of one standard full-time occupancy. Details of how to calculate FTE occupancy are given in the LEED reference guides.

A variety of strategies can be employed to reduce indoor water use, including

- specifying water-conserving or waterless fixtures, including faucets, sinks, showers, toilets, and urinals
- using graywater for flushing toilets

Energy and Atmosphere: Issues and Approaches

A building's components—from the foundation to the roof—can either be detrimental to the building's energy efficiency or enhance its performance and increase the comfort of its occupants. In 2008, USGBC hired the New Buildings Institute to conduct a study of 121 buildings which were LEED certified under the LEED NC v2.0 rating system. NBI's findings, summarized in a report entitled *Energy Performance of LEED for New Construction Buildings*, revealed that projects that have attained LEED certification perform significantly better in energy use tests than comparable buildings designed and constructed with traditional techniques. On average, a LEED-certified building in the study uses 25% to 30% less energy than the national average; this study suggests that actual performance of these buildings is similar to that predicted with energy modeling.

Many new energy-saving components are coming to market that can perform their primary job—protecting the building's occupants from the external environment—while at the same time also saving energy. For example, roof shingles are available that are faced with heat-reflective coatings. Instead of absorbing the sun's heat, these shingles send it away from the building. Roof shingles with integrated photovoltaic cells can generate electricity for use in the building. Compact fluorescent lights use less energy and put less heat into the building, and advances in HVAC technology and efficiency result in more comfortable spaces that use less energy to maintain a suitable indoor environment.

The benefits of these components won't be realized unless they are fully integrated into the whole-building design. Building components influence each other. To make sure they perform optimally, component performance and interaction should be modeled during the design phase. This applies to new construction as well as building renovations.

Building components include

- the building envelope: windows, doors, insulation, foundations, framing, and roofs
- sources of electricity: photovoltaic (PV) cells and other renewable energy sources, such as cogeneration, wind turbines, alternative fuels, and purchasing green power
- heating and cooling systems: passive and active solar heating and cooling, heat pumps, geothermal energy, alternative fuels, and alternative methods of ventilation
- water heating: solar hot water, point-of-use, and other energy-saving systems
- lighting and daylighting: selection and placement of glazing, natural lighting techniques, and energy efficient lamps and luminaires
- appliances and equipment: Energy Star-rated office equipment and appliances

The Building Envelope

The building envelope is a critical component of any facility. It protects the building's occupants and plays a major role in regulating the indoor environment. Consisting of the building's foundation, roof, walls, windows, and doors, the building envelope controls the flow of energy between the interior and exterior of the building. The building envelope can be considered the *selective pathway* by which a building works with the climate, responding to heating, cooling, ventilation, and natural lighting needs.

In a new building project, consideration of the elements that make up the building envelope should begin during the pre-design phase. Optimal design of the building envelope may lead to significant reductions in heating and cooling loads—which in turn can allow downsizing of mechanical equipment. When the right strategies are integrated, the extra cost for a high-performance envelope may be recouped through savings achieved by installing smaller HVAC equipment.

In existing facilities, facility managers have much less opportunity to change most envelope components. Insulation of the building envelope can sometimes be improved as a part of repair or maintenance projects. During reroofing, extra insulation can typically be added with little difficulty. Windows and insulation can be upgraded during more significant building improvements and renovations. The make-up of the existing wall assembly generally remains unchanged.

It is usually quite feasible to reduce the infiltration of outside air into the building by improving the tightness of the building envelope. Air infiltration can be reduced in a variety of ways.

- Replace existing door weatherstripping
- Apply air sealant foam products to any gaps in the exterior wall. Likely locations for air infiltration include the roof/wall connection (eaves), improperly installed ridge vents, penetrations through the roof or wall, and other locations where there is a change in materials.

The envelope design must balance requirements for ventilation and daylight while providing thermal and moisture protection appropriate to climatic conditions. Envelope design is a major factor in determining the amount of energy a building will use in its operation. Also, the overall environmental life cycle impacts and energy costs associated with the production and transportation of different envelope materials vary greatly.

In keeping with the whole-building approach, the entire design team must consider design of the envelope in conjunction with other design elements, including selection of materials, the use of daylighting and other passive solar design strategies, strategies for heating, ventilating, and air conditioning (HVAC), and project performance goals. One of the most important factors affecting envelope design is climate. Hot/dry, hot/moist, temperate, and cold climates will suggest different design strategies. Specific designs and materials can take advantage of a climate's beneficial aspects and mitigate its drawbacks.

A second important factor in envelope design is what occurs inside the building. A building's thermal loads may be primarily internal (generated from people and equipment) or external (generated from the sun and weather). This affects the rate at which a building gains or loses heat. Building volume and siting also have significant impacts upon the efficiency and requirements of the building envelope. Careful study is required to arrive at a building footprint and orientation that works in combination with the building envelope to maximize energy benefit.

Openings are located in the building envelope to provide physical access to a building, create views to the outside, admit daylight for lighting and solar energy for heating, and supply natural ventilation. The form, size, and location of the openings vary depending on the role they play in the building envelope. Window glazing can be used to affect heating and cooling requirements and occupant comfort by controlling the type and amount of light that passes through windows.

Decisions about construction details and specified materials also play a crucial role in design of the building envelope. Building materials conduct heat at different rates. Components of the envelope, such as foundation walls, sills, studs, joists, and connectors, can create *thermal bridges* or paths for the transfer of thermal energy across the wall assembly. Wise detailing decisions, including appropriate choice and placement of insulation material, are essential to assure thermal efficiency.

For buildings dominated by cooling loads, it makes sense to provide exterior finishes with high reflectivity or wall-shading devices that reduce solar gain. Reflective roofing products help reduce cooling loads because the roof is exposed to the sun for the entire operating day. Specify roofing products that carry the Energy Star roof label—low-slope roofing products with this label have an initial reflectivity of at least 65%. Energy Star roof products are widely available in single-ply and other types of roofing systems.

Wall shading can reduce solar heat gain significantly—use roof overhangs, window shades, awnings, a canopy of mature trees, or other vegetative plantings such as trellises with deciduous vines. To reduce cooling loads, wall shading on the east and west facades is most important. The south facade of a building with year-round cooling loads will benefit from shading as well. In new construction, providing architectural features that shade walls and glazing should be considered. In existing buildings, vegetative shading options are generally more feasible.

All the following play into design decisions about the building envelope.

- climate considerations
- insulation
- fenestration: doors, windows, and openings
- foundations
- framing and wall systems
- roofs

- thermal efficiency
- reflectivity
- moisture buildup

Climate Considerations

Assess the local climate (using typical meteorological year data) to determine appropriate envelope materials and building designs. Solar gain on roofs and walls and in the building's interior through window openings can be either a benefit or a hindrance to heating, cooling, and occupant comfort; a thorough understanding of solar geometry specific to the site is crucial to proper envelope design. The climate of the project area determines the appropriate strategies for envelope design.

Strategies for Hot/Dry Climates

Use materials with high thermal mass. Buildings in hot/dry climates with significant day-to-night temperature swings have traditionally employed thick walls constructed from materials with high mass, such as adobe and masonry. Openings on the north and west facades are limited, and large southern openings are detailed to exclude direct sun in the summer and admit it in winter. Often this is accomplished with the use of overhangs "tuned" to the sun's location in the sky at different times of the year.

Specifying building materials with high thermal mass and adequate thickness will lessen and delay the impact of temperature variations from outside the wall to the wall's interior. The material's high thermal capacity allows heat to penetrate slowly through the wall or roof. Because the temperature in hot/dry climates tends to fall considerably after sunset, the result is a thermal "flywheel effect"—the building interior is cooler than the exterior during the day and warmer than the exterior at night.

Strategies for Hot/Moist Climates

In hot/moist climates, use materials with low thermal capacity. In these environments, where nighttime temperatures do not drop considerably below daytime highs, light materials with little thermal capacity are preferred. In some hot/moist climates, masonry is a common building material because it functions as a dessicant. Roofs and walls should be protected by plant material or overhangs. Large openings should be located primarily on the north and south sides of the envelope to catch breezes or encourage stack ventilation; these openings should be protected from the summer sun.

Strategies for Temperate Climates

Select materials based on the building's location and the heating/cooling strategy to be used. Determine the thermal capacity of materials for buildings in temperate climates based on the specific location and the heating/cooling strategy employed. Walls should be well insulated. Openings in the skin should be shaded during hot times of the year and unshaded during cool months. This can be accomplished by designing roof overhangs sized to respond to solar geometries at the site, or by specifying operable awnings.

Strategies for Cold Climates

Design wind-tight and well-insulated building envelopes. The thermal capacity of materials that should be used in colder climates will depend on the use of the building and the heating strategy employed. A building that is conventionally heated and occupied intermittently should not be constructed with high-mass materials because it will take longer to reheat the space to a comfortable temperature. Conversely, a solar heating strategy will necessitate the incorporation of massive materials, either in the envelope or in other building elements. Where solar gain is not used for heating, the floor plan should be as compact as possible to minimize the area of building skin.

Insulation

The amount of wall insulation can be increased at a relatively low cost in new construction. Consider as well the hot-cold pathway and ways to reduce *thermal bridging*, which can significantly degrade the rated performance of cavity-fill insulation. For example, when framing the building with highly conductive steel, specify a layer of rigid insulation to interrupt heat transfer through the wall.

Boosting wall insulation levels in existing buildings is difficult without expensive building modifications. One option for increasing the *R*-value of existing buildings' envelopes is to add an exterior insulation and finish system (EIFS) on the outside of the current building skin. Such a strategy may be objectionable for aesthetic reasons. An EIFS system should include a drainage layer to accommodate small leaks that may occur over time and prevent water from being trapped within the assembly.

Another strategy that does not affect the existing appearance of the building is to install blown-in insulation in the wall cavities and seal any points where air infiltration has been identified. Typically, air infiltrates a building at roof gables, eaves, and anywhere that building equipment penetrates the building envelope. Insulation and infiltration are two different issues; simply increasing insulation without providing an air barrier will not solve infiltration problems.

Roof insulation can typically be increased relatively easily during reroofing. At the time of reroofing, consider switching to a protected-membrane roofing system, which will allow reuse of the rigid insulation during future reroofing—thus greatly cutting down on the amount of material directed to the landfill.

While we naturally think of insulation as a strategy for cold climates, it also makes sense in warm climates where high levels of cooling are required. The addition of insulation can significantly reduce air conditioning costs and should be considered during any major renovation project. Roofs and attics should receive priority attention for insulation retrofits because of the ease of installation and the relatively low cost.

Fenestration

When choosing the size and position of doors, windows, and vents in the building envelope, carefully consider daylighting, heating, and ventilating strategies. The prescribed form, size, and location of openings may vary depending on how each affects the building envelope and the objective of the opening. A window meant only to provide a view need not open, but a window intended for ventilation must do so. High windows are preferable because they can bring light deeper into the interior of a space and eliminate glare. Another strategy is to place light shelves below those high windows to help reflect the light into the space and illuminate the ceiling plane.

Vestibules at building entrances should be designed to avoid the loss of cooled or heated air to the exterior. The negative impact of door openings on heating or cooling loads can be reduced with airlocks—two sets of doors placed in succession to prevent outdoor air from interacting directly with conditioned air within the building. Weatherstripping materials should be installed at the interior set of doors.

Openings in the building envelope can be shaded during hot weather to reduce the amount of direct sunlight that penetrates to the interior of the building. Overhangs or deciduous plant materials on southern orientations shade exterior walls during warmer seasons. Be aware, however, that even though deciduous plants lose their leaves in the winter, the remaining structure of the tree or vine can cut solar gains in the winter by 20% or more. Shade window openings or use light shelves at work areas at any time of year to minimize thermal discomfort from direct radiation and visual discomfort from glare.

In all but the mildest climates, select double- or triple-paned windows with as high an *R*-value as possible and specify proper shading coefficients for the windows' locations. (As *R*-values increase, costs go up, so it is important to consider this decision relative to the project's budget.) *R*-value is a measure of resistance to heat flow across a wall or window assembly; the higher the *R*-value, the more resistant it is and the lower the energy loss. A *shading coefficient* is a ratio used to simplify comparisons among different types of heat-reducing glass. The shading coefficient of clear double-strength glass is 1.0, so a product with a shading coefficient of 0.75 transmits three-quarters of the solar energy permitted through its clear counterpart.

Select the proper type of glazing for windows. Glazings that contain layers of metallic coatings or tints can be specified to either absorb or reflect specific wavelengths in the solar spectrum. The combination of layers in the glazing allows wavelengths in the visible spectrum (daylight) to pass through the window, while other wavelengths, such as near-infrared (which provides heat) and ultraviolet (which can damage fabric), are reflected. In this way, the admission of excess heat and damaging ultraviolet light can be reduced while the benefits of natural lighting are retained. More advanced windows use glazings that adapt to changing environmental conditions, such as windows with tinting that increases under direct sunlight and decreases as light levels are reduced. Research is being conducted on windows that can be adjusted by the building occupants to allow more or less heat into a building space.

Glazing systems have a huge impact on energy consumption, and glazing modifications are one of the most effective strategies for improving the energy efficiency of a building. Appropriate glazing choices vary greatly depending on the location of the facility, the uses of the building, and the glazing's placement on the building's facade. In hot climates, the primary strategy is to control heat gain by keeping solar energy from entering the interior space while allowing reasonable visible light transmittance for views and daylighting. Solar screens that intercept solar radiation, or films that prevent infrared and ultraviolet transmission while allowing good visibility, are useful retrofits for hot climates. In colder climates, the focus shifts to reducing heat loss to the outdoors and (in some cases) allowing desirable solar radiation to enter. Windows with two or three glazing layers that utilize low-emissivity coatings will minimize the transmission of conductive energy. Filling the spaces between the glazing layers with an inert, low-conductivity gas such as argon will further reduce heat flow.

Much heat is also lost through a window's frame. For optimal energy performance, specify a frame material with low conductivity, such as wood or vinyl. If metal frames are used, make sure the frame design includes thermal breaks. In addition to reducing heat loss, a good window frame will help prevent condensation within the airspaces between panes; even the most expensive high-performance glazings may suffer from condensation problems if panes are mounted in inappropriate frames or window sashes.

The light pouring through the building's windows can be a source of visual discomfort when solar gain and glare increase contrast and interfere with workstation visibility. The benefits of daylighting will be negated if the glare forces occupants to close blinds and turn on electric lights. This is especially important to consider when building occupants will be using computer screens or must perform visually demanding tasks. If known, also consider the lighting conditions those employees currently have in their workspaces; people are extremely sensitive to changes in light levels, and if they all declare it "too dark" and bring in incandescent lamps, the strategy has failed.

Designers should choose appropriate window technologies that are cost effective for the project's unique climate conditions. Computer modeling can help to determine which glazing system is most appropriate for a particular climate. In coastal California, for example, single-paned glazing may be all that can be economically justified, while in both hotter and colder climates, more sophisticated glazing systems are likely to be much more effective.

Foundations

For each type of building foundation—basement, slab on grade, and crawl space—there are several construction systems and products from which to choose.

- cast-in-place concrete
- concrete or masonry blocks
- insulating concrete forms
- precast concrete
- permanent wood foundations

Most of these foundation systems can be designed to meet necessary structural, thermal, radon, and moisture control requirements. In a whole-building design strategy, considering the climate and the source of the materials will help determine an appropriate choice. (Moisture control is also a factor in durability planning. See the section on durability planning and management in the previous chapter.)

Cast-in-Place Concrete

Cast-in-place concrete construction involves setting up removable forms for the pouring of concrete foundation walls. Cast-in-place concrete can be used to construct all three types of foundations—basement, slab on grade, and crawl space. Rigid foam board insulation is usually placed between the removable forms and held in place with a system of nonconductive ties. Then concrete is poured on either side of the foam. This allows the assembly to achieve a greater R-value than poured concrete alone. Steel rebar is used to add strength to the wall. Once the concrete has cured, the forms can be removed and reused as many as 3000 times with minimum maintenance.

Concrete Masonry Units

Another common foundation system is the use of concrete or masonry blocks, which are often referred to as *concrete masonry units* (CMU). When using blocks to build a foundation wall, the block cores should be filled with insulation as the wall is constructed. Filling the cores with high-pressure foam works better than most other block-filling methods, such as poured-in insulations like polystyrene beads or vermiculite. Foam inserts for the block cores are also available. These are slipped inside the cavities of the blocks as they are mortared into place.

Some concrete block manufacturers attempt to increase the thermal resistance of their product by adding materials such as polystyrene or wood chips to the concrete mix. Although insulating the block cavities and specifying special block designs can improve a block wall's thermal characteristics, it doesn't reduce heat movement through the wall very much in comparison to rigid insulation installed over the surface of the blocks, either on the exterior or interior of the foundation walls.

Insulating Concrete Forms

Insulating concrete forms (ICFs) serve as both foundation structure and insulation. ICFs are forms for poured concrete walls that stay in place as a permanent part of the wall assembly. The forms, made of rigid foam insulation, are either preformed interlocking blocks or separate panels connected with plastic ties. The forms are left in place to provide both continuous insulation and a substrate for installing drywall on the inside.

Although all ICFs are identical in principle, various brands differ widely in the details of their shapes, cavities, and component parts. Currently, about one-third of all ICFs sold are used in residential basements.

Precast Concrete

Precast concrete panels provide high *R*-values, structural integrity, and termite protection, and minimize air infiltration as well. Precast concrete foundation walls and panels are manufactured off site. Most are pre-insulated with rigid foamboard. Additional insulation usually can be added inside the wall cavity to achieve a higher *R*-value. The panels typically come in lengths of up to 16 feet (4.9 m) and in standard heights of 4 feet (1.2 m), 8 feet (2.4 m), and 10 feet (3.0 m). Once constructed, they're transported to the building site, where a crane lifts them into place.

Permanent Wood Foundation

Permanent wood foundation (PWF) construction is similar to wood-framed exterior wall construction. Any type of insulation product may be installed in conjunction with this foundation system. However, because PWF walls are used below grade, all lumber and plywood must be pressure-treated with preservatives to ward against decay and termites. This is a potential disadvantage of this type of system, as the preservatives injected into the wood can cause indoor air quality issues. In addition, wood foundations don't have the same degree of structural integrity as concrete foundation systems.

Framing and Wall Systems

A whole-building design strategy should include consideration of a variety of framing materials and products. When selecting a framing system and material, it's important to consider the structural properties of the framing materials and the type of insulation that will be used with the structural elements.

Wood

Traditionally, "stick-built" buildings—those entirely or mostly constructed on the site—use a framing system consisting of dimensional lumber covered by some type of sheathing. Wood construction makes it possible for a small crew to construct a large project and is popular because of the ease of construction, flexibility, availability of materials and components, and economy of the system.

Builders can choose from a variety of wood sheathing products that vary in cost, strength, insulation value, and ease of installation. Plywood and oriented strand board (OSB) are the strongest and most durable. Wood sheathing panels add shear and racking strength—important characteristics that help a structure withstand the forces of high winds and earthquakes. Wood-sheathed walls are also easy to build and easy to insulate to achieve high *R*-values.

While manufactured wood products often perform as well or better than dimensional lumber, the glues used in the manufacturing process can contribute to indoor air quality problems. Engineered wood products made with exterior-type glues (phenolic resins) and urethane (polyurea) adhesives give off some of the lowest emissions. However, because they're susceptible to damage from termites and dry rot, some wood products also are pressure-treated with preservatives. These glues and preservatives can negatively affect indoor air quality if not used properly.

Structural Insulated Panels

Structural insulated panels (SIPs) have both structural and insulative properties. They consist of engineered laminate with a foam core 4 inches to 8 inches (10 cm to 20 cm) thick, sandwiched between structural facings on each side. The most common types of facings are drywall and structural wood sheathing such as plywood and oriented strand board (OSB).

R-values for SIPs range from about R-4 to R-6 per inch (2.5 cm) of thickness, depending on the type of foam core used. Most SIPs contain expanded polystyrene (EPS) foam cores (also known as beadboard), but some manufacturers choose to use polyurethane or isocyanurate as the insulating material.

Although SIPs cost more than traditional building materials, installation is less labor intensive. Therefore, the total cost is roughly the same.

Steel

Steel is commonly used in the construction of commercial buildings, and it can also be used in residential construction. Steel buildings that utilize light-gage steel stud framing make use of nearly the same framing techniques employed in wood-framed buildings. Construction costs for both materials are typically about the same, but the relative costs of wood and steel in the marketplace at the time of construction may skew this one way or the other.

Unlike wood, steel is impervious to termites. It provides added resistance to fire and earthquake. Steel ceiling joists can span greater distances than wooden ones, allowing new design possibilities for architects and builders.

Steel conducts heat more than 300 times faster than wood, so steel studs can create thermal bridges to the outside of the building and must be carefully detailed to prevent heat loss. Even the fasteners used to attach building materials to one another can become a heat loss issue. Screws attached to steel studs can reduce the insulating value of the foam sheathing by 39%. Therefore, when steel framing is used, it is important to insulate properly and to detail connections carefully. In cold climates, the additional insulation needed to prevent heat transfer might reduce the cost-effectiveness of steel framing.

Concrete

Concrete framing provides structural integrity, termite protection, and thermal insulation, and reduces air infiltration. It also readily absorbs heat, making it ideal for use as thermal mass in passive solar building design. There are many concrete framing options and products.

Masonry

Masonry refers to a system of concrete masonry units assembled with mortar. (See the section on foundations earlier in this chapter for more information on masonry.)

A Trombe wall is a special type of masonry wall used for thermal storage in passive solar building design. A typical Trombe wall consists of an 8 inch to 16 inch (20 cm to 41 cm) thick masonry wall coated with a dark, heat-absorbing material and faced with a single or double layer of glass. The glass is placed $^3/_4$ inch to 6 inches (2 cm to 15 cm) from the masonry wall to create a small airspace. Heat from sunlight passing through the glass is absorbed by the dark surface, stored in the wall, and conducted slowly inward through the masonry.

Applying a *selective surface* to a Trombe wall improves its performance by reducing the amount of infrared energy radiated back through the glass. A selective surface is a sheet of metal foil glued to the outside surface of the wall. It absorbs almost all the radiation in the visible portion of the solar spectrum and emits very little in the infrared range. High absorbency turns the light into heat at the wall's surface, and low emittance prevents the heat from radiating back toward the glass. Although less effective than a selective surface, painting the wall with black, absorptive paint will also help the wall absorb the sun's heat.

Heat will take about eight to ten hours to reach the interior of the building through an 8 inch (20 cm) thick Trombe wall (heat travels through a concrete wall at rate of about 1 inch (2.5 cm) per hour). This means that rooms remain comfortable through the day and receive slow, even heating for many hours after the sun sets, greatly reducing the need for conventional heating. Rooms heated by Trombe walls often feel more comfortable than those heated by forced-air furnaces because of the wall's radiantly warm surface, even at lower air temperatures.

Architects can use Trombe walls in conjunction with windows, eaves, and other building design elements to evenly balance the delivery of solar heat. Strategically placed windows will heat a building during the day with direct solar gains. At the same time, the Trombe wall absorbs and stores heat for evening use. Properly sized overhangs shade the Trombe wall during the summer when the sun is high. Shading the Trombe wall keeps it from getting hot during the time of the year when heating is not needed.

Autoclaved Aerated Concrete

Autoclaved aerated concrete comes in the form of planks or blocks. These units are much lighter than traditional concrete blocks because they use a special mixture of sand, limestone, cement, and an expanding agent.

Insulating Concrete Forms

An insulating concrete form (ICF) is made from concrete poured into a foam form that is left in place to provide insulation. Walls are constructed by stacking ICFs and cutting them where needed to fit windows, corners, and so on. Steel rebar is placed horizontally and vertically within the form to provide strength. Although all ICFs are identical in principle, the various brands differ widely in the details of their shapes, cavities, and component parts. (See the section on foundations earlier in this chapter for more information on ICFs.)

Cast-in-Place Concrete

Cast-in-place concrete construction involves setting up removable or temporary forms for the pouring of concrete walls. Unlike ICFs, the forms are removed after the concrete hardens. Before the concrete is poured, rigid foamboard insulation is usually placed within the empty space between the forms and steadied with nonconductive ties; the concrete is then poured into the forms so that the insulation board is encased in the concrete. Steel rebar is also generally used to add strength to the wall. Cast-in-place concrete buildings are typically constructed in one of three ways.

- Only the exterior walls are cast-in-place concrete, with interior walls and floor and ceiling assemblies constructed of other materials
- Both the exterior and interior walls are cast-in-place concrete, with floor and ceiling assemblies constructed of other materials
- Floors, ceilings, exterior walls, and interior walls are all constructed of cast-in-place concrete

Precast Concrete

Precast concrete walls and panels are manufactured in a factory and transported to the project site. Most are pre-insulated with rigid foamboard, but additional insulation can be added inside the wall cavity to achieve a higher R-value. The panels typically come in lengths of up to 16 feet (4.9 m) and in standard heights of 4 feet (1.2 m), 8 feet (2.4 m), and 10 feet (3.0 m). A crane is needed to lift them into place. Precast concrete walls have been shown to be very effective in passive solar design. Precast construction is also used for building elements, such as prison cells, for which continuity of construction is a primary concern. (See the section on foundations earlier in this chapter for more information on precast concrete.)

Thermal Mass and High-Mass Materials (Including Straw Bale Construction)

Thermal mass can reduce energy use in climates where buildings need to be cooled during the day and heated at night. To optimize the effects of the thermal mass, additional insulation materials are typically added. Therefore, insulating a building using a thermal mass system usually costs more than insulating a typical wood-framed building. This increase is often offset by other lowered construction costs, such as reduced use of drywall and a shorter construction period. The R-values of concrete construction methods typically range from R-1 to R-2 per inch of thickness.

Straw bale construction can yield about R-2.4 per inch (2.5 cm) of thickness. Straw panels are also available, which are usually 2 inches to 4 inches (5 cm to 10 cm) thick and faced with heavyweight kraft paper on each side. Although manufacturers' claims vary, R-values range from about R-1.4 to R-2 per inch (2.5 cm) of thickness. They also make effective sound-absorbing panels for interior partitions. Some manufacturers have developed structural insulated panels from multiple-layered, compressed-straw panels.

Roofs

Roofs play a key role in protecting building occupants and interiors from outside weather conditions, keeping the inside of the building dry and comfortable. The roof, insulation, and ventilation systems must all work together to keep the building free of moisture. Roofs also provide protection from the sun. In fact, if designed correctly, roof overhangs can protect the building's exterior walls from moisture and sun and help achieve a successful passive solar design.

Different roof designs and materials are used for residential and commercial buildings. Commercial buildings typically have low-slope or flat roofs, while the roofs on most homes are pitched at a slope greater than 3:12. The concerns regarding moisture, standing water, durability, and appearance are different for the two kinds of buildings, and this is reflected in the choices of roofing materials. Commercial projects often use rubber or built-up roofing materials, while residential projects are more likely to use asphalt shingles or metal.

Roof design can affect the building's thermal performance. For example, in a metal-framed building, the metal eaves can act as thermal fins, moving heat out of the building, which is not desirable in cool climates.

A number of roofing choices are available for high-performance buildings. New roof shingles on the market today produce electricity using solar technology and photovoltaic cells. Reflective roofing materials or coatings help send the heat back into the sky rather than into the building. Plastic shingles are available that look like slate or wood but are made from recycled content. The choice of roofing materials should be considered as a part of the overall design of the building and can depend as much on aesthetic preferences as on the desired energy attributes.

A number of types of roofing materials are available.

- asphalt shingles
- metal, such as steel, galvalume, copper, or aluminum
- wood shakes or shingles
- concrete or clay tiles
- single-ply rubber or vinyl membranes, such as ethylene propylene diene monomer (EPDM), polyvinyl chloride (PVC), or thermoplastic polyolefin (TPO)
- solar shingles (containing PV cells)
- recycled-content shingles or shakes, generally composed of a combination of vinyl and cellulose
- built-up roofing, consisting of multiple layers of asphalt-saturated felts laminated with bitumen

Thermal Efficiency

Determine the building's function and what equipment will be used in it. The type of activity and the amount of equipment in a building affect how much internal heat will be generated. The rate at which a building gains or loses heat through its skin is directly proportional to the difference in air temperature between the inside and outside. For example, a large commercial building with significant internal heat loads would be less influenced by heat exchanges at the skin than a residence with far fewer internal sources of heat generation.

In general, build walls, roofs, and floors of adequate thermal resistance to provide human comfort and energy efficiency. Roofs are especially vulnerable to solar gain in summer and heat loss in winter. Avoid insulation materials that require chlorofluorocarbons (CFCs) or hydrochlorofluorocarbons (HCFCs) in their production, as these are ozone-depleting compounds. Consider insulation made from recycled materials such as cellulose or mineral wool, if such items meet the project's performance criteria and budget. If the framing system is made of a highly conductive material, install a layer of insulation or sheathing to limit thermal bridging.

Specify building materials and details and landscaping techniques that reduce heat transfer across the building envelope, which can occur through conduction, radiation, or convection. Building materials conduct heat at different rates. Metals have a high rate of thermal conductance. Masonry has a lower rate; the rate for wood is lower still. This means that, where all other components are the same, a wall framed with metal studs would have a much greater tendency to transmit heat from one side to the other than would a wall framed with wood studs. Insulating materials, either installed in the spaces between framing members or applied to the envelope, resist heat flow through walls and ceilings.

Consider the following principles in construction detailing.

- To reduce thermal transfer from conduction, develop details that eliminate or minimize thermal bridges.
- To reduce thermal transfer from convection, develop details that minimize opportunities for air infiltration or exfiltration.
- Plug, caulk, or putty all holes in sills, studs, and joists.
- Where possible, specify sealants with low environmental impact that do not compromise indoor air quality.

Incorporate solar controls on the building exterior to reduce heat gain. Radiant gains can have a significant impact on heating and cooling loads. A surface that is highly reflective of solar radiation will gain much less heat than one that is absorptive. This is important in selecting roofing materials because of the large amount of radiation they will be exposed to over the course of a day. Color may also play a role in selecting thermal storage materials in passive solar buildings; in general, light colors decrease solar gain while dark ones increase it. Overhangs are effective on south-facing facades, while a combination of vertical fins and overhangs is needed on east and west exposures and, in warmer areas during summer months, on north-facing facades.

Consider using earth berms to reduce heat transmission and radiant loads on the building envelope. Burying part of a building with earth berms or sod roofs will minimize both solar gain and wind-driven air infiltration. It will also lessen thermal transfer caused by extremely high or low temperatures.

Landscape is integral to a building's performance. Make landscaping decisions that coordinate with building strategy.

- Coordinate decisions about the building envelope with existing and new landscaping schemes on a year-round basis.
- Reduce paved areas to lessen heat buildup around the building and reduce the load on the building envelope.
- Consider selecting a paving color with a high albedo (high reflectance) to minimize heat gain.
- Mitigate glare with landscaping.

In regions with significant cooling loads, select exterior finish materials with light colors and high reflectivity. Consider the impact of decisions on neighboring buildings. A highly reflective envelope may result in a smaller cooling load for that particular building, but glare from the surface may significantly increase cooling loads in adjacent buildings—as well as the number of complaints from their occupants.

Moisture Buildup within the Envelope

Under certain conditions, water vapor can condense within the building envelope. When this occurs, the materials that make up the wall can become wet, lessening their performance and contributing to their deterioration. To prevent this, place a vapor-tight sheet of plastic or metal foil, known as a *vapor barrier*, as near as possible to the warmer side of the wall construction. For example, in an area with a meaningful heating load, the vapor barrier should go near the inside of the wall assembly, just underneath the gypsum board. This placement can lessen or eliminate the problem of condensing water vapor.

Careful detailing, weatherstripping, and sealing of the envelope is required to eliminate sources of convective losses. Convective losses can occur from wind loads on exterior walls. They also occur through openings around windows and doors and through small openings in floor, wall, and roof assemblies. Occupants can experience these convective paths as drafts. Weatherstrip all doors and place sealing gaskets and latches on all operable windows; inspect the weatherstripping and seals periodically to ensure that they are airtight. Tiny leaks in buildings can cause significant energy loss and added fuel and pollution costs.

Sources of Electricity

Buildings that are designed using a whole-building approach and that incorporate energy efficient building components use much less electricity than conventional buildings. After all energy saving measures have been implemented, consider achieving the next level of sustainability by buying green power or generating clean energy on-site.

Guide to Purchasing Green Power: Renewable Electricity, Renewable Energy Certificates and On-Site Renewable Generation, published by the U.S. Department of Energy's Energy Efficiency and Renewable Energy Program, EPA's Green Power Partnership, the World Resources Institute Sustainable Enterprise Program, and the Center for Resource Solutions, is a guide to the types, benefits, costs, and availability of green power. A current link to this document can be found at **www.ppi2pass.com/LEEDreferences**.

Purchase of green power can help an organization reduce its reliance on traditional methods of power generation, such as the use of fossil fuels. This provides some insulation against energy price instability and fuel supply disruptions. In addition, this progressive approach can help a firm achieve sustainability goals, demonstrate civic leadership, and differentiate its products and services. Today, renewable energy is typically more expensive than conventional sources of power; it is anticipated that this margin will grow smaller as additional technologies are introduced and adoption becomes more widespread.

Green power can be purchased in a variety of ways, distinguished by the location of the power generation equipment (on site or on the power grid). Not every option is available in or appropriate for every location, so it is important to research available technologies before deciding which LEED credits to pursue.

- Renewable energy products can be purchased either as a fixed energy quantity block or as a percentage of monthly use. The project must be located in a region that offers this option to purchase this type of green power.
- Renewable energy certificates (RECs) can often be purchased even if the local utility does not offer renewable energy products. However, RECs are not yet offered in all areas. The *Guide to Purchasing Green Power* describes an REC as a representation of "the environmental, social, and other positive attributes of power generated by renewable resources" that "may be sold separately from the underlying commodity electricity."
- On-site renewable generation requires the purchase and installation of some sort of equipment that generates electricity. This can take the form of solar cells, wind turbines, a steam turbine powered by burning biomass, fuel cells, or equipment that converts methane gas derived from landfills, sewage treatment plants, or agricultural waste into electricity.
- Off-site renewable energy is produced by equipment owned and operated by the utility company or its subsidiaries at a location other than the project site. The energy can be produced through the use of a variety of technologies, such as wind or photovoltaics. It is then sold in the form of renewable energy certificates, or *green tags*, by Green-e providers, which are organizations that have been certified by an independent third-party to meet the Green-e requirements for sale of the RECs.

The *Guide to Purchasing Green Power* explains the process of gathering information to determine an appropriate green power option for an organization, development of a procurement plan, and the planning process for an on-site renewable generation project.

A growing trend in the power industry is *distributed generation*. Distributed generation involves placing small, modular electricity generators close to where the power is used, which helps utilities defer or eliminate costly investments in transmission and distribution system upgrades while providing customers with better quality, more reliable energy supplies and a cleaner environment. Technologies used for distributed electricity generation include wind, solar, bioenergy, fuel cells, gas microturbines, hydrogen, combined heat and power, and hybrid power systems.

Heating and Cooling Systems

HVAC (heating, ventilating, and air conditioning) refers to the equipment, distribution network, and terminals that provide the heating, ventilating, and air conditioning processes to a building. HVAC accounts for 40% to 60% of the total energy used in U.S. commercial and residential buildings; this represents a great opportunity for energy savings using proven technologies and design concepts.

In addition, HVAC systems have a significant effect on the health, comfort, and productivity of occupants. "Sick building" issues like user discomfort, improper ventilation, and poor indoor air quality are linked to HVAC system design and operation and can be improved by better mechanical and ventilation systems. In existing buildings, upgrades to the building envelope that reduce leakage are often necessary to maximize comfort and energy efficiency, and may require tweaking the HVAC system to allow it to perform optimally.

The best HVAC design considers all the interrelated building systems while addressing issues of indoor air quality, energy consumption, and environmental benefits. To optimize the design and the benefits, the mechanical system designer and the architect must consider these issues early in the schematic design phase and continually revise their decisions throughout the remaining design process. Well-designed commissioning activities should be scheduled for the building after construction and throughout its life cycle, and routine preventative maintenance programs should be implemented by the building management.

To select the most efficient and cost-effective mechanical and ventilation systems, perform an energy analysis early in the process, preferably during the schematic design phase. Several design and analysis software programs include building simulations that can predict hour by hour the energy behavior of the building's structure, air conditioning system, and central plant equipment. A variety of techniques can be used to improve buildings' energy performance, and there is room in the LEED rating systems for incorporation of the technologies that make the most sense for a specific project.

Passive Solar Design

Passive solar systems harvest solar energy to provide space heating, natural ventilation, water heating, and daylighting. They can also lower cooling loads. This design approach integrates building components—exterior walls, windows, and building materials—to provide solar collection, heat storage, and heat distribution. Passive solar design considers the synergy of different building components and systems. For example, consider these questions.

- Can natural daylighting reduce the need for electric light?
- If less electric light generates less heat, will there be a lower cooling load?
- If the cooling load is lower, can the fans be smaller?
- Will natural ventilation allow fans and other cooling equipment to be turned off at times?

Passive solar design is often more challenging than designing a traditional mechanical system to accomplish the same functions. When using the building components themselves to regulate temperature, a rigorous analytical approach is needed in order to optimize performance while avoiding problems such as overheating and glare. Building occupants must be educated about the system and how they can manipulate building elements such as shades or operable windows to achieve the most comfortable indoor environment.

Generic design solutions are of limited value in passive solar design. Rules of thumb may be useful in anticipating system size and type, but only early in the design process. Computer simulation provides much more accurate guidance because of the complexity of system combinations and interactions. The variables involved include

- climate (sun, wind, air temperature, and humidity)
- building orientation (glazing and room layout)
- building use type (occupancy schedules and use profiles)
- lighting and daylighting (electric and natural light sources)
- building envelope (geometry, insulation, fenestration, air leakage, ventilation, shading, thermal mass, and color)
- internal heat gains (from lighting, office equipment, machinery, and people)
- HVAC (plant, systems, and controls)
- energy costs (fuel source, demand charges, and conversion efficiency)

An hour-by-hour simulation analysis uses all these parameters to evaluate annual energy use or annual operating cost.

The interaction of many energy efficient strategies must be considered in passive solar design. These include passive solar heating, glazing, thermal mass, insulation, shading, daylighting, energy efficient lighting, lighting controls, air leakage control, natural ventilation, and mechanical system options such as economizer cycle, exhaust air heat recovery, high-efficiency HVAC, HVAC controls, and evaporative cooling. Passive solar heating systems are typically categorized as sun-tempered, direct-gain, sunspaces, and thermal storage walls (Trombe walls).

Cost and technical analyses are conducted in passive solar design to find the best ways of investing resources that will be repaid in energy cost savings. It is rarely feasible to satisfy 100% of the building load with a passive solar system, so an optimal design is based on minimizing life-cycle cost: the sum of initial cost and life-cycle operating costs. It is often difficult to separate the cost of many passive solar systems and components from other building costs, because many passive solar features such as windows and wall systems serve so many other building functions.

New construction projects offer the greatest opportunities for incorporating passive solar design, but any renovation or addition to a building envelope can integrate passive methods. It is important to consider passive solar design as early as possible in the site planning and design process. Ideally, an energy budget will be included in the building design specifications, and the requests for proposal should require the design team to demonstrate their commitment to whole-building performance and their ability to respond to the energy targets. Approaches to meeting these goals in new buildings include

- passive solar design
- passive solar cooling
- thermal storage

- active solar design
- lighting design incorporating daylighting techniques

For retrofit projects, consider

- daylighting strategies, such as making atriums out of courtyards and adding clerestories, along with modifying the electric lighting system to ensure energy savings
- heat control techniques, such as adding exterior shades or overhangs
- using passive solar heating strategies to allow modification of HVAC systems, perhaps downsizing mechanical equipment if the passive strategies sufficiently reduce energy loads
- determining whether passive features that have been disabled can be reactivated

Passive solar design is most effective when the building's type, use, and design allow passive solar strategies to be effective. For example, large multistory core zones are hard to reach with passive solar design and might not be an appropriate place to use this strategy. Building requirements such as privacy and security may also limit the types of passive solar heating system that can be used.

Reducing energy costs to 30% to 50% below national averages is realistic in new office design if an optimal mix of energy conservation and passive solar design strategies is applied to the building design. Annual savings of $0.45 to $0.75 per square foot ($5 to $8 per square meter) is a reasonable estimate of achievable cost savings.

Passive Solar Heating

The following are some strategies for passive solar heating.

Analyze building thermal-load patterns. An important concept of passive solar design is matching the times when the sun can provide daylight and heat to a building with the times when the building needs light and heat. Facilities in operation 24 hours a day, for example, may not be good candidates for passive approaches, but a typical office building open from 7 a.m. to 7 p.m. is a good prospect. This principle will also determine which passive solar design strategies will be most effective. Commercial buildings have complicated demands for heating, cooling, and lighting; therefore, their design strategies require computer analysis.

Integrate passive solar heating with daylighting design. A passive solar building that uses sunlight as a heating source can be designed to use the sunlight as a lighting source as well. However, each use has different design requirements that need to be addressed. In general, passive solar heating is most effective when sunlight directly strikes dark-colored surfaces. Daylighting, on the other hand, benefits from the gentle diffusion of sunlight over large, light-colored surfaces. Integrating the two approaches requires an understanding and coordination of daylighting, passive design, electric lighting, and mechanical heating systems and controls.

Design the building's floor plan to optimize passive solar heating. Orient the solar collection surfaces within 15 degrees of true south, if possible. South-facing surfaces do not all have to be along the same wall. Because of the sun's path, the optimal orientation for passive solar buildings in the Northern Hemisphere is due south. The efficiency of the system and the ability to control shading and summer overheating decline dramatically as the solar collection surface shifts away from due south.

Identify appropriate locations for exposure to beam sunlight. Overheating and glare can occur when sunlight penetrates directly into a building, and these must be addressed through proper design. A "direct gain" space can overheat in full sunlight and is many times brighter than normal indoor lighting, causing intense glare. Generally, rooms and spaces where people stay in one place for more than a few minutes are inappropriate for direct gain systems, but lobbies, atriums, or lounges can be located along the south wall where direct sun penetrates. Choose glazings that are best for the desired levels of heat gain, daylighting, and reduction of cooling loads.

Avoid glare from low sun angles. As the sun rises in the early morning and sets in the late afternoon, the low angle allows the sun's beams to penetrate deep into the building beyond the normal direct gain area. If the building's occupied spaces are not designed to control the impact of the sun's penetration, the occupants will experience discomfort from glare. Careful analysis is needed to find the design strategies that will best address the low sun angles. For example, light shelves can be used, or workstations can be oriented north-south so that walls or high partitions intercept and diffuse the light.

Locate thermal mass so that it will be illuminated by low winter sun angles. Building design should incorporate a sufficient amount of correctly located thermal mass to effectively contribute to the heating requirements and provide cooling benefits in the summer.

Passive Solar Cooling

Buildings should be designed to minimize cooling load, whether passive solar strategies or conventional cooling strategies are being considered. Design strategies that minimize the need for mechanical cooling systems include proper window placement and daylighting design, selection of appropriate glazings for windows and skylights, proper shading of glass when heat gains are not desired, use of light-colored materials for the building envelope and roof, careful siting and orientation decisions, and good landscaping design.

Here are some shading strategies.

Install fixed shading devices, use correctly sized overhangs or porches, or design the building to be "self-shading." Fixed shading devices such as awnings, trellises, or overhangs will shade windows throughout the solar cycle. They are most effective on the south-facing windows. The depth and position of fixed shading devices must be carefully engineered to allow the sun to penetrate only during particular times of the year. In the winter, overhangs allow the low winter sun to enter south-facing windows. In the summer, the overhangs block the higher sun.

Plant trees and bushes to shade the windows at the right time of day and season. Deciduous vegetation is often an attractive and inexpensive form of shading, because it follows the local seasons, not the calendar. In the warm south, where more shading is needed, trees leaf out earlier, while in the cold north, where solar heat is beneficial late into spring, leaves appear later. Trees can be strategically planted on east and west sides to block the rising and setting sun. Bushes can be positioned to block undesirable low sun angles from the east or west. Deciduous vines trained to grow over trellises make easily controlled shading systems.

Use evergreen trees. When they are trimmed so that their canopies allow low winter sun underneath but block the high summer sun, evergreen trees can be very effective. Properly placed vegetation can also guide airflows toward buildings for natural ventilation and can block cold winter winds. Vegetation and ground cover also contribute to evaporative cooling around a building.

Choose locations for shading carefully. Vegetation used for shading should be located so as not to interfere with solar gain to buildings in winter. Deciduous trees can reduce winter solar gain by 20% or more and should not be placed in the solar access zone. Take in account that trees will need maintenance, pruning, watering, and feeding. As they grow, their shading pattern changes. They may be damaged or killed, leaving the building exposed.

Consider awnings that can be extended or removed. Traditional movable awnings are an excellent solution to the variation between seasons and the calendar year. When rolled out in the summer, they not only provide deep shade but also lend a colorful touch to a building's facade. When rolled up in winter, they allow more sun into the building and are protected from snow loads and excessive weathering.

Consider exterior roll-down shades or shutters. Operable shutters are the most traditional option, but a variety of vertical shading devices are available. Also available are many exterior-grade fiberglass and plastic fabrics that cut out a significant amount of sunlight but still allow a clear view through the window; however, these products do not prevent the glare problems caused by low-angle sun. Opaque steel or plastic roll-down shutters have proved to be reliable and long lasting and can help protect against storms and vandalism as well as shading the building. They can be expensive, however, and their appearance may not be a good fit for the aesthetics of some buildings.

Limit glazing on the east and west facades. Glass on these exposures is harder to shade from low-angle morning or evening sun. Vertical or eggcrate fixed shading works well if the shading projections are fairly deep or close together; however, these may limit views. North-facing glass receives little direct solar gain, but does provide diffuse daylight.

Other cooling strategies include the following.

Design the building to take advantage of natural ventilation. Natural ventilation uses passive stack effect and pressure differentials to bring fresh, cooling air through a building without the use of mechanical systems. This process cools the occupants and provides comfort even in humid climates. Buildings using this design strategy incorporate operable windows or other ways of taking in outdoor air. Wingwalls are sometimes used to increase the convective airflow. Other features include fresh air inlets located near floor level, use of ceiling fans, and the use of atriums and stairwell towers to enhance the stack effect. Care should be taken not to increase the *latent load*, the cooling load resulting from condensation, by bringing in moist outside air.

Consider radiative cooling in appropriate climates. Radiative cooling (also known as nocturnal radiative cooling) is the release of stored heat to the outside. This cooling strategy is particularly effective in climates and during seasons of the year when the temperature differences between day and night are significant. Night flushing of buildings uses radiative cooling principles. The building mass serves as a heat sink during the day, but releases the heat at night while being cooled with night air.

Consider ground-coupled cooling. Ground coupling is achieved by conductive contact between the building and the earth. The most common strategy is to cool air by channeling it through an underground tunnel. Another strategy provides cool air by installing a tube in the ground and dripping water into the tube. This reduces the air temperature through evaporation.

Consider evaporative cooling strategies. This cooling method works because water evaporating into the atmosphere extracts heat from the air. Evaporative cooling is most appropriate in dry climates such as the Southwest.

Use dehumidification in humid climates. Dehumidification removes moisture from the air and is necessary in climates with high humidity levels, and therefore high latent loads, during portions of the year. Common strategies include dilution of interior moisture by ventilating with less humid air, collecting condensation on cooled surfaces connected to a heat sink, and desiccant systems.

Thermal Storage

Thermal mass in a passive solar building is intended to meet two needs. It should absorb solar heat quickly for use throughout the day and night, and release the stored heat slowly when the sun is no longer shining. It must also be designed to avoid overheating. Depending on the local climate and the use of the building, the delayed release of heat may be timed to occur a few hours later or slowly over days. Careful selection of the thermal storage medium, its location in the building, and its quantity are important design and cost decisions.

Venting, another solution for handling stored heat, can rid the building of late afternoon heat or exhaust heat when the building's thermal mass is already saturated. Venting can also be viewed as a form of economizer cooling, using outside air to cool the building when the outside air is cooler than the building's thermostat setting. The building can be flushed either by a mechanical exhaust fan tied to a thermostatic control or through the use of natural ventilation.

Two basic thermal storage strategies utilize thermal mass.

- With *direct thermal storage*, high mass materials such as concrete masonry or tiles are placed directly in the sunlight so that intense solar energy enters them quickly.
- With *diffuse thermal storage*, materials are placed throughout the building. They can absorb heat by radiation, by the reflectance of sunlight as it bounces around a room, and by the movement of air heated elsewhere in the building (such as in sunspaces and atriums).

Active Solar Design

Active solar energy systems should be integrated with a building's design and systems only after passive solar and energy-conserving strategies are considered. Active solar collector systems take advantage of the sun to provide energy for domestic water heating, pool heating, ventilation air preheating, and space heating.

Water heating for domestic use is generally the most economical application of active solar systems. The demand for hot water is fairly constant throughout the year, so the solar system provides energy savings year-round. Successful use of solar water heating systems requires careful selection of components and proper sizing. Major components of a system include collectors, the circulation system that moves the fluid between the collectors and storage, the storage tank, a control system, and a backup heating system.

An active solar water heating system can be designed with components sized large enough to provide heating for pools or to provide a combined function of both domestic water and space heating. Space heating requires a heat-storage system and additional hardware to connect with a space heat distribution system. An active solar space heating system makes economic sense if it can offset considerable amounts of heating energy that would be required from conventional systems over the life of the building or the life of the system. The system equipment, which can be costly, should be evaluated on a life-cycle basis, using established project financial criteria acceptable to the building owner. The following should be considered in analysis of the economy and practicality of an active solar system.

- Determine if the climate and building usage is appropriate for an active solar collection system. The energy savings for active solar systems depend on the amount of available solar radiation, the projected uses of the system, and the proper system design.

- Determine the financial feasibility of an active solar system through a life-cycle cost analysis. This analysis should consider the upfront and operational costs and expected energy savings of the active solar system in comparison to conventional systems. The financial analysis should be performed over the projected life of the system, which should be assumed to be a minimum of 10 years. Based on the resulting estimates, the project owner can determine the financial feasibility of investment in the active solar system.

If an active solar system is financially feasible, the next step is to determine an appropriate location for solar collectors on or near the building. Keep in mind these general design guidelines.

Locate collectors to maximize exposure to the sun. Solar engineering texts describe how to optimize the orientation (ideally due south) and tilt of the collector according to latitude, climate, and usage. Collectors intended for winter space heating should have a steeper slope than collectors designed for year-round hot water heating. Vertically mounted wall collectors and horizontal roof collectors have also been used.

Locate collectors to avoid shading from nearby buildings and vegetation. A study of sun angles and local sky obstructions should help determine the best location on the site. For large commercial buildings, the most common location for good solar access is the highest flat roof.

Locate collectors to avoid vandalism and safety hazards. Collectors can be attractive targets for vandals. Their flat surfaces are well suited to graffiti, and glass cover plates can be broken. The more visible the collectors, the more likely they are to attract the attention of vandals.

Locate collectors to avoid blinding hazards from reflected sunlight. In addition to absorbing the sun's energy, almost all collectors reflect light at certain angles. This reflection is undesirable if directed at the occupants of another building, and can be hazardous if directed toward a road or a machine operator.

Collectors must be designed to withstand all weather conditions. Heavy snow loads, ice storms, and especially hailstorms can damage collector glass. Tempered or reinforced glass is often used to increase strength. The structures supporting the collectors have to be designed to survive wind loads from all directions. A structural engineer should be consulted to ensure compliance with all structural codes.

Design and locate collectors to make it easier to keep their surfaces clean. Dirt and dust on collector glazing can easily reduce the efficiency of the system by 50% or more. Insist on a location and system materials that will minimize dirt collection. A regular maintenance schedule is aided by easy access to the collectors, a convenient source of water, and a nearby drainage system. Very large, tall, or horizontal collectors may need to be designed to support the weight of maintenance personnel. In some cases, rainwater may provide adequate surface cleaning.

Minimize the distance from the collectors to the storage unit. The longer the distance, the greater the potential for heat loss and reduced system efficiency. For solar heating, locate storage near the central heating system.

Optimize insulation of collectors, ducts, pipes, and storage. Greater insulation should be installed for higher-temperature collection levels.

Place duct and piping runs within conditioned space. This strategy can be advantageous during the heating season, but may be disadvantageous during the cooling season.

Minimize controls, and educate maintenance staff to optimize systems operations. Control technology, along with computer and sensor technology, has advanced significantly in recent years, and older models have been made obsolete quickly. New systems provide higher efficiencies and greater returns on investment.

Minimize maintenance. A system that is self-maintaining is likely to have a higher efficiency and lower failure rate, and thus the best economic payback. Generally, fewer moving parts mean less maintenance. Active solar space heating systems generally do not operate year-round, so their moving parts must be reliable enough to work intermittently. Pressure relief valves, self-cleaning surfaces, and overheating sensors quickly pay for themselves by extending the life of the system.

Maximize access to collectors, pipes, ducts, and storage areas. Assume that all parts of a system will have to be maintained and may have to be replaced in the future, and make sure that maintenance and replacement will not be difficult. Pipes and ducts buried in walls and under concrete slabs will be costly to fix, and thus the active solar system is more likely to be abandoned than repaired.

Lighting

Lighting is an important component of whole-building design. Improvements to traditional lighting elements such as lamps (like fluorescent bulbs) and ballasts (which transform and control electrical power to the light) help improve the efficiency and effectiveness of electrical lighting strategies.

Additional energy savings can result from the installation of lighting control devices such as timers and sensors that turn lights off when not needed, and from the use of daylighting. When properly designed and effectively integrated with the electric lighting system, daylighting can offer significant energy savings by offsetting a portion of the electric lighting load. A related benefit is the reduction in cooling capacity and amount of use required of the HVAC system by lowering a significant component of internal heat gains. In addition to saving energy, daylighting generally improves occupant satisfaction and comfort. Recent studies show a connection between daylighting levels and improvements in productivity and health in schools and offices. Windows also provide visual relief, a contact with nature, time orientation, the possibility of ventilation, and emergency egress.

Incorporating daylighting techniques into building design requires consideration of

- the daylight zone
- window design
- effective aperture
- light shelves
- toplighting strategies
- daylighting controls
- design coordination
- modeling daylighting

The Daylight Zone

The best opportunities for daylighting are present in those spaces that are occupied predominantly during the daytime. Site solar analysis should assess the access to daylight by considering what is "seen" from the various potential window orientations. How much of the sky is seen from typical task locations in the room? What are the exterior obstructions and glare sources? Will the building shade a neighboring building or landscape feature that depends on daylight?

It is important to establish which spaces will most benefit from daylight and which will not. Within the spaces that can use daylight, place the most critical visual tasks near the windows. Try to group tasks by similar lighting requirements and occupancy patterns. Avoid placing a window in the direct line of sight of an occupant, as this can cause extreme contrast and glare. It is best to orient the occupant at a 90-degree angle to the window. Where privacy is not a major concern, consider interior glazing (known as relights or borrow lights) that allows light from one space to be shared with another. If privacy is required, this can be achieved with transoms, obscured glass, or translucent panels.

The floor plan should maximize the perimeter daylight zone. This may result in a building with a higher skin-to-volume ratio than a typical compact building design. A standard window can produce useful illumination to a depth of about 1.5 times the height of the window. With light shelves or other reflector systems, this depth can be increased to 2.0 times or more. As a general rule, the higher the window is placed on the wall, the deeper the daylight penetration.

Window Design

The daylight that arrives at a work surface has three components that come from different sources.

- *The exterior reflected component.* This includes light reflected from ground surfaces, pavement, adjacent buildings, wide windowsills, and objects. Remember that excessive ground reflectance will result in glare.
- *The direct sun/sky component.* Typically, the lighting design will block the direct sun component from occupied spaces because of heat gain, glare, and UV degradation issues. The diffuse light of the sky dome then becomes an important contributor to daylighting the space.
- *The internal reflected component.* Once the daylight enters the room, the surrounding wall, ceiling, and floor surfaces are important reflectors. Using high-reflectance surfaces will better bounce the daylight around the room and will reduce extremes of brightness and contrast. Window frame materials should be light-colored to reduce contrast with the view, and should have a non-specular finish to eliminate glare spots. The window jambs and sills can play a role as light reflectors. Deep jambs should be splayed (angled toward the interior) to reduce the level of contrast around the perimeter of the window.

Remember that the most important interior light-reflecting surface is the ceiling. Paints and ceiling tiles are available with reflectance values of 0.90 and higher. Tilting the ceiling plane toward the daylight source increases the amount of daylight that is reflected from this surface. In small rooms, the rear wall is the next most important surface because it directly faces the window. This surface should also have a high-reflectance matte finish. The side walls and the floor have less impact on the reflected daylight in the space. Major room furnishings such as office cubicles and partitions can have a significant impact on reflected light, so select light-colored materials and finishes when possible.

The proportions of a daylighted room are more important than its dimensions. A room with a higher ratio of ceiling height to depth will have deeper penetration of daylight, whether that daylight enters through sidelighting (windows) or toplighting (skylights and clerestories). Raising the window head height will also result in deeper penetration and more even illumination in the room. Punched window openings, such as small, square windows separated by wall area, result in uneven illumination and harsh contrasts between the window and adjacent wall surfaces. A more even distribution can be achieved with horizontal strip windows.

Effective Aperture

One method of assessing the relationship between visible light and the size of the window is the effective aperture method. The *effective aperture* (EA) is defined as the product of the visible transmittance (VT) and the window-to-wall ratio (WWR). The *window-to-wall ratio* is the proportion of window area compared to the total area of the wall where the window is located. For example, if a window covers 25 sq ft in a 100 sq ft wall (25 sq m in a 100 sq m wall), then the WWR is 25/100 or 0.25. A good starting target for EA is in the 0.20 to 0.30 range. For a given EA number, a higher WWR (that is, a larger window) results in a lower visible transmittance.

Examples:

> If WWR = 0.5 (half the wall is glazing) and VT = 0.6, then EA = (0.5)(0.6) = 0.3.
> If WWR = 0.75 and VT = 0.4, then EA = (0.75)(0.4) = 0.3.

Lowering the visible transmittance will usually lower the shading coefficient as well, but this is not always the case; it must be verified with the glazing manufacturer's data.

Light Shelves

Because the luminance ratio, or brightness, is a major consideration in view windows, it is often wise to separate the view aperture from the daylight aperture. This allows a higher visible transmittance glazing to be used in the daylight aperture if it is located outside of normal sight lines. Because the ceiling is the most important light-reflecting surface, using the ceiling to bounce daylight deep into the room can be highly effective. Both of these strategies are utilized in light shelf designs. A *light shelf* is a horizontal, light-reflecting overhang placed above eye level, with a transom window placed above it. This design, which is most effective for windows with southern orientations, improves daylight penetration, creates shading near the window, and helps reduce window glare. Exterior light shelves are more effective shading devices than interior light shelves. A combination of exterior and interior light shelves will work best to provide an even illumination gradient.

Toplighting Strategies

Large single-level floor areas and the top floors of multistory buildings can benefit from toplighting. Toplighting strategies include skylights, clerestories, monitors, and sawtooth roofs.

Skylights

Horizontal skylights can be an energy problem because they tend to receive the most solar gain at the peak of the day, when the sun is at its highest position in the sky. The daylight contribution also peaks at midday and is much less in the morning and afternoon. High-performance skylight designs incorporate reflectors or prismatic lenses that reduce the peak daylight and heat gain while increasing early morning and late afternoon daylight contributions. Another option is a *light pipe* or *light tube*, a high-reflectance duct that channels the light from a skylight down to a diffusing lens in the room. These strategies may be advantageous in deep roof constructions.

Clerestory Windows

A clerestory window is vertical glazing located high on an exterior wall. South-facing clerestories can be effectively shaded from direct sunlight by a properly designed horizontal overhang. In this type of design, the interior north wall can be sloped to better reflect the light down into the room. Use light-colored overhangs and adjacent roof surfaces to improve the reflected component. If exterior shading is not possible, consider interior vertical baffles to better diffuse the light. A south-facing clerestory will produce higher levels of daylight illumination than a north-facing one. East- and west-facing clerestories have the same problems as east- and west-facing windows: they are difficult to shade and can produce high levels of heat gain.

Roof Monitors

A roof monitor consists of a flat roof section raised above the adjacent roof with vertical glazing on all sides. This design often results in excessive glazing area, which results in higher heat losses and gains than a clerestory design. The multiple orientations of the glazing can also create shading problems.

Sawtooth Roofs

A sawtooth roof is an old design often seen in industrial buildings. Typically, one sloped surface is opaque and the other is glazed. A contemporary sawtooth roof may have solar collectors or photovoltaic cells on the south-facing slope and daylight glazing on the north-facing slope.

Unprotected glazing on the south-facing sawtooth surface may result in high heat gains. In these applications, an insulated diffusing panel may be a good choice.

Daylighting Controls

A building designed for daylighting that does not include an integrated electric lighting system will be a net energy loser because of the increased thermal loads. Only when the electric lighting load is reduced in response to the amount of light entering the space through the daylighting techniques will there be more than offsetting savings in electrical and cooling loads. The benefits from daylighting are maximized when both occupancy and lighting sensors are used to control the electric lighting system.

- *Occupancy sensors* detect when a space is occupied by using passive infrared or ultrasonic technologies or a combination of the two. When the heat or movement of the occupant is no longer detected, and after a preset delay time, the sensor will emit a signal to extinguish the lights. Occupancy sensors used alone are good for low or intermittent use areas such as storage rooms, restrooms, and even corridors.
- *Light-level sensors* have a photoelectric "eye" that measures the illumination in a room. Threshold on and off values can be set to respond to specific lighting conditions. These sensors can operate on/off switching of various luminaires or lamps within luminaires and they can also operate a continuous dimming system. A continuous dimming system will obviously cost more than a switching system, but can produce greater user satisfaction because the change in lighting levels is not as noticeable.

Fluorescent lighting systems are the most common daylight control lamp source because of the availability of step switching and dimming systems. High intensity discharge (HID) sources are typically not a good choice for daylight switching because of the extended strike and restrike times. There are now two-step HID sources available that may be useful in some step switching applications where the "off" mode is not needed during a typical day.

Lighting design in a building that employs daylighting techniques should utilize both occupancy and light sensors. With these two control strategies in place, the lights will come on only when the room is occupied and only if there is insufficient daylight. In most designs, a manual override is provided for user convenience.

Design Coordination

When using daylighting, the electrical lighting and interior design require special consideration.

Electric Lighting Design Coordination

The coordination of the electrical lighting system with the daylighting design is critical for the success of the system. The layout and circuiting of the lighting should coordinate with the locations of the daylight apertures. For example, in a typical sidelighting design with windows along one wall, it is best to place the luminaires in rows parallel to the window wall and circuit them so that the row nearest the windows will be the first to dim or switch off followed by successive rows.

Interior Design Coordination

In order to maintain the designed performance of the daylighting system, the person responsible for interior finishes and furnishing must be aware of the desired reflectance values. Dark interior finishes can compromise an otherwise great daylighting design.

Modeling Daylighting

Physical models are a very effective way to analyze daylighting performance. Even simple models can give an idea of how daylight will behave in the building. It is important that the daylight apertures be accurately modeled and that the materials used to construct the model are assigned the reflectance values used in the design. The model can then be tested on the actual site or under artificial sky conditions in a daylighting laboratory. A sundial indicating 36° north latitude can be attached to the model base to enable the designer to simulate various dates and times of the year.

Computer analysis is another method of testing a daylighting solution. Typically, a three-dimensional digital model is constructed with the use of computer-aided design software and is imported into the lighting software. The operator then defines all surface characteristics, sky conditions, the location, and the date and time. Many of these programs can produce photorealistic renderings of the proposed design.

Water Heating

Water heating constitutes 14% of the total energy consumption of residential buildings. In commercial buildings where large amounts of hot water are used, the energy tied up in heating water can be a significant component of the building's total energy consumption. For example, in the lodging industry, 42% of energy use is attributed to water heating. Other commercial buildings with heavy demand for hot water include restaurants, commercial laundries, high-density housing facilities such as dormitories and apartment buildings, and plants or factories housing industrial processes that use hot water.

A number of technologies are available for heating water efficiently. However, before implementing these technologies, it's important to first reduce the demand for hot water with water-saving fixtures and appliances. Both conserving water and heating it efficiently should be addressed during the whole-building design process. Water-heating technologies include drainwater heat recovery, heat-pump water heating, on-demand (tankless or instantaneous) water heating systems, and solar hot water heating.

Refrigerant Management

Traditional HVAC & R systems have used refrigerants to chill water, which, in turn, cools buildings. Over time, however, the environmental effects of using these substances has become apparent, and the use of refrigerants has been found to deplete ozone found in the atmosphere and so contribute to global warming. To address this issue, the Montreal Protocol on Substances Which Deplete the Ozone Layer, a treaty among almost all the member nations of the United Nations, was introduced in 1987 and has undergone subsequent amendments. This treaty restricts the use of certain chlorofluorocarbons (CFCs) and hydrochlorofluorocarbons (HCFCs).

The Montreal Protocol bans the use of CFCs completely, and schedules a phase-out of the use of all HCFCs by 2030. But it does not restrict the use of hydrofluorocarbons (HFCs), which are often substituted for CFCs. HCFCs and HFCs cause less ozone depletion than the now-banned CFCs (HFCs, because they contain no chlorine, are believed to have no effect on ozone at all), but both chemicals are now known to accelerate global warming. USGBC's report *The Treatment by LEED of the Environmental Impact of HVAC Refrigerants* summarizes the results of a study conducted in 2004 on the request of the LEED Steering Committee.

In the LEED rating systems, credits are awarded to projects that do not use refrigerants at all, and to projects that strike an acceptable balance between global warming potential and ozone depletion potential and are under the threshold for combined contributions to these effects.

Materials and Resources: Issues and Approaches

Materials

Sustainable building materials should be selected whenever possible. The best construction materials are durable and long lasting. They should also be

- nontoxic
- recyclable or made from recycled material
- renewable
- obtained from local sources
- certified, labeled, or otherwise recognized as compliant with sustainability standards

Nontoxic

The Indoor Environmental Quality category of the LEED rating systems addresses low-emitting materials. Select materials within prescribed volatile organic compound (VOC) limits.

- Select adhesives, sealants, and primers that meet or exceed the VOC limits of South Coast Air Quality Management District Rule #1168.
- Select paints and coatings that meet or exceed the VOC and chemical component limits of applicable Green Seal requirements.
- Select carpet systems that meet or exceed the Carpet and Rug Institute Green Label and Green Label Plus Test Programs.
- Select composite wood and agrifiber products that do not contain added ureaformaldehyde resin.

Recycled

The recycled content of a material is classified as either post-consumer or pre-consumer (which was called "postindustrial" in previous versions of the rating systems). Specifying materials made with recycled content is another method of saving processing or manufacturing energy. Building materials that can contain a high percentage of recycled material include reinforcing and framing steel, concrete masonry units, gypsum wallboard and facing paper, and acoustic ceiling panels and their suspension systems.

Use recycled materials to reduce the use of raw materials and divert material from landfills. LEED credits may be awarded to projects that use salvaged or refurbished materials and those that integrate products that contain a combination of post-consumer and pre-consumer recycled content.

Recyclable

During the design phase, identify the potential waste streams that the facility will produce. All LEED-certified projects must provide facilities to handle the separation, collection, and storage of common recyclable materials such as paper, glass, plastics, and metals. The collection points should be easily accessible to the occupants. A multistory building might have separate trash chutes for various recyclables. Low-rise buildings should provide at least one collection point on each floor. Care should be taken to design the loading dock or trash collection area for easy central access. All these elements should be identified on the building plans.

Renewable

To reduce the depletion of virgin materials and the use of petroleum-based materials, use *rapidly renewable materials*. A rapidly renewable material is one that is made from plants that are harvested within a ten-year cycle. Examples include bamboo flooring, cotton batt insulation, linoleum flooring, panels made of sunflower seed board, wheatboard, wool carpeting, and cork flooring. To achieve LEED credit for use of rapidly renewable materials, specify that a minimum of 2.5% of the total value of all building materials be made from these plant materials.

Local

Specifying materials mined, harvested, salvaged, or manufactured within a 500-mile (805 km) radius from the project can reduce the costs and the associated environmental impacts of transportation. Designing with regional materials also encourages use of local natural resources and can have the added benefit of helping the local economy. LEED credits may be awarded to projects that use at least 10% regionally produced materials. Regional material opportunities should be researched early in the design process to maximize the potential benefits.

Certified, Labeled, or Recognized by Sustainability Standards

The Forest Stewardship Council is a nonprofit organization that encourages responsible management of forests worldwide. The group certifies products, such as building materials and paper, that are made from trees grown in accordance with FSC forest management guidelines. A hallmark of FSC certification is the chain-of-custody document that accompanies each product and details its path from forest to job site, documenting that all growers, harvesters, processors, and sellers of that wood product are in compliance with FSC regulations. Achievement of LEED credits requires use of a minimum of 50% wood-based materials that are certified in accordance with the Forest Stewardship Council principles and criteria.

Indoor Environmental Quality: Issues and Approaches

Designing a building with good indoor environmental quality (IEQ) requires consideration of the future inhabitants and the characteristics of the facility that will optimize their level of comfort while they are in the building. These characteristics make a building a healthy and pleasant place to spend time.

- ventilation
- protection from environmental tobacco smoke
- protection from potential contaminants in building materials
- protection from pollutants
- occupants' ability to control temperature and lighting
- access to natural light and views

All these factors contribute to occupants' sense of well-being. While scientific methods and instrumentation can measure levels of pollution (which includes carbon dioxide, carbon monoxide, volatile organics, ozone, particulates, and other air emissions), light, noise, and indices of comfort such as mean radiant temperature, the most telling indicator of design success is how employees feel when they are in the space. Employees can be surveyed to determine their reactions to their indoor environment and their perceptions of its effects on their performance and sense of satisfaction. Some of the statistics that may be examined include absenteeism, sick days, and drops in productivity. To make sense of this information, the data must be collected for a significant period of time, both before and after the changes.

The Rocky Mountain Institute and Pacific Gas and Electric have conducted several studies linking improvements in IEQ to improvements in productivity. In most federal facilities, for example, the cost per square foot (square meter) of the workforce is twenty times greater than the cost per square foot (square meter) of the building. This huge difference readily demonstrates that investments in IEQ that improve productivity are likely to be rapidly recovered.

Ventilation

LEED-certified buildings are required to include mechanical or natural ventilation systems that comply with ASHRAE Standard 62.1, which describes a method for verifying the ability of the ventilation system to provide fresh air to all interior spaces at a prescribed rate. Projects that exceed the minimum requirements of this standard and incorporate mechanisms for monitoring the flow of outdoor air into the building may earn additional credits. Such ventilation systems must be in operation when the building is occupied. Additional credits may be awarded to projects that include measures for protecting the HVAC system during the construction phase and those that flush the building with a high volume of outdoor air in combination with replacement of all filtration media. All these techniques are used to evacuate dust, odors, or potentially harmful fumes from the building after the completion of construction operations but before the building is occupied.

Environmental Tobacco Smoke

All LEED-certified buildings must prohibit smoking in the building and within 25 feet (7.6 m) of building openings, or provide designated smoking rooms. Smoking rooms must be equipped with exhaust systems and the smoking room must be negatively pressurized so that smoke does not enter the nonsmoking areas of the building.

Contaminants in Building Materials

The chemicals used in production of some building materials, such as VOCs and formaldehydes, can have a negative impact on human health, causing headaches, sore throats, dizziness, eye irritation, nausea, and other ill effects. Products that often contain such chemicals include paints and strippers, solvents, adhesives, sealants, flooring materials, and composite wood products. The IEQ section of the LEED rating systems references standards for controlling the amount of potentially harmful substances included in building materials. During the design and specification phase, it is important to research the characteristics of building materials and choose those which meet or exceed the requirements of the LEED referenced standards.

Pollutants

Pollutants may enter a building from a variety of sources. LEED credits address the following types of interior pollution and prescribe ways to minimize the amount of chemicals or particulates that enter the interior space.

- Entryway systems at exterior doors help catch dirt and materials that may be on the shoes of people entering the building.
- Exhaust systems are recommended in areas where chemicals may be used or odors may be generated, such as copy rooms, garages, and housekeeping or laundry areas.
- Filtration media should be changed before occupancy and periodically after the building is occupied to capture particulates in the air entering and leaving the building.
- Any hazardous liquid wastes generated on site should be appropriately contained and disposed of off site.

Occupant Control of Lighting and Temperature

People are happy when they have control over their environment. Office workers constantly battle over the temperature in their space; half probably think it's too hot, the other half are always shivering. LEED credits may be awarded to projects that provide individual comfort controls such as thermostats or operable windows to at least half of the building occupants. In addition to temperature controls, LEED credits may also be given to projects that allow most occupants to adjust light levels in their workspaces through lighting controls or task lighting. A challenge in providing both of these controls is to design a system that allows occupants to adjust light levels and temperature to their personal liking but does not compromise energy conservation strategies employed in the building as a whole.

Access to Natural Light and Views

Access to windows is important for a variety of reasons; windows allow ventilation, light, a connection to the outdoors and a way to monitor the progression of time. In addition, provisions for admission of natural light and ventilation can reduce a building's dependence on mechanical systems. LEED credits may be awarded to projects that incorporate daylighting strategies and direct lines of sight to the outdoors in the majority of regularly occupied interior spaces.

Putting It All Together: Construction, Operations, and Maintenance

The Construction Phase

The building's impact on the environment begins during the construction phase. Before that time, a building is just a concept on paper; during construction, that design assumes physical form and begins consuming resources. While the design team will continue to be involved with the project, the day-to-day operations on site are now the responsibility of the general contractor, who must be an integral part of the project team and who will implement the strategy developed in the design phase. A sustainable approach to construction leads to reduced resource use, reduced disturbance of the site, and can also lower costs. Attention to environmental issues during construction also leads to a safer, healthier working environment, first for those who construct the building, and later for those who occupy it.

Environmental guidelines can be established as a part of the construction documents and contract for the project. If contractors are required to follow specific environmental guidelines during the construction process, these requirements must be included in the contract, drawings, and specifications for the project. To develop and implement the guidelines, work with the entire team, including the architect, engineers, and contractors, to consider the best ways to educate contractors about sustainability issues and to get their early commitment to follow sustainability guidance.

Integrating construction guidelines with other sustainability guidelines is an essential part of the whole-building design process. As the project moves from design to construction, much of the responsibility for documentation of products and approaches is transferred to the builder, who will put design strategies discussed earlier in this chapter into effect. Therefore, to complete the requirements of the LEED credits and achieve the associated points, design features must be understood and properly implemented by the construction team. The contractor and subcontractors may be responsible for the following activities while building construction is under way.

- Collaborate with the design team to understand sustainability practices to be implemented on this project.
- Locate trailers, equipment, storage, and construction traffic, including the locations of site entrances and exits, to minimize site impact.

- Implement the erosion and sedimentation plan and comply with all applicable regulations.
- Specify which areas of the site should be kept free of traffic, equipment, and storage and limit site disturbance to only those areas where work is to be performed.
- Implement the stormwater management plan and comply with all applicable regulations.
- Provide and install specified equipment or propose substitutions, as required, that meet the design intent and comply with LEED requirements.
- Work with the commissioning authority to provide access to the site as required for verification of building systems.
- Make sure the infrastructure for recycling construction and demolition materials is in place and operating at the beginning of the project. Set up an on-site system to collect and sort waste for recycling or for reuse, and monitor the system consistently throughout all phases of construction. (Also see the next section on construction waste management.)
- Create a waste management plan that sets goals to recycle or salvage a minimum of 50% (by weight) of construction, demolition, and land-clearing waste. Aim for 75%.
- If possible, purchase products and materials with minimal or no packaging.
- Purchase materials in the sizes necessary, rather than cutting them to size.
- Consistently track and monitor the amount of waste production during construction and measure it against pre-existing goals and guidelines.
- Coordinate acquisition of salvaged, refurbished, or reused materials.
- Identify suppliers who can provide recycled-content materials and document the cost of these materials and that building materials used for the project contain specified levels of recycled content.
- Identify regional suppliers who can provide locally-produced materials and document the point of origin, distance to the project site, cost, and quantities of materials used.
- Coordinate acquisition of rapidly renewable materials as specified and document the quantity and cost of the materials used for the project.
- Document the chain-of-custody and cost of any certified wood products incorporated into the building.
- Prohibit smoking on the jobsite during construction.
- Implement the IAQ management plan designed to protect HVAC systems during construction and preoccupancy.
- Keep the site and interiors clean and free of debris in order to keep dust down. Storing polluting materials in a specified storage area will protect the building from pollutants.
- Meet or exceed the minimum requirements of the Sheet Metal and Air Conditioning Contractors' National Association (SMACNA) *IAQ Guidelines for Occupied Buildings Under Construction.*
- Protect stored on-site or installed absorptive materials from moisture damage.
- Put up barriers to keep noise and pollutants from migrating.
- Ventilate using the building's HVAC system, once installed, and with temporary exhaust systems before installation.

- Increase the amount of outside air coming into the building during construction to reduce pollutants.

- Schedule construction activities at the end of the day so that they will ventilate overnight while site and surroundings are unoccupied.

- Be aware of air quality throughout the project, not just during times of activities that create high amounts of airborne pollutants and emissions.

- Regularly monitor IAQ with tests and inspections and adjust the ventilation and scheduling if necessary to improve IAQ.

- Prevent poor IAQ by selecting materials and products designed for less off-gassing, such as low-VOC paints and sealants and formaldehyde-free particleboard.

- Replace all filters in the mechanical system immediately prior to occupancy. Filtration should have a Minimum Efficiency Reporting Value (MERV) of 13 as determined by ASHRAE Standard 52.2.

- Conduct a minimum two-week building flush-out with new filtration media at 100% outside air after construction ends and before occupancy, or conduct a baseline IAQ testing procedure consistent with current EPA-RTP environmental specification 01445, Testing for Indoor Air Quality, Baseline IAQ, and Materials. This specification can be found on the EPA website, www.epa.gov.

- Verify and document that all materials used in the building are in compliance with the specifications and meet or exceed the LEED-referenced standards for VOC content.

- Support the LEED submission by keeping thorough, organized records and assisting in compiling information needed to verify compliance with LEED requirements.

- Develop a plan for the abatement of any hazardous substances or materials that may be present in the building, including polychlorinated biphenyl (PCBs) and asbestos. PCBs, which are toxic and can be readily absorbed through the skin, were used until the 1970s in materials such as coolants, paints, coatings, sealants, and adhesives. Asbestos was used as an insulator and fireproofing material until it was banned in 1978. Serious health risks have been associated with the disturbance of existing asbestos in buildings, so the removal of materials that contain asbestos must be undertaken only by those trained in abatement techniques.

Construction Waste Management

During the construction phase, a large amount of waste material is generated through construction, demolition, and land-clearing procedures. LEED credits addressing construction waste management and reuse of materials encourage a variety of approaches to keep building materials out of landfills. The primary waste products in building construction, in descending percentages, are wood, asphalt/concrete/masonry, drywall, roofing, metals, and paper products. Recycling on the jobsite is becoming more economical as the cost of disposal increases, regulations get more stringent, and material costs rise. Developing a waste management plan in writing in the early planning stages can help realize cost and environmental savings. This plan should identify local waste haulers and recyclers, examine the local market in salvage materials, identify and clearly label site spaces for storage of various waste materials, and require a reporting system that will quantify the results.

Projects that require demolition of existing buildings or parts of buildings may be able to donate salvaged or deconstructed materials to charitable organizations in the local community or sell the items privately to keep them out of the waste stream. Leftover new construction materials, such as scraps of lumber, plywood, paint, or other odds and ends may be welcomed by a school or Scout troop. Significant quantities of materials suitable for reuse are accepted by groups such as Habitat for Humanity for use in their own construction projects or for resale to raise money to finance other projects. As an added bonus, contributions may be tax-deductable.

LEED credits may be awarded for recycling and/or salvaging at least 50% of the project's nonhazardous construction and demolition waste. The waste management plan must identify what materials are to be recycled or salvaged, and whether the materials will be sorted on site or commingled. Amounts and percentages must be calculated consistently, either always by volume or always by weight. Reductions of 75% and 95% will earn additional credits.

Operations and Maintenance

The best efforts to reduce negative environmental impacts in the built environment are doomed to failure unless well-crafted operations and maintenance (O&M) procedures are implemented. Furthermore, even the best O&M procedures are of no use unless they are understood and followed by building O&M personnel.

Facility managers play the key role in ensuring that this happens. An integrated team approach can be a big help. In this process, O&M personnel are active participants in the design of a facility and the development of O&M procedures. This integrated team promotes useful procedures that are efficient and—most important—faithfully executed.

Building operation and maintenance programs specifically designed to enhance operating efficiency of HVAC and lighting systems can reduce energy bills by 5% to 20% without significant capital investment. Addressing O&M considerations at the start of a project can contribute greatly to improved working environments, higher productivity, and reduced energy and resource costs.

There are tremendous opportunities in most existing buildings and facilities to improve O&M procedures and make them more environmentally responsible. With new buildings, there are opportunities during design and construction to facilitate easy, low-environmental-impact O&M. In all buildings there are opportunities to derive multiple benefits from simple maintenance or upgrades. Energy savings and improved indoor air quality can be achieved by tuning up older oil-fired boilers, for example. Improved indoor air quality and less hazardous effluent from a building can be achieved by switching to more benign cleaning chemicals. If implemented effectively, the multiple benefits of O&M practices should include reduced operating costs.

To create an effective O&M program, these general procedures should be followed.

- Ensure that up-to-date operational procedures and manuals are available.
- Obtain up-to-date documentation on all building systems, including system drawings.
- Implement preventive maintenance programs complete with maintenance schedules and records of all maintenance performed for all building equipment and systems.
- Create a well-trained maintenance staff and offer professional development and training opportunities for each staff member.

- Implement a monitoring program that tracks and documents building systems performance to identify and diagnose potential problems and track the effectiveness of the O&M program. Include cost and performance tracking in this analysis.

Specific elements addressed in an effective O&M program include the following.

HVAC Systems and Equipment

Energy consumption and conservation are tied heavily to O&M procedures. HVAC equipment must be well maintained in order for the complex array of chillers, boilers, air handlers, controls, and other hardware to function at peak performance. Easy access to HVAC systems for ongoing maintenance and repair is critical and should be considered during the design phase of a new building project. A well-conceived, well-executed O&M program can provide huge savings in equipment and energy costs.

Indoor Air Quality (IAQ) Systems and Equipment

Air ventilation and distribution systems should be well maintained and frequently checked for optimal performance. Coordination between air distribution systems and furniture layouts is especially important. In addition, regular inspection for biological and chemical contaminants is crucial. Poor IAQ lowers productivity, can cause illness, and has resulted in numerous lawsuits.

Cleaning Equipment and Products

Using biodegradable and least-toxic cleaning products and equipment can reduce both O&M costs and pollution to air and wastewater streams while improving both indoor air quality and worker productivity. The need for chemical cleaning products can also be reduced through environmentally conscious design and material choices. New requirements for cleaning contracts must be clearly specified.

Materials

Facilities should maintain an attentive and proactive stance with regard to the environmental impacts of their material choices. Every day, new products, systems, and equipment become available that have fewer adverse environmental impacts. All these choices should be carefully scrutinized in terms of O&M.

Water Fixtures and Systems

Routine inspections and maintenance programs for water fixtures and systems are crucial. Population growth and development have reduced the availability of high-quality, potable water in many regions of the country. Along with increased water prices, reduced supply often leads to usage restrictions. An O&M program will reduce operating costs when it verifies that fixtures and systems are functioning effectively and ensures that leaks or components are quickly repaired.

Waste Systems

Recycling and waste-reduction programs and their supporting hardware need frequent attention and maintenance in order to function at peak performance.

Landscape Maintenance

Use of native plantings can significantly reduce landscape O&M requirements and costs. Although natural vegetation may take several years to become established, once it is established there is usually less need for water. Integrated pest management can also reduce overall O&M costs by reducing the need for hazardous chemicals and pesticides.

Building Commissioning

The commissioning process is the mechanism used to ensure that the interface between the trades is working properly. It affects all dynamically operated components, equipment, systems, and features as well as the environmental performance aspects of selected static materials and systems.

Enhanced commissioning supplements fundamental commissioning and focuses on review of the building design and construction documents to identify areas for improvement as well as areas where recommissioning of building systems might be appropriate after occupancy.

Commissioning Report

Complete a commissioning report for each identified component, equipment, system, and feature, including the results of installation observation, start-up and checkout, operation sampling, functional performance testing, and performance criteria verification.

Training

Assemble written verification that training was conducted for appropriate personnel on all commissioned features and systems.

Operation and Maintenance Manuals

Review operation and maintenance manuals for completeness, including instructions for installation, maintenance, replacement, and start-up; replacement sources; parts list; special tools; performance data; and warranty details.

Recommissioning Management Manual

Develop an indexed recommissioning management manual with components such as guidelines for establishing and tracking benchmarks for whole-building energy use and equipment efficiencies, recommendations for recalibration frequency of sensors, a list of all user-adjustable set points and reset schedules, and a list of diagnostic tools.

Measuring Performance

When an organization makes a commitment to reducing energy costs and protecting the environment, it is important to measure the results of these efforts. Senior managers need this information to justify budgets for capital improvements to produce long-term benefits and to determine the benefits received from these investments. These measurements can provide feedback on whether investments are producing the anticipated benefits. If they are not, monitoring may identify reasons for the shortfalls and help facility managers improve performance with other projects.

Some of these measurements are relatively easy to quantify. For example, quantities of energy and water and their associated costs are provided monthly to the facility manager, and the cost-benefit ratio of some energy and water reduction measures can be readily determined from those bills. Levels of specific indoor air pollutants can be measured, but the cost-benefit determination is less straightforward. Many issues are not so readily quantified, such as durability, maintenance, drought-tolerant landscaping, and indoor environmental quality.

For a project financed by an energy savings performance contract (ESPC), an annual verification of cost savings should be provided. Instrumentation and measurement plays a role throughout the process, from measuring baseline energy use, to commissioning new systems, to optimizing long-term performance and serving as the basis of performance metrics and contractor payments.

The International Performance Measurement & Verification Protocol (IPMVP) provides a wide range of measurement and verification (M&V) alternatives, including stipulation based on engineering calculations, metering, and using the results of a short-term test to calibrate computer models. In general, more detailed and labor-intensive efforts yield more information, but the value of the information must be weighed against the cost of the M&V program. Simple, low-cost measurements are often adequate and cost effective. Energy management system tracking features are an effective way to collect consumption and demand information. Three volumes have been published by IPMVP: *Volume I—Concepts and Options for Determining Energy Savings, Volume II—Concepts and Practices for Improved Indoor Environmental Quality,* and *Volume III—Applications.* They are available to download from the Efficiency Valuation Organization website (www.evo-world.org).

Factors affecting the costs of measurement and verification include

- number of energy measures implemented
- size and complexity of energy conservation measures
- interactions between energy conservation measures
- how risk is allocated between the owner and the contractor in a performance contract

The appropriate M&V strategy can be determined by assessing the project's complexity and the way risk is allocated between an energy service company and its customer. Risk allocation refers to whether the contractor (a) is responsible only for equipment performance (efficiency), or (b) also bears some risk related to operational factors, such as uncertainty in the load.

In an ESPC, the M&V program would evaluate all measures of performance in the contract. For example, a lighting contract might include measurements of both electric power consumption and lighting levels.

Electrical Energy

Determining electrical energy consumption is relatively straightforward, and an ordinary electrical meter is adequate for simple daily, weekly, or other regular electrical energy determinations. If consumption versus time is required, either the manual method of taking frequent meter readings or automated data collection is necessary. For the collection of time-based information, split-core current transducers and power transducers can be installed without disconnecting power. Data loggers can be used to collect data, which can then be downloaded as needed.

Electrical Demand

Time-based information is essential if electrical demand is to be determined. For this purpose, it is essential to have the appropriate software to determine the "peak" value. The peak can be a time-averaged value over a sliding 15- or 30-minute time frame in which single or multiple spikes are not indicative of the peak as measured by the local utility. Others simply measure the highest demand in a month and base demand charges on that value.

Chilled Water and Hot Water

Btu meters can be installed to determine the energy consumption of HVAC equipment lines: chilled water, hot water, and steam. Simple, reasonably accurate meters can be installed "hot"; that is, without the need to turn off the water system.

Referenced Standards

The credit descriptions in the LEED rating systems make frequent reference to other documents or resources published by a variety of organizations to establish the requirements for earning LEED points. The standards referenced by the rating systems are chosen because USGBC has determined that they support and standardize the incorporation of green building strategies. Standards may be developed by trade associations, standards writing organizations, or government agencies. By themselves, standards have no legal standing, but when incorporated into a building code adopted by a local agency having jurisdiction, the standards may be enforced by the local code official.

The standards referenced by the LEED rating systems are the benchmark against which a project team and LEED certification reviewers can measure the performance of a particular project. These standards and resources provide the foundation for the technical analysis of planned or implemented green building strategies. Some of the standards are descriptions of minimum performance levels, others are labeling or accreditation mechanisms, and others are computer programs or other interactive technologies that facilitate modeling, simulation and calculations that provide additional building data and assist in assessing the effectiveness of the selected strategies.

Although the LEED Green Associate exam will not require in-depth knowledge of the standards referenced by the rating systems, it is important to be familiar with the organizations that write the standards, what these documents are intended to accomplish, and how the requirements of the standards may be applied. The following documents are common to the LEED for New Construction, Commercial Interiors, Core & Shell, and Existing Buildings: Operations & Maintenance rating systems. After the description of each document is a list of the credits in these systems that make reference to it. (As a general rule, similar standards are referenced by LEED for Schools, Retail, and Healthcare. A very different set of standards is used by LEED for Homes and LEED for Neighborhood Development, but overlapping requirements have been noted.)

Occasionally standards are written as a cooperative effort of two or more independent organizations; an example is ANSI/ASHRAE/IESNA Standard 90.1. In the LEED rating systems, they may be referred to in two different ways; either by the primary agency alone (e.g., ASHRAE Standard 90.1) or by listing the collective agencies (e.g., ANSI/ASHRAE/IESNA Standard 90.1).

This chapter lists standards by the name of the organization that published the standard, the title of the reference, a brief description, and a list of related LEED credits. Where more than one organization participated in development of the standard, the reference is listed by the primary agency.

Many of these standards and other documents can be found on the internet. Those available online are indicated. A list of links to the current URLs for these standards is maintained at **www.ppi2pass/LEEDreferences**.

ANSI (www.ansi.org)

The American National Standards Institute (ANSI) oversees the creation and application of thousands of guidelines for the application of a variety of types of building products and technologies. The organization provides accrediting programs that assess conformance to standards and ensure that the requirements of quality standards are met. ANSI often partners with other organizations who write standards to ensure that appropriate, objective methodology is used to develop the testing requirements.

ASHRAE (www.ashrae.org)

The American Society of Heating, Refrigerating and Air-Conditioning Engineers (ASHRAE) produces standards related to building mechanical systems, often in cooperation with IESNA and ANSI. LEED frequently references ASHRAE standards to establish guidelines for acceptable indoor air quality and energy use.

ANSI/ASHRAE 52.2-1999, *Method of Testing General Ventilation Air Cleaning Devices for Removal Efficiency by Particle Size* (with errata but without addenda). This standard establishes the *minimum efficiency reporting value* (MERV) system. After laboratory testing is completed, the filter's minimum efficiency values at various particle sizes are recorded. These efficiency values are then used to assign a MERV to the filter. Designations range from MERV 1 (typically a low-efficiency, throwaway filter) up to MERV 16 (a filter removing more than 95% of particles tested). Designating the minimum efficiency (as opposed to average efficiency) allows contractors and building owners to select filters knowing their "worst case" efficiency. Using the results of this testing, it is possible to select a filter to remove a specific contaminant if the size range of that contaminant's particles is known. ASHRAE Standard 52.2-1999 groups airborne particles into 12 different size ranges, from 0.3 microns to 10.0 microns in diameter. Further information on particle sizes of contaminants is available from ASHRAE and from leading filter manufacturers. LEED generally requires filtration media with a MERV value of at least 8 to be used during construction, and for filters with a MERV value of 13 or better to be installed prior to occupancy.

Related Credits: *NC IEQc3.1, NC IEQc5, CI IEQc3.1, CI IEQc5, CS IEQc3, CS IEQc5, EBO&M IEQc1.4, EBO&M IEQc1.5*

ASHRAE 55-2004, *Thermal Environmental Conditions for Human Occupancy* (with errata but without addenda). The purpose of this standard is to specify the combination of environmental and personal factors within the interior spaces of a building which will produce thermal environmental conditions acceptable to 80% or more of the occupants of the space.

Related Credits: *NC IEQc6.2, NC IEQc7.1, NC IEQc7.2, CI IEQc6.2, CI IEQc7.1, CI IEQc7.2, CS IEQc6, CS IEQc7, EBO&M IEQc2.3*

ANSI/ASHRAE 62.1-2007, *Ventilation for Acceptable Indoor Air Quality* (with errata but without addenda). Most building codes incorporate all or part of this ASHRAE standard by reference, giving it the force of law and making the requirements of this standard not just the level of performance required for LEED certification, but the minimum level of performance required for code compliance. In addition to setting minimum requirements for indoor ventilation, the standard includes provisions for managing sources of contamination, controlling indoor humidity, and filtering building air, as well as requirements for HVAC system construction and startup, and operation and maintenance of systems. The standard outlines two alternative procedures that may be used to obtain acceptable air quality: the ventilation rate procedure and the indoor air quality procedure.

- *Ventilation Rate Procedure:* Acceptable air quality is achieved by providing ventilation rates equivalent to the specified quantity to the space. For example, a ventilation rate of 20 cu ft per minute per person (0.6 cu meter per minute per person) is required for the average (not peak) occupancy in offices.
- *Indoor Air Quality Procedure:* Acceptable air quality is achieved by controlling known contaminants in the space. This procedure incorporates both quantitative and subjective evaluation of contaminants. Indoor carbon dioxide (CO_2) levels are often monitored as an indicator of the concentration of human bioeffluents with this procedure. An indoor-to-outdoor differential concentration not greater than 700 parts per million of CO_2 indicates that the comfort (odor) criteria related to human bioeffluents are likely to be satisfied.

Related Credits: *NC IEQp1, NC IEQc1, NC IEQc2, NC IEQc6.2, CI IEQp1, CI IEQc1, CI IEQc2, CI IEQc6.2, CS IEQp1, CS IEQc1, CS IEQc2, CS IEQc6, EBO&M IEQp1, EBO&M IEQc1.2, EBO&M IEQc1.3*

ANSI/ASHRAE/IESNA 90.1-2007, *Energy Standard for Buildings Except Low-Rise Residential Buildings* (with errata but without addenda). Sections 5 through 10 of this standard establish maximum energy use requirements and restrictions for the building envelope, ventilations, heating, and air conditioning systems, service water heating, power, lighting (including exterior lighting), and other equipment. The standard also provides methods for comparing energy efficiency design strategies. Each section contains both mandatory provisions and prescriptive requirements for compliance, and some sections contain a performance alternative for compliance. All LEED projects must meet the mandatory measures; project teams may choose between using a prescriptive compliance or a performance compliance approach. Documentation for these two approaches differs significantly.

- *Prescriptive Method:* For buildings where the team chooses to use the prescriptive method, the designers strictly follow the guidelines laid out in the standard, such as providing a recommended constant level of ventilation air to a space. In conjunction with the requirements of ASHRAE Standard 90.1, certain project types selecting the prescriptive compliance path must meet the criteria outlined in *Advanced Energy Design Guide for Small Office Buildings*, 2004; *Advanced Energy Design Guide for Small Retail Buildings*, 2006; *Advanced Energy Design Guide for Small Warehouses and Self-Storage Buildings*, 2008. These guides provide climate- and project type specific approaches to exceeding ASHRAE 90.1 requirements. Recommendations relate to the building envelope, interior lighting, and HVAC & R systems.
- *Performance Method:* In buildings where the performance method of evaluation has been selected, the overall building performance is designed to meet the intent of the standard but may not follow a strict set of requirements. For example, a designer using the performance method may specify more or less ventilation air be provided

to a space at various times than the levels recommended in the prescriptive portion of the standard, because he or she knows that occupant levels in the space will fluctuate during the day (such as in a high school cafeteria). Complying with the intent of the standards using the performance method and adapting the requirements for the specific needs of a particular project often results in buildings that consume less energy while maintaining healthy and comfortable indoor conditions.

Projects in California are permitted to substitute Title 24, Part 6 of the California Code of Regulations, *California's Energy Efficiency Standards for Residential and Non-Residential Buildings*, in place of ASHRAE Standard 90.1.

Related Credits: *NC SSc8, NC EAp2, NC EAc1, CI EAp2, CI EAc1.1, CI EAc1.2, CI EAc1.3, CS SSc8, CS EAp2, CS EAc1*

ASTM (www.astm.org)

ASTM International, originally known as the American Society for Testing and Materials, is one of the largest voluntary standards development organizations in the world and is the source of many technical standards for materials, products, systems, and services. ASTM standards are frequently referenced in building codes to provide a benchmark against which products can be evaluated.

Manufacturers pay ASTM or other similar testing agencies to evaluate their products based upon the criteria established by the standard. If the product passes the test, the manufacturer earns the right to claim that the material meets the requirements. Often, a single product will be tested according to a variety of ASTM standards, each of which addresses specific properties of the material. ASTM standards are a tool that designers can use to fairly evaluate products sold by a variety of manufacturers to determine whether one brand of product will perform in a similar way to another.

ASTM C1371, *Standard Test Method for Determination of Emittance of Materials Near Room Temperature Using Portable Emissometers*. This test method provides a comparative means of quantifying the emittance, or emissivity, of opaque, highly thermally conductive materials near room temperature. This information can be used to evaluate temperatures, heat flows, and derived thermal resistances of materials.

Related Credits: *NC SSc7.1, NC SSc7.2, CI SSc1, CS SSc7.1, CS SSc7.2, EBO&M SSc7.1, EBO&M SSc7.2*

ASTM C1549, *Standard Test Method for Determination of Solar Reflectance Near Ambient Temperature Using a Portable Solar Reflectometer*. This test method measures the solar reflectance of a flat opaque surface. The temperatures of opaque surfaces exposed to solar radiation are generally higher than adjacent air temperatures. Where roofs or walls enclose conditioned spaces, increased inward heat flows result. In the case of equipment or storage containers exposed to the sun, internal operating temperatures are usually increased. The extent to which solar radiation affects surface temperatures depends on the solar reflectance of the exposed surface. A solar reflectance of 1.0 (100% reflected) would result in no effect on surface temperature, while a solar reflectance of zero (none reflected, all absorbed) would result in the maximum effect. Coatings and finishes with specific solar reflectance values can be used to change the temperature of surfaces exposed to sunlight. The initial (clean) solar reflectance value must be maintained during the life of the coating or finish to have the expected thermal performance.

Therefore, these coatings must be capable of withstanding environmental effects that may cause them to discolor, peel, or otherwise degrade.

The test method provides a means for periodic testing of surfaces in the field or in the laboratory. The precision of the average of several measurements is usually governed by the variability of reflectances on the surface being tested.

The value for solar reflectance determined by this method can be used to calculate the solar energy absorbed by an opaque surface using the equation $Q_{abs} = Aq_{solar}(1 - r)$. It is then possible to combine the absorbed solar energy with conductive, convective and other radiative terms to construct a heat balance around an element or calculate a Solar Reflectance Index (SRI).

Related Credits: *NC SSc7.1, NC SSc7.2, CI SSc1, CS SSc7.1, CS SSc7.2, EBO&M SSc7.1, EBO&M SSc7.2*

ASTM D1003, *Standard Test Method for Haze and Luminous Transmittance of Transparent Plastics*. This test method measures the amount of light that is scattered upon passing through a transparent material. It is used to evaluate the amount of light admitted by a skylight.

Related Credits: *NC IEQc8.1, CI IEQc8.1, CS IEQc8.1, EBO&M IEQc2.4*

ASTM E408, *Standard Test Methods for Total Normal Emittance of Surfaces Using Inspection Meter Techniques*. These nondestructive test methods rapidly determine the total normal emittance, or emmissivity, of surfaces by means of portable, inspection-meter instruments. *Total normal emittance* (N) is defined as the ratio of the normal radiance of a specimen to that of a blackbody radiator at the same temperature. *Emittance* measures a material's ability to shed heat, and values can be from 0 to 1. The *emittance value* is used to calculate a material's solar reflective index.

Related Credits: *NC SSc7.1, NC SSc7.2, CI SSc1, CS SSc7.1, CS SSc7.2, EBO&M SSc7.1, EBO&M SSc7.2*

ANSI/ASTM E779-03, *Standard Test Method for Determining Air Leakage Rate by Fan Pressurization*. Air leakage, both into and out of the building envelope, accounts for a significant portion of the thermal space conditioning load. Infiltration can affect occupant comfort, indoor air quality, and the efficiency and energy consumption rates of mechanical equipment.

In most commercial or industrial buildings, some outdoor air is introduced by design; however, air leakage can be a significant addition to the designed outdoor airflow. In most residential buildings, indoor-outdoor air exchange is attributable primarily to air leakage through cracks and construction joints; the problem can be exacerbated by pressure differences due to temperature differences, wind, operation of auxiliary fans (for example, kitchen and bathroom exhausts), and operation of combustion equipment in the building.

The *fan pressurization method* evaluates the airtightness of the building envelope. It can be used to compare the relative air tightness of several similar buildings, identify the leakage sources and rates of leakage from different components of the same building envelope, determine the air leakage reduction for individual retrofit measures applied incrementally to an existing building, and determine ventilation rates when combined with weather and leak location information.

This ANSI/ASTM standard is referenced in the Environmental Tobacco Smoke Control prerequisites and is used to restrict the amount of space that can allow air to pass from one room to another to less than 1.25 sq in (8.1 sq cm) per 100 sq ft (9.3 sq m) of wall area.

Related Credits: *NC IEQp2, CI IEQp2, CS IEQp2, EBO&M IEQp2*

ASTM E903, *Standard Test Method for Solar Absorptance, Reflectance, and Transmittance of Materials Using Integrating Spheres.* This test method covers the measurement of spectral absorptance, reflectance, and transmittance of materials using spectrophotometers equipped with integrating spheres. Methods of computing solar weighted properties from the measured spectral values are specified. The standard is referenced in the Energy Star roofing method, which also allows the use of reflectometers to measure solar reflectance of roofing materials. *Solar reflectance* (also called albedo) measures a material's ability to reflect light and is measured as a percentage. A value of 0% equals total absorption (the definition of a black body), and 100% is a perfect reflective surface. The reflectance value is used to calculate a material's SRI.

Related Credits: *NC SSc7.1, NC SSc7.2, CI SSc1, CS SSc7.1, CS SSc7.2, EBO&M SSc7.1, SSc7.2*

ASTM E1903-97, *Phase II Environmental Site Assessment Process.* A Phase II Environmental Site Assessment (ESA) is conducted to provide testing guidelines and mitigation measures for contaminated soils (prioritizing CERCLA— Comprehensive Environmental Response, Compensation, and Liability Act, or "Superfund"—contaminants) identified in a Phase I ESA. Upon completion, the environmental professional should be able to confirm or deny the presence of hazardous substances or petroleum products that have been improperly disposed of or released on the site. Depending upon the scope of the work, the environmental professional may also be able to provide guidance on the nature and extent of contamination, as well as mitigation measures, which may assist the property owner in making business decisions regarding the property.

This guide to the Phase II Environmental Site Assessment process has twelve sections and one appendix. Section 1 is the Scope section. Section 2 is Referenced Documents. Section 3, Terminology, contains definitions of terms and acronyms used in the guide. Section 4 is Significance and Use of this guide. Section 5 is Contracting Considerations. Sections 6 to 11 constitute the main body of the guide and include objectives (Section 6), developing the scope of work (Section 7), assessment activities (Section 8), evaluation of data (Section 9), interpretation of results (Section 10), and recommended report preparation (Section 11). Section 12 provides additional information regarding non-scope considerations. This book's appendix provides a sample table of contents and report format for a written Phase II Environmental Site Assessment Report.

Related Credits: *NC SSc3, CI SSc1, CS SSc3 (also cited in ND SSLc2)*

ASTM E1918-06, *Standard Test Method for Measuring Solar Reflectance of Horizontal and Low-Sloped Surfaces in the Field.* This test method facilitates measurement of solar reflectance of various horizontal and low-sloped surfaces and materials in the field. Measurements are taken using a pyranometer when the sun angle relative to the normal from a surface is less than 45 degrees.

Related Credits: *NC SSc7.1, NC SSc7.2, CI SSc1, CS SSc7.1, CS SSc7.2, EBO&M SSc7.2*

ASTM E1980-01, *Standard Practice for Calculating Solar Reflectance Index of Horizontal and Low-Sloped Opaque Surfaces*. Solar reflectance and thermal emittance (or thermal emissivity) are important factors affecting surface and near-surface ambient air temperature. Surfaces with low solar reflectance absorb a large fraction of the incoming solar energy. Of this absorbed energy, part is conducted into the ground and buildings, part is convected to air (raising air temperatures), and part is radiated to the sky. When conditions are equivalent, the lower the emissivity of a surface, the higher its steady-state temperature. Surfaces with low emissivity cannot effectively radiate to the sky; therefore, they get hot. Determination of solar reflectance and thermal emittance, and subsequent calculation of the relative temperature of the surfaces with respect to black and white reference temperature (defined as solar reflectance index, or SRI), may help designers and consumers to choose the proper materials to make their buildings and communities energy efficient. The method described by the standard gives the SRI of surfaces based on measured solar reflectances and thermal emissivities of the surfaces.

Related Credits: *NC SSc7.1, NC SSc7.2, CI SSc1, CS SSc7.1, CS SSc7.2, EBO&M SSc7.2*

U.S. Code of Federal Regulations (CFR) (www.gpoaccess.gov/cfr/index.html)

The CFR is the codification of the general and permanent rules published in the Federal Register by the executive departments and agencies of the federal government (e.g., DOE, EPA). It is divided into 50 titles that represent broad areas subject to federal regulation. LEED has adopted the following CFR definitions.

Wetlands: Defined by U.S. Code of Federal Regulations 40 CFR, Parts 230-233 and Part 22.

Wetlands are areas inundated or saturated by surface or groundwater at a frequency and duration sufficient to support, and that under normal circumstances do support, a prevalence of vegetation typically adapted for life in saturated soil conditions.

Related Credits: *NC SSc1, CS SSc1 (this definition is also used in H LLc2)*

Prime farmland: Defined by the U.S. Department of Agriculture in the United States Code of Federal Regulations, Title 7, Volume 6, Parts 400 to 699, Section 657.5 (citation 7CFR657.5). Land that has the best combination of physical and chemical characteristics for producing food, feed, forage, fiber, and oilseed crops, and is also available for these uses. (The land can be cropland, pastureland, rangeland, forest land, or other land, but not urban built-up land or water.) It has the soil quality, growing season, and moisture supply needed to economically produce sustained high yields of crops when treated and managed, including water management, according to acceptable farming methods. In general, prime farmlands have an adequate and dependable water supply from precipitation or irrigation, a favorable temperature and growing season, acceptable acidity or alkalinity, acceptable salt and sodium content, and few or no rocks. They are permeable to water and air. Prime farmlands are not excessively erodible or saturated with water for a long period of time, and they either do not flood frequently or are protected from flooding. Examples of soils that qualify as prime farmland are Palouse silt loam, 0 to 7 percent slopes; Brookston silty clay loam, drained; and Tama silty clay loam, 0 to 5 percent slopes.

Related Credits: *NC SSc1, CS SSc1*

U.S. Department of Energy (DOE) (www.doe.gov)

The U.S. Department of Energy (DOE), through the Office of Energy Efficiency and Renewable Energy's (EERE) Building Technologies Program, works closely with the building industry and manufacturers to research and development technologies and practices for energy efficiency. The department also promotes energy and money-saving opportunities to builders and consumers and works with state and local regulatory groups to improve building codes and appliance standards. In addition, the DOE Office of Hearings and Appeals plays a regulatory role in the area of energy efficiency as it relates to the Energy Policy and Conservation Act (EPAct).

Commercial Buildings Energy Consumption Survey. This is a nationwide survey conducted every four years that assesses the average energy consumption and expenditures of commercial buildings. It is available online at **www.ppi2pass/LEEDreferences**.

Related Credits: *NC EAc2, NC EAc6, CS EAc2, CS EAc6*

Energy Policy Acts (EPAct) of 1992 and 2005. EPAct was passed by Congress in 1992 to reduce U.S. dependence on imported petroleum and improve air quality. Officially known as Public Law 102-486, EPAct includes provisions that address all aspects of energy supply and demand, such as encouraging use of alternative fuels and introducing regulatory approaches for encouraging the fundamental changes necessary to building a self-sustaining alternative fuel market.

Congress established several regulatory activities within EPAct that focus on building an inventory of alternative fuel vehicles (AFVs) in large, centrally fueled fleets in metropolitan areas. EPAct requires certain fleets to purchase a percentage of light-duty AFVs, which can run on alternative fuels, each year. Some types of vehicles are excluded.

Most of the citations of EPAct in the LEED rating systems deal with water consumption and conservation. The Act addresses energy and water use in commercial, institutional, and residential projects, and prescribes maximum water usage (flow) requirements for water closets, urinals, showerheads, faucets, replacement aerators, and metering faucets.

EPAct also provides guidance on the following systems.

- *Buildings:* Requires states to establish minimum commercial building energy codes and to consider minimum residential codes based on current voluntary codes. This gave impetus to the creation and modification of ANSI/ASHRAE/IESNA Standard 90.1-1999 and -2001, ANSI/ASHRAE/IESNA Standard 90.2, and development of the International Energy Conservation Code by the International Code Council.
- *Utilities:* Requires states to consider new regulatory standards that would require utilities to undertake integrated resource planning; allows energy efficiency programs to be at least as profitable as new supply options; and encourages improvements in supply system efficiency.
- *Equipment Standards:* Establishes efficiency standards for commercial heating and air conditioning equipment, electric motors, and lamps.
- *Renewable Energy:* Establishes a program for providing federal support on a competitive basis for renewable energy technologies.
- *Electricity:* Removes obstacles to wholesale power competition in the Public Utilities Holding Company Act (PUHCA).

The Energy Policy Act of 2005 provides tax incentives and subsidies for energy conservation and the production and use of wind energy and other alternative energies, and authorized loan guarantees for the development of innovative energy technologies.

Related Credits: *NC WEp1, NC WEc3, CI WEp1, CI WEc1, CS WEp1, CS WEc3 (also cited in ND GIBp3)*

Standard Process for Commercial Energy Code Determination. This provides the Department of Energy's current opinion on the latest version of ASHRAE Standard 90.1. Each edition of the standard is evaluated to determine if buildings constructed in accordance with the new requirements will have greater energy efficiency than those built according to the prior criteria. It is available online at **www.ppi2pass/LEEDreferences**.

Related Credits: *NC EAp2, NC EAc1, CI EAp2, CS EAp2, CS EAc1*

EcoLogo (www.ecologo.org)

EcoLogo is the sponsor of the Environmental Choice Certification Criteria Documents cited in the requirements for cleaning products prescribed by LEED EBO&M IEQc3.3.

Environmental Choice CCD-082: *Toilet Tissue.*
Related Credits: *EBO&M IEQc3.3*

Environmental Choice CCD-086: *Hand Towels.*
Related Credits: *EBO&M IEQc3.3*

Environmental Choice CCD-104: *Hand Cleaners—Industrial & Institutional.*
Related Credits: *EBO&M IEQc3.3*

Environmental Choice CCD-110: *Cleaning and Degreasing Compounds, Biologically-Based.*
Related Credits: *EBO&M IEQc3.3*

Environmental Choice CCD-112: *Biological Digestion Additives for Cleaning and Odor Control.*
Related Credits: *EBO&M IEQc3.3*

Environmental Choice CCD-113: *Drain and/or Grease Trap Additives—Alternative.*
Related Credits: *EBO&M IEQc3.3*

Environmental Choice CCD-115: *Odor Control Additives—Alternative.*
Related Credits: *EBO&M IEQc3.3*

Environmental Choice CCD-146: *Hardsurface Cleaners.*
Related Credits: *EBO&M IEQc3.3*

Environmental Choice CCD-147: *Floor Care Products.*
Related Credits: *EBO&M IEQc3.3*

Environmental Choice CCD-148: *Carpet and Upholstery Cleaners.*
Related Credits: *EBO&M IEQc3.3*

Energy Star (www.energystar.gov)

Energy Star is a joint program of the U.S. Department of Energy and the U.S. Environmental Protection Agency that identifies energy efficient products and practices, such as high-albedo roofs and appliances.

Related Credits: *NC SSc7.2, CI EAp2, CI EAc1.4, EBO&M SSc7.2, EBO&M EAp2, EBO&M EAc1, EBO&M EAc6, EBO&M MRc2*

Energy Star Portfolio Manager. This is an interactive property management tool that allows facility managers to track and monitor energy and water consumption at all buildings in the company's portfolio. It can be used to evaluate building performance, set goals for improvement, or verify information for Energy Star building recognition. More information is available online at www.energystar.gov.

Related Credits: *EBO&M EAp2, EBO&M EAc1*

Environmental Protection Agency (EPA) (www.epa.gov)

The EPA is a Federal agency formed to develop and enforce regulations implemented by environmental laws enacted by Congress. The agency is responsible for researching and setting national standards for a variety of environmental programs. It delegates to states and (through the American Indian Environmental Office) to tribes the responsibility for issuing permits and for monitoring and enforcing compliance. Where national standards are not met, the EPA can issue sanctions and take other steps to assist the states and tribes in reaching desired levels of environmental quality. The EPA also conducts research to advance environmental education.

EPA, *Compendium of Methods for the Determination of Air Pollutants in Indoor Air*. This guide provides a standard format for the active and passive sampling and on- and off-site analysis of indoor air.

Related Credits: *NC IEQc3.2, CI IEQc3.2*

EPA, *Comprehensive Procurement Guidelines*. These guidelines encourage the purchase of recycled-content products. Available online: See **www.ppi2pass/LEEDreferences**.

Related Credits: *EBO&M IEQc3.3*

EPA, *Construction General Permit*. This stormwater management guide establishes requirements for discharge of stormwater from construction sites greater than one acre. LEED considers it applicable to sites of all sizes. Available online: See **www.ppi2pass/LEEDreferences**.

Related Credits: *NC SSp1, CS SSp1*

Research Triangle Institute/EPA, *Environmental Technology Verification: Large Chamber Test Protocol for Measuring Emissions of VOCs and Aldehydes, September 1999*. This test method measures emissions from products under conditions simulating indoor use. The use of systems furniture and seating that has been tested by this protocol and that does not exceed emission limits can help a project meet the requirements of LEED CI IEQ Credit 4.5. Available online: See **www.ppi2pass/LEEDreferences**.

Related Credits: *CI IEQc4.5*

EPA, *Guidance Specifying Management Measures for Sources of Nonpoint Pollution in Coastal Waters, January 1993 (EPA 840-B-92-002).* This guide suggests strategies for post-construction stormwater management and treatment, including structural and nonstructural measures. Available online: See **www.ppi2pass/LEEDreferences**.

Related Credits: *CI SSc1*

EPA, *Indoor Air Quality Building Education and Assessment Model (I-BEAM), EPA Reference Number 402-C-01-001, December 2002.* This is a computer software program that can be used by building managers to develop an indoor air quality improvement and maintenance program. Available online: See **www.ppi2pass/LEEDreferences**.

Related Credits: *EBO&M IEQc1.1*

Green Seal (www.greenseal.org)

Green Seal tests and evaluates products and materials based on standards developed to recognize environmental sustainability leadership. Green Seal Standards are often cited in the LEED rating systems to define VOC limits. Like the Environmental Choice CCDs, many of the Green Seal Standards are also cited in the requirements for cleaning products.

Green Seal GS-1, *Tissue Paper.*
Related Credits: *EBO&M IEQc3.3*

Green Seal GS-9, *Paper Towels and Napkins.*
Related Credits: *EBO&M IEQc3.3*

Green Seal GS-11, *Paints, 1st Edition, May 20, 1993.* This standard sets VOC limits for commercial paints. (Note that LEED refers to a document that is not the most current version of this standard.)
Related Credits: *NC IEQc4.2, CI IEQc4.2, CS IEQc4.2, EBO&M MRc3 (also cited in H MRc2)*

Green Seal GS-03, *Anti-Corrosive Paints, 2nd Edition, January 7, 1997.* This standard sets VOC limits for anti-corrosive and anti-rust paints and coatings. (Note that LEED refers to a document that is not the most current version of this standard. The most current version of GS-11 supersedes and eliminates GS-03. The credit descriptions in the LEED NC and CS rating systems erroneously refer to this as "GC-03.")
Related Credits: *NC IEQc4.2, CI IEQc4.2, CS IEQc4.2*

Green Seal GS-36, *Commercial Adhesives.* This standard sets VOC limitations for aerosol adhesives, which are measured as the percentage of VOCs by weight.
Related Credits: *NC IEQc4.1, CI IEQc4.1, CS IEQc4.1*

Green Seal GS-37, *Industrial and Institutional Cleaners.* This standard sets limits for general purpose, bathroom, glass, and carpet cleaners.
Related Credits: *EBO&M IEQc3.3*

Green Seal GS-40, *Industrial and Institutional Floor Finish and Floor Finish Strippers.*
Related Credits: *EBO&M IEQc3.3*

Green Seal GS-41, *Hand Cleaners and Hand Soaps Used for Industrial and Institutional Purposes.*
Related Credits: *EBO&M IEQc3.3*

Other Referenced Standards & Resources

ANSI/BIFMA M 7.1-2007, *Standard Test Method for Determining VOC Emissions from Office Furniture Systems, Components, and Seating.* (BIFMA stands for the Business and Institutional Manufacturer's Association.)

Related Credits: *CI IEQc4.5*

ANSI/BIFMA X 7.1-2007, *Standard for Formaldehyde and TVOC Emissions of Low-Emitting Office Furniture Systems and Seating.*

Related Credits: *CI IEQc4.5*

ANSI/BOMA Z 65.1-98, *Standard Methods for Measuring Floor Area in Office Buildings.* This standard defines usable area, floor rentable area, building common area, gross rentable area, and load factor for commercial office buildings. (BOMA stands for Building Owners and Managers Association.)

Related Credits: *CS EAc6*

ANSI/SMACNA 008-2008, *IAQ Guidelines for Occupied Buildings Under Construction,* 2nd Edition 2007. This standard provides an overview of air pollutants associated with construction, their control measures, management of construction process quality control, and more. SMACNA stands for Sheet Metal and Air Conditioning Contractors' National Association.

Related Credits: *NC IEQc3.1, CI IEQc3.1, CS IEQc3, EBO&M IEQc1.5*

APPA/Leadership in Educational Facilities, *Custodial Staffing Guidelines.* This rating system is used to determine a facility's level of cleanliness and effectiveness of the custodial staff. Defines five levels of clean: 1—Orderly Spotlessness, 2—Ordinary Tidiness, 3—Casual Inattention, 4—Moderate Dinginess, 5—Unkempt Neglect. LEED EBO&M requires a maximum score of 3.

Related Credits: *EBO&M IEQc3.2*

ASME A112.18.1-2005, *Plumbing Supply Fittings.* This publication by the American Society of Mechanical Engineers defines standards and performance requirements for plumbing fixture fittings, materials, and equipment.

Related Credits: *NC WEp1, NC WEc3, CI WEp1, WEc1, CS WEp1, CS WEc3 (also referred to in H WEc3 and ND GIBp3)*

Bay Area Air Quality Management District Regulation 8, Rule 51. This rule establishes the maximum levels of VOC permitted in adhesives and sealants. Available online: See **www.ppi2pass/LEEDreferences**.

Related Credits: *EBO&M MRc3*

California Code of Regulations, Title 24, Part 6, *Residential Alternative Calculation Method Approval Manual*. Available online: See **www.ppi2pass/LEEDreferences**.

Related Credits: *CI IEQp2*

California Department of Health Services Standard Practice for the Testing of Volatile Organic Emissions from Various Sources Using Small-Scale Environmental Chambers, including 2004 Addenda (Section 1350). Available online: See **www.ppi2pass/ LEEDreferences**.

Related Credits: *NC IEQc4.3, CS IEQc4.3*

Carbon Trust, Good Practice Guide 237, *Natural Ventilation in Non-Domestic Buildings,* 1998. This guide summarizes the benefits of natural ventilation and considers the commercial implications, illustrating the issues with case studies. (In EBO&M IEQc1.3, this is erroneously referred to as the "CIBSE Good Practice Guide 237".)

Related Credits: *NC IEQc2, CI IEQc2, CS IEQc2, EBO&M IEQc1.3*

Carpet and Rug Institute, Green Label and Green Label Plus Testing Programs. These labeling programs' standards set VOC limits for carpets and carpet cushioning. Measurements are in micrograms per square meter per hour. Available online: See **www.ppi2pass/LEEDreferences**.

Related Credits: *NC IEQc4.3, CI IEQc4.3, CS IEQc4.3, EBO&M MRc3, EBO&M IEQc3.4*

Center for Resource Solutions, Green-e Product Certification Requirements. The Green-e program certifies and verifies green electricity products. Qualifying criteria include renewable source (e.g., wind, solar, geothermal, biomass, and low-impact hydro facilities), low emissions, non-nuclear, and others (which may be regionally specific). Information on the program is available at www.green-e.org.

Related Credits: *NC EAc6, CI EAc4, CS EAc6, EBO&M EAc4*

Chartered Institution of Building Services Engineers (CIBSE), Applications Manual 10, *Natural Ventilation in Non-domestic Buildings,* 2005. This guide presents design strategies for natural ventilation, components and system integration, and calculations for establishing required airflow rates.

Related Credits: *NC IEQc2, CI IEQc2, CS IEQc2, EBO&M IEQc1.3*

Clean Air Act, Title VI, Rule 608. Congress passed the Clean Air Act in 1963, with an extension in 1970 and amendments in 1977 and 1990. The 1990 amendment was made in response to the Montreal Protocol. Title VI, Sec. 608, of the Clean Air Act regulates stationary air conditioning and refrigeration appliances, excluding air conditioners for motor vehicles. Available online: See **www.ppi2pass/LEEDreferences**.

Related Credits: *EBO&M EAp3*

Clean Water Act. The Clean Water Act was passed by Congress in 1972, with major amendments in the Clean Water Act of 1977 and the Water Quality Act of 1987. Water bodies are defined as "seas, lakes, rivers, streams, and tributaries which support or could support fish, recreation, or industrial use, consistent with the terminology of the Clean Water Act." Small human-made water bodies constructed for stormwater retention, fire suppression, or recreation are not included, but human-made water bodies and wetlands are included if they were constructed for the purpose of restoring an area's natural ecology. Available online: See **www.ppi2pass/LEEDreferences**.

Related Credits: *NC SSc1, CS SSc1*

Federal Emergency Management Agency. LEED has adopted FEMA's definition of a 100-year flood, which is the flood elevation that has a 1% chance of being equaled or exceeded in any given year. A 100-year flood doesn't necessarily happen once every hundred years, and a better term might have been a "one chance in a hundred years" flood. It is possible for two 100-year floods to happen in consecutive years, or for a 100-year period to contain none at all.

Related Credits: *NC SSc1, CS SSc1 (also referenced in H LLc2 and ND SLLp6)*

Forest Stewardship Council, *Principles and Criteria.* Forest Management Certification from the FSC confirms responsible forest management and operations. Wood from such a source is "FSC certified." FSC Chain of Custody Certification may be awarded to companies that use FSC-certified wood. Available online: See **www.ppi2pass/LEEDreferences**.

Related Credits: *NC MRc7, CI MRc7, CS MRc6, EBO&M MRc1, EBO&M MRc2 (also cited in H MRc2)*

Greenguard Environmental Institute, *Greenguard Indoor Air Quality Certification Program.* Products that are Greenguard Indoor Air Quality Certified meet standards for low chemical and particle emissions for use indoors. More information is available at www.greenguard. com.

Related Credits: *CI IEQc4.5*

IESNA RP-33-99, "*Lighting for Exterior Environments.*" Establishes limits for lighting levels and requirements for luminaire types, mounting heights, and aiming angles in outdoor areas such as parking lots.

Related Credits: *NC SSc8, CS SSc8*

International Association of Plumbing and Mechanical Officials, Uniform Plumbing Code, 2006 ed. and **International Code Council, International Plumbing Code, 2006 ed.** These are plumbing codes widely adopted by jurisdictions in the United States and around the world. The LEED rating systems refer to these publications to define water use baseline requirements.

Related Credits: *NC WEp1, NC WEc3, CI WEp1, CI WEc1, CS WEp1, CS WEc3, EBO&M WEc2*

International Performance Measurement and Verification Protocol (IPMVP), *Volume I: Concepts and Options for Determining Energy and Water Savings,* January 2001. This volume of the IPMVP defines terms and general procedures for measuring and verifying savings due to energy efficiency, water efficiency, and renewable energy use. Available online: See **www. ppi2pass/LEEDreferences**.

Related Credits: *CI EAc3*

International Performance Measurement and Verification Protocol (IPMVP), *Volume III: Concepts and Options for Determining Energy Savings in New Construction*, April 2003. This guide describes best-practice methods for measuring and verifying (M&V) energy performance for new construction, including development of theoretical baseline usage and the M&V plan. Available online: See **www.ppi2pass/LEEDreferences**.

Related Credits: *NC EAc5, CS EAc5.1*

ISO 14021:1999, *Environmental Labels and Declarations—Self-Declared Environmental Claims (Type II Environmental Labeling)*. In addition to describing the evaluation and verification methods for self-declared environmental claims, this international standard also defines requirements for environmental products. (ISO stands for International Organization of Standards.)

A helpful document called *Best Practices of ISO 14021* is available online; see **www.ppi2pass/LEEDreferences**.

- *assembly recycled content:* determined by dividing the weight of the pre- and post-consumer recycled content by the overall weight of the assembly
- *post-consumer waste:* waste collected after the end user has used a product and disposed of it
- *pre-consumer content:* material recovered from a waste stream somewhere in the manufacturing process prior to reaching the end user

Related Credits: *NC MRc4, CI MRc4, CS MRc4*

Montreal Protocol. The U.S. Congress passed the Clean Air Act in 1963, with an extension in 1970 and amendments in 1977 and 1990. The 1990 amendment was made in response to the Montreal Protocol, an international treaty that entered into force in 1989. Countries that signed the Montreal Protocol, including the United States, agreed to protect the ozone layer by phasing out the production of a number of substances connected to ozone depletion, including chlorofluorocarbons (CFCs). According to the terms of the Montreal Protocol, the use of CFCs was to be phased out beginning in 1991 and was to reach zero by 1996.

Related Credits: *NC EAc4, CS EAc4, EBO&M EAc5*

NEMA LL 8-2008, *Limits on Mercury Content in Self-Ballasted Compact Fluorescent Lamps.* This set the voluntary maximum limit on mercury content in self-ballasted compact fluorescent lamps. (NEMA stands for National Electrical Manufacturers Association.) Available online: See **www.ppi2pass/LEEDreferences**.

Related Credits: *EBO&M MRc4*

New Building Institute, *Advanced Buildings Core Performance Guide.* This guide outlines a step-by-step simplified approach to achieve predictable energy savings in small- to medium-sized buildings without the need for modeling. The Core Performance program brings together over 30 criteria defining high performance in building envelope, lighting, HVAC, power systems and controls, and includes quantitative and descriptive specifications for exceeding state and national energy standards such as ANSI/ASHRAE/IESNA Standard 90.1-2004 by 20% to 30%. More information is available at www.advancedbuildings.net.

Related Credits: *CI EAc1.3*

National Institute of Standards and Technology, *NIST CONTAM Multizone Modeling Software* and *LoopDA Natural Ventilation Sizing Tool.* This software is used to model and analyze indoor environmental conditions. Available online: See **www.ppi2pass/LEEDreferences**.

Related Credits: *NC IEQc2, CI IEQc2, CS IEQc2, EBO&M IEQc1.3*

Residential Manual for Compliance with California's 2001 Energy Efficiency Standards. (Note that LEED refers to a document that is not the most current version of this standard; the 2005 Standards supersede this edition.) Available online: See **www.ppi2pass/LEEDreferences**.

Related Credits: *NC IEQp2, CS IEQp2*

Resilient Floor Covering Institute, FloorScore Testing Program. This standard sets VOC limits for flooring products, including vinyl, linoleum, laminate, wood, ceramic, rubber, wall base, and related accessories. Available online: See **www.ppi2pass/LEEDreferences**.

Related Credits: *NC IEQc4.3, CI IEQc4.3, CS IEQc4.3, EBO&M MRc3*

South Coast Air Quality Management District (SCAQMD) Rule 1113, "Architectural Coatings," rules in effect on January 1, 2004. This standard sets VOC limits for architectural coatings. Available online: See **www.ppi2pass/LEEDreferences**.

Related Credits: *NC IEQc4.2, NC IEQc4.3, CI IEQc4.2, CI IEQc4.3, CS IEQ c4.2, CS IEQc4.3*

South Coast Air Quality Management District (SCAQMD) Rule 1168, "Adhesive and Sealant Applications," rules amended on January 7, 2005, and in effect on July 1, 2005. This standard sets VOC limits for adhesives. Limits for architectural adhesives are below 100 g/L, sealants are below 450 g/L, sealant primers are below 775 g/L, and specialty application limits are as high as 850 g/L. These limits can be compared to the Green Seal VOC limitations, which are the percentage of VOCs by weight. Available online: See **www.ppi2pass/LEEDreferences**.

Related Credits: *NC IEQc4.1, NC IEQc4.3, CI IEQc4.1, CI IEQc4.3, CS IEQc4.1, CS IEQc4.3, EBO&M MRc3*

U.S. Fish and Wildlife Service, List of endangered and threatened wildlife and plants. This site provides federal and state lists of threatened and endangered species (both plants and animals). Available online: See **www.ppi2pass/LEEDreferences**.

Related Credits: *NC SSc1, CS SSc1*

WaterSense, A labeling program of the U.S. Environmental Protection Agency used to identify water-efficient products and programs. The WaterSense label identifies approved lavatory fixtures as well as irrigation systems. More information available at www.epa.gov (search for "WaterSense").

Related Credits: *NC WEp1, NC WEc1, CI WEp1, CI WEc1, CS WEp1, CS WEc1 (also referenced in H WEc3)*

Terminology

List of Abbreviations

A/E/C	architecture, engineering, and construction
ACCA	Air Conditioning Contractors of America
ACEEE	American Council for an Energy Efficient Economy
ACH	air changes per hour
AE	Awareness and Education (LEED for Homes credit category)
A/E	architecture/engineering
AFUV	annual fuel utilization efficiency
AFV	alternative fuel vehicle
AHJ	authority having jurisdiction
AIA	American Institute of Architects
ANSI	American National Standards Institute
ASHRAE	American Society of Heating, Refrigerating and Air-Conditioning Engineers
ASME	American Society of Mechanical Engineers
ASTM	American Society for Testing and Materials
ATV	advanced technology vehicle
BAS	building automation system
BD+C	Building Design and Construction (LEED AP specialty)
BIFMA	Business and Institutional Furniture Manufacturer's Association
BIPV	building integrated photovoltaics
BIM	building information modeling
BMP	best management practice
BOD	basis of design
BOMA	Building Owners and Managers Association
BRI	building related illness
CAE	combined annual efficiency
CARB	California Air Resources Board

CARE	Carpet America Recovery Effort
CBECS	Commercial Building Energy Consumption Survey (conducted by the Department of Energy)
C&D	construction and demolition
CCD	certification criteria document
CDL	construction, demolition, and land clearing
CDVR	corrected design ventilation rate
CERCLA	Comprehensive Environmental Response Compensation and Liability Act (also known as "Superfund")
CFA	conditioned floor area
CFC	chlorofluorocarbon
CFL	compact fluorescent lamp (or light)
CFM	cubic feet per minute
CFR	U.S. Code of Federal Regulations
CI	Commercial Interiors (LEED CI)
CIBSE	Chartered Institution of Building Services Engineers
CIR	Credit Interpretation Request or Credit Interpretation Ruling
CITES	Convention on International Trade in Endangered Species of Wild Fauna and Flora
CMP	Credentialing Maintenance Program
CO	carbon monoxide
CO$_2$	carbon dioxide
COC	chain of custody
COP	coefficient of performance
CRI	Carpet and Rug Institute
CRS	Center for Resource Solutions
CS	Core & Shell Development (LEED CS rating system)
CSI	Construction Specifications Institute
CWMP	construction waste management plan
Cx	commissioning
CxA	commissioning agent
CZ	climate zone
D-B	design-build
dBA	decibels (adjusted)
DBB	design-bid-build
DBIA	Design-Build Institute of America
DCV	demand controlled ventilation
DF	daylight factor
DHW	domestic hot water
DOE	U.S. Department of Energy
DU	distribution uniformity
EA	effective aperture
EA	Energy and Atmosphere (credit category)
EBO&M	Existing Buildings: Operation & Maintenance (LEED EBO&M rating system)

ECB	energy cost budget
ECM	energy conservation measures
EER	energy efficiency rating
EERE	U.S. Office of Energy Efficiency and Renewable Energy
EF	energy factor
EIFS	exterior insulation and finish system
EPA	U.S. Environmental Protection Agency
EPAct	U.S. Energy Policy Act of 1992 or 2005
EPDM	ethylene propylene diene monomer
EPEAT	electronic product environmental assessment tools
EPP	environmentally preferable purchasing
EPS	expanded polystyrene
ESA	environmental site assessment
ESC	erosion and sedimentation control
ESPC	energy savings performance contract
ET	evapotranspiration
ETS	environmental tobacco smoke
ETV	environmental technology verification
FEMA	U.S. Federal Emergency Management Agency
FF&E	fixtures, furnishings, and equipment
FSC	Forest Stewardship Council
FTE	full-time equivalent
GBCI	Green Building Certification Institute
GF	glazing factor
GHG	greenhouse gas
GIB	Green Infrastructure and Building (LEED for Neighborhood Development credit category)
GWP	global warming potential
GPF	gallons per flush
GPM	gallons per minute
HCFC	hydrochlorofluorocarbon
HD+C	Home Design and Construction (LEED AP specialty)
HEPA	high-efficiency particulate air (filter)
HERS	Home Energy Rating System
HET	high-efficiency toilet
HFC	hydrofluorocarbon
HOA	homeowners' association
HSPF	heating season performance factor
HVAC	heating, ventilating, and air conditioning
HVAC & R	heating, ventilating, air conditioning, and refrigeration
IAP	(Energy Star) Indoor Air Package
IAQ	indoor air quality
IBC	International Building Code
I-BEAM	Indoor Air Quality Building Education and Assessment Model (software program sponsored by U.S. EPA)

ICC	International Code Council
ICF	insulating concrete form
ID	Innovation in Design (credit category)
ID+C	Interior Design and Construction (LEED AP specialty)
IDP	Innovation and Design Process (LEED for Neighborhood Development credit category)
IDR	Innovative Design Request (LEED for Homes credit category)
IEBC	International Existing Building Code
IECC	International Energy Conservation Code
IFC	International Fire Code
IEQ	Indoor Environmental Quality (credit category)
IESNA	Illuminating Engineering Society of North America
IFGC	International Fuel Gas Code
IMC	International Mechanical Code
IPC	International Plumbing Code
IPD	integrated project delivery
IPLV	integrated part load value
IPM	integrated pest management
IPMC	International Property Maintenance Code
IPMVP	International Performance Measurement and Verification Protocol
IPSC	International Private Sewage Code
IQ	irrigation quality
IRC	International Residential Code
ISO	International Organization for Standardization (*Organisation internationale de normalisation*)
IWUC	International Wildland Urban Code
IZC	International Zoning Code
kW	kilowatt
kWh	kilowatt hour
LCA	life-cycle assessment/analysis
LCC	life-cycle cost
LCGWP	life-cycle direct global warming potential
LCM	life-cycle management
LCODP	life-cycle ozone depletion potential
LED	light emitting diode
LEED	Leadership in Energy and Environmental Design
LEED AP	LEED Accredited Professional
LID	low-impact development
LL	Location and Linkages (LEED for Homes credit category)
LPD	lighting power density
LZ	lighting zone
MDF	medium-density fiberboard
MEF	modified energy factor
MERV	minimum efficiency reporting value
MPR	minimum program requirement

MR	Materials and Resources (credit category)
MSDS	material safety data sheet
M&V	measurement and verification
NBI	New Building Institute
NC	New Construction (LEED NC rating system)
ND	Neighborhood Development (LEED AP specialty)
NEMA	National Electrical Manufacturers Association
NFRC	National Fenestration Rating Council
NIBS	National Institute of Building Sciences
NIOSH	National Institute for Occupational Safety and Health
NIST	National Institute of Standards and Technology
NPD	Neighborhood Pattern and Design (LEED for Neighborhood Development credit category)
NPDES	National Pollutant Discharge Elimination System
OA	outside air
ODP	ozone depletion potential
O&M	operations and maintenance
O+M	Operations and Maintenance (LEED AP specialty)
OPR	owner's project requirements
OSB	oriented strand board
OSHA	Occupational Safety and Health Administration
OSWER	U.S. EPA Office of Solid Waste and Emergency Response
PCB	polychlorinated biphenyl
PRM	performance rating method
PUHCA	Public Utilities Holding Company Act
PV	photovoltaic
PVC	polyvinyl chloride
PWF	permanent wood foundation
REC	renewable energy certificate
RESNET	Residential Energy Services Network
RFP	request for proposal
RP	Regional Priority (credit category)
SAD	seasonal affective disorder
SBS	sick building syndrome
SCAQMD	South Coast Air Quality Management District
SCS	Scientific Certification Systems
SEER	seasonal energy efficiency rating
SHGC	solar heat gain coefficient
SIP	structural insulated panel
SLL	Smart Location and Linkage (LEED for Neighborhood Development credit category)
SMACNA	Sheet Metal and Air Conditioning Contractors' National Association
SOP	standard operating procedure
SOW	statement of work

SRI	solar reflectance index
SS	Sustainable Sites (credit category)
TAG	Technical Advisory Group
TARP	Technology Acceptance Reciprocity Partnership
TASC	Technical Advisory Subcommittee
TCE	trichloroethylene
TCLP	toxicity characteristic leaching procedure
TP	total phosphorus
TPO	thermoplastic polyolefin
TRACI	Tool for the Reduction and Assessment of Chemical and other Environmental Impacts
TRC	tradable renewable certificate
TSS	total suspended solids
TVOC	total volatile organic compounds
Tvis	visible transmittance
TWA	total water applied
UL	Underwriters Laboratory
UPC	Uniform Plumbing Code
USDA	United States Department of Agriculture
USGBC	United States Green Building Council
VAV	variable air volume
VFD	variable frequency drive
VOC	volatile organic compound
VLT	visible light transmittance
VT	visible transmittance
WDF	wood derived fuel
WE	Water Efficiency (credit category)
WF	water factor
WFR	window-to-floor area ratio
WWR	window-to-wall area ratio
ZEV	zero emission vehicles (defined by the California Air Resources Board)

Glossary

A

accreditation profile: An individual's listing in the LEED Professional Credentialing Directory at www.gbci.org.

acid rain: Acidic precipitation in the form of rain.

adapted plants: Plants indigenous to a locality or cultivars of native plants that are adapted to the local climate and are not considered invasive species or noxious weeds, and which require only limited irrigation following establishment, do not require active maintenance such as mowing, and provide habitat value and promote biodiversity through avoidance of monoculture plantings.

adaptive reuse: The process of adapting old structures for new purposes.

adhesive: A substance used to bond two materials.

advanced technology vehicle (ATV): A type of alternative vehicle that uses advanced technologies for powertrains, emissions controls, and other vehicle features that allow for improved environmental performance. Electric hybrid vehicles and fuel cell vehicles are examples of ATVs.

agrifiber product: Products made from agricultural fiber.

air changes per hour (ACH): A value representing the number of times each hour that an enclosure's total volume of air is exchanged with fresh or filtered air.

albedo: Reflective power; *specifically*: the fraction of incident radiation (as light) that is reflected by a surface or body (as the moon or a cloud). (See also *solar reflectance*.)

alternative fuel vehicle (AFV): A vehicle that uses low-polluting, non-gasoline fuel such as electricity, hydrogen, propane or compressed natural gas, liquid natural gas, methanol, or ethanol. Efficient gas-electric hybrid vehicles are included in this group for LEED purposes.

angle of maximum candela: The direction in which a luminaire emits the greatest luminous intensity.

anticorrosive paints: Coatings formulated and recommended for use in preventing the corrosion of ferrous metal substrates.

aquatic system: Ecologically designed treatment systems that utilize a diverse community of biological organisms (e.g., bacteria, plants, and fish) to treat wastewater to advanced levels.

aquifer: An underground water-bearing stratum of permeable rock, sand, or gravel that supplies groundwater, wells, or springs.

aromatic compounds: Defined by Green Seal Standard GS-11 as "hydrocarbon compounds containing one or more 6-carbon benzene rings in the molecular structure."

assembly recycled content: Includes the percentages of post-consumer and pre-consumer content of a specific assembly or product. The determination is made by dividing the weight of the recycled content by the overall weight of the assembly.

B

balancing damper: An adjustable plate used to regulate airflow in a duct.

baseline building performance: The annual energy cost for a building design intended for use as a baseline for rating above standard design, as defined in ANSI/ASHRAE/IESNA Standard 90.1-2004, Informative App. G.

basis of design (BOD): Includes design information necessary to accomplish the owner's project requirements, including system descriptions, indoor environmental quality criteria, other pertinent design assumptions (such as weather data), and references to applicable codes, standards, regulations, and guidelines.

bedroom: Defined in LEED for Homes as "any room or space that could be used or is intended to be used for sleeping purposes and meets local fire and building code requirements."

best management practice (BMP): In the context of stormwater management, best management practices (BMPs) are effective, practical, structural or nonstructural methods that prevent or reduce the movement of sediment, nutrients, pesticides and other pollutants from the land to surfacewater or groundwater, or that otherwise protect water quality from potential adverse effects of construction activities. These practices are developed to achieve a balance between water quality protection and construction within natural and economic limitations.

bioaccumulants: Substances that increase in concentration in the living organisms exposed to them because they are very slowly metabolized or excreted.

biodiversity: Biological diversity in an environment as indicated by numbers of different species of plants and animals. The variety of life in all forms, levels and combinations, including ecosystem diversity, species diversity, and genetic diversity.

biomass: Plant materials such as trees, grasses, and crops that can be converted to heat energy to produce electricity.

bioremediation: The treatment of pollutants or waste (as in an oil spill, contaminated groundwater, or an industrial process) by the use of microorganisms (as bacteria) that break down the undesirable substances. Bioremediation is generally a form of *in situ* remediation, and can be a viable alternative to disposal in a landfill or incineration.

bioretention: A best management practice (BMP) for stormwater management that utilizes soils and both woody and herbaceous plants to remove pollutants from stormwater runoff.

blackwater: Wastewater containing biological material such as feces or food waste, which must be treated before it can be safely released or reused. Wastewater from toilets and urinals is always considered blackwater. Wastewater from kitchen sinks (perhaps differentiated by the use of a garbage disposal), showers, or bathtubs may be considered blackwater by state or local codes.

borate: Chemical used as a wood preservative; it is nontoxic to humans and pets, but kills termites, carpenter ants, and cockroaches and prevents fungal decay.

breathing zone: The region within an occupied space between planes 3 feet (0.9 m) and 6 feet (1.8 m) above the floor and more than 2 feet (0.6 m) from the walls or fixed air conditioning equipment.

brownfield site: With certain legal exclusions and additions, the term "brownfield site" means real property, the expansion, redevelopment, or reuse of which may be complicated by the presence or potential presence of a hazardous substance, pollutant, or contaminant (source: Public Law 107-118, H.R. 2869—"Small Business Liability Relief and Brownfields Revitalization Act").

buildable land: Portion of a site suited for construction and not occupied by public streets, roads, or rights-of-way, existing structures, or parks.

building density: The floor area of the building divided by the total area of the site (square foot per acre).

building energy performance baseline: The average building performance for the specific type of building. For building types covered by Energy Star, this is a score of 50. For building types not covered by Energy Star, the building energy performance baseline is established with historic building energy use data and/or energy use data from other, similar buildings.

building envelope: The exterior surface of a building's construction—the walls, windows, roof and floor. Also referred to as the *building shell*.

building footprint: The area on a project site that is used by the building structure and is defined by the perimeter of the building plan. Parking lots, landscapes, and other non-building facilities are not included in the building footprint.

building integrated photovoltaics (BIPV): Photovoltaic systems integrated into building's external materials, such as its facade or roof.

building-related illness: Diagnosable illnesses that can be directly attributed to airborne building contaminants.

built environment: Human-made additions to or alterations of a site.

C

candela: The base unit of luminous intensity in the International System of Units. A candela is equal to the luminous intensity, in a given direction, of a source that emits monochromatic radiation of frequency 540×10^{12} hertz and has a radiant intensity in that direction of watt 1/683 per steradian. Abbreviated cd; called also *candle*.

car sharing: A system under which multiple households share a pool of automobiles, either through cooperative ownership or through some other mechanism.

carbon dioxide (CO_2): A heavy colorless gas that does not support combustion, dissolves in water to form carbonic acid, is formed especially in animal respiration and in the decay or combustion of animal and vegetable matter, is absorbed from the air by plants in photosynthesis, and is used in the carbonation of beverages.

carbon dioxide monitoring: An indicator of ventilation effectiveness inside buildings. Carbon dioxide concentrations greater than 530 parts per million above outdoor carbon dioxide conditions are generally considered an indicator of inadequate ventilation. Absolute concentrations of carbon dioxide greater than 800 to 1000 parts per million are generally considered an indicator of poor breathing air quality.

catchment area: Surface area of a roof that captures water to be used in a rainwater harvesting system.

central vacuum system: Built-in vacuum system used for removing dirt and debris from floors and capturing it in a remote receptacle.

chain of custody: A document that tracks the movement of a wood product from the forest to a vendor and is used to verify compliance with FSC guidelines. A *vendor* is defined as the company that supplies wood products to project contractors or subcontractors for on-site installation.

charrette: Collaborative design effort undertaken in a short period of time that brings together members of a project team to brainstorm and evaluate design opportunities and approaches.

chemical component restriction: A set of restrictions set by the Green Seal Standard GS-11 requiring that the manufacturer demonstrate that the chemical compounds included on the Chemical Component Restrictions list are not used as ingredients in the manufacture of the product.

chlorofluorocarbon (CFC): Any of several simple gaseous compounds that contain carbon, chlorine, fluorine, and sometimes hydrogen, that are used as refrigerants, cleaning solvents, and aerosol propellants and in the manufacture of plastic foams, and that are believed to be a major cause of stratospheric ozone depletion.

circulation loop: Part of a building's plumbing system that returns cold water to a heating element rather than down the drain until hot water reaches the faucet.

climate zone: Temperature region defined by the International Energy Conservation Code.

combustion exhaust gases: Gases resulting from fossil fuel combustion, such as carbon dioxide, carbon monoxide, sulfur dioxide and nitrogen oxide.

cogeneration: The simultaneous production of electrical or mechanical energy (power) and useful thermal energy from the same fuel/energy source such as oil, coal, gas, biomass, or solar.

comfort criteria: Specific original design conditions that shall at a minimum include temperature (air radiant and surface), humidity, and air speed, as well as outdoor temperature design conditions, outdoor humidity design conditions, clothing (seasonal), and activity expected. (ASHRAE 55-2004.)

commissioning (Cx): The process of ensuring that systems are designed, installed, functionally tested, and capable of being operated and maintained to perform in conformity with the owner's project requirements.

commissioning authority (CxA): Person or team that acts as a commissioning agent.

commissioning plan: A document defining the commissioning process that is developed in increasing detail as the project progresses through its various stages.

commissioning report: The document that records the results of the commissioning process, including the as-built performance of the HVAC system and unresolved issues.

commissioning specification: The contract document that details the objective, scope, and implementation of the construction and acceptance phases of the commissioning process as developed in the design-phase commissioning plan.

commissioning team: Includes people responsible for working together to carry out the commissioning process.

compensating shower valve: A valve that keeps water temperature in the shower constant when other household appliances, such as a dishwasher or washing machine, are in use.

completed design area: The total area of finished ceilings, finished floors, full height walls and demountable partitions, interior doors, and built-in case goods in the space when the project is completed; exterior windows and exterior doors are not included.

composite panel: Panels made from several materials. Plywood and oriented strand board are two examples of composite panels.

composite wood: A product consisting of wood or plant particles or fibers bonded together by a synthetic resin or binder (i.e., plywood, particleboard, oriented strand board, medium density fiberboard, composite door cores). For the purposes of LEED requirements, products must comply with the following conditions.

    a.   The product is inside the building's waterproofing system.

    b.   Composite wood components used in assemblies are included (e.g., door cores, panel substrates, plywood sections of I-beams).

    c.   The product is part of the base building system.

composting toilet system: Dry plumbing fixtures that contain and treat human waste by means of microbiological processes.

Comprehensive Environmental Response, Compensation, and Liability Act (CERCLA): Commonly known as Superfund, this act addresses abandoned or historical waste sites and contamination. It was enacted in 1980 to create a tax on the chemical and petroleum industries and provided federal authority to respond to releases of hazardous substances.

concentrate: A product that must be diluted by at least eight parts by volume water (1:8 dilution ratio) prior to its intended use. (Green Seal GS-37.)

conditioned space: The part of a building that is heated, cooled, or both, for the comfort of occupants. (ASHRAE 62.1-2004.)

constructed wetland: An engineered system designed to stimulate natural wetland functions and remove contaminants from wastewater.

construction and demolition (C&D) waste: Includes waste and recyclables generated from the construction, renovation, and demolition or deconstruction of pre-existing structures. Debris from land clearing, including soil, vegetation, rocks, and so forth, is not included.

construction, demolition, and land clearing (CDL) waste: Includes waste and recyclables generated from the construction, land clearing (e.g., vegetation but not soil), renovation, and demolition or deconstructing of pre-existing structures.

construction IAQ management plan: A document specific to a building project that outlines measures to minimize contamination in the building during construction, and to flush the building of contaminants prior to occupancy.

contaminant: An unwanted airborne constituent that may reduce the acceptability of the air. (ASHRAE 62.1-2004.)

conventional irrigation: The most common irrigation system used in the region where the building is located. A common conventional irrigation system uses pressure to deliver water and distributes it through sprinkler heads above the ground.

conventional turf: Grass; a lawn that must be watered, fertilized, and mowed.

corrected design ventilation rate (CDVR): The design ventilation rate divided by the air change effectiveness.

Credentialing Maintenance Program (CMP): Continuing education required to keep LEED AP credentials in good standing. LEED Green Associates are required to complete 15 hours of training biennially, 3 hours of which must be LEED specific. LEED APs with specialty must complete 30 hours of training biennially, 6 hours of which must be LEED specific.

curfew hours: Locally determined times when greater lighting restrictions are imposed. When no local or regional restrictions are in place, 10:00 p.m. is generally regarded as a default curfew time.

D

daylight factor (DF): The ratio of exterior illumination to interior illumination, expressed as a percentage. The variables used to determine the daylight factor include the floor area, window area, window geometry, visible transmittance, and window height.

daylight glazing: Vertical window area that is located 7 feet 6 inches (2.3 m) above the floor of the room. Glazing at this height is the most effective at distributing daylight deep into the interior space.

daylighting: The controlled admission of natural light into a space through glazing with the intent of reducing or eliminating electric lighting. By utilizing solar light, daylighting creates a stimulating and productive environment for building occupants.

demand-controlled circulation: Allows hot water to be immediately available through use of a looped system.

density: Number of structures on a site or in an area. LEED measures residential density as dwellings per acre of buildable land available for residential use, and commercial density as floor area ratio per net acre of available buildable land.

design light output: The light output of light bulbs at 40% of their useful life.

detention pond: A pond that captures stormwater runoff and allows pollutants to drop out before release to a stormwater or waterbody. A variety of detention pond designs are available, with some utilizing only gravity while others use mechanical equipment such as pipes and pumps to facilitate transport. Some ponds are dry except during storm events, while other ponds store water permanently.

development footprint: The area within the project site that has been impacted by any development activity. Hardscape, access roads, parking lots, non-building facilities, and building-structures are all included in the development footprint.

direct line of sight to perimeter vision glazing: The approach used to determine the calculated area of regularly occupied areas with direct line of sight to perimeter vision glazing. The area determination includes full height partitions and other fixed construction prior to installation of furniture.

distribution uniformity: Measures how uniformly water is applied to an area from an irrigation system.

disturbed lot area: Part of a site directly affected by construction.

diverted waste: Trash or construction debris that is not sent to a landfill, but is disposed of through recycling or other reuse measures.

drip irrigation: A high-efficiency irrigation method in which water is delivered at low pressure through buried mains and sub-mains. From the submains, water is distributed to the soil from a network of perforated tubes or emitters. Drip irrigation is a type of micro-irrigation.

dry well: Underground cistern that collects runoff and distributes it over a large area to increase absorption into the soil and minimize erision.

dual-flush toilet: Fixture with two flush volumes. Dual-flush toilets use less water to dispose of liquid waste than solid waste. The user specifies the volume of water used.

durability: Defined by LEED for Homes as "the ability of a building or any of its components to perform its required function in its service environment over the period of time without unforeseen cost for maintenance or repair."

E

ecological restoration: The process of assisting in the recovery and management of ecological integrity, which includes a critical range of variability in biodiversity, ecological processes and structures, regional and historical context, and sustainable cultural practices.

ecologically appropriate site feature: Natural site elements that maintain or restore the ecological integrity of the site, which may include native/adapted vegetation, waterbodies, exposed rock, unvegetated ground, and other features that are part of the historic natural landscape within the region and provide habitat value.

ecosystem: A basic unit of nature that includes a community of organisms and their non-living environment linked by biological, chemical, and physical processes.

edge development: Defined by LEED for Homes as "a group of homes that extend an existing community beyond its borders but remain connected to it"; at least 25% of the edge development perimeter must border an existing neighborhood.

embodied energy: The total energy used during the entire life cycle of a commodity for its manufacture, transportation, and disposal, as well as the inherent energy captured within the product itself.

emissions offset: Emissions reductions from one set of actions that are used to offset emissions caused by another set of actions.

emissivity: The ratio of the radiation emitted by a surface to the radiation emitted by a black body at the same temperature. Also called *emittance*.

energy conservation measure (ECM): Installation of equipment or systems, or modification of equipment or systems, for the purpose of reducing energy use and/or costs.

Energy Star®: U.S. Department of Energy initiative to indicate appliances and products which use acceptable amounts of energy or contribute to energy efficiency.

Energy Star Home: A home that uses 15% less energy than it would if it were constructed to the requirements of the 2004 International Energy Efficiency Code. To be labeled an "Energy Star Home" the project must submit data to Energy Star for evaluation.

Energy Star Portfolio Manager: Rating system that allows a building manager to compare and monitor building energy performance of all buildings in a company's portfolio.

environmental attributes of green power: Emission reduction benefits that result when green power is used instead of conventional power sources.

environmental tobacco smoke (ETS): Secondhand smoke. Airborne particles emitted from the burning ends of cigarettes, pipes, and cigars, or exhaled by smokers. These particles contain about 4000 different compounds, up to 40 of which are known to cause cancer. The particles can be inhaled by persons located nearby.

environmentally preferable products: Products identified as having a lesser or reduced effect on health and the environment when compared with competing products that serve the same purpose.

environmentally preferable purchasing: A United States federal-wide program (Executive Order 13101) that encourages and assists executive agencies in the purchasing of environmentally preferable products and services.

erosion: A combination of processes through which materials of the earth's surface are loosened, dissolved, or worn away, and transported from one place to another by natural agents (such as water, wind, or gravity).

eutrophication: The process by which lakes and ponds age. Water, through natural or human sources, becomes rich in nutrients (such as phosphates) and promotes the proliferation of plant life (especially algae) that reduces the dissolved oxygen content of the water and often causes the extinction of other organisms within the waterbody.

evapotranspiration: Loss of water from the soil both by evaporation and by transpiration from the plants growing thereon.

exfiltration: Uncontrolled outward air leakage from conditioned spaces through unintentional openings in ceilings, floors and walls to unconditioned spaces or the outdoors caused by pressure differences across these openings due to wind, inside-outside temperature differences (stack effect), and imbalances between supply and exhaust airflow rates. (ASHRAE 62.1-2004.)

exhaust air: The air removed from a space and discharged to outside the building by means of mechanical or natural ventilation systems.

existing building commissioning: Developing a building operation plan that identifies current building operating requirements and needs, conducting tests to proactively determine if the building and fundamental systems are operating in accordance with the building operation plan, and making any repairs needed so that the building and fundamental systems are operating according to the plan.

***ex situ* remediation:** Remediation of contaminated soil and groundwater by removing it to another location, typically a treatment facility. Pump-and-treat technology is a traditional method of *ex situ* remediation that uses carbon filters and incineration. More advanced methods of *ex situ* remediation include chemical treatment and use of biological reactors.

F

filtration basin: A basin that removes sediment and pollutants from stormwater runoff using a filter medium such as sand or gravel to avoid clogging, a sediment trap is usually included to remove sediment from stormwater before filtering.

fixture sensors: Motion sensors that automatically turn lavatories, sinks, water closets, and urinals on and off. Sensors may be hard-wired or battery operated.

flat coatings: Coatings that register a gloss of less than 15 on an 85-degree meter, or less than 5 on a 60-degree meter.

floodplain: Level land that may be submerged by floodwaters.

fly ash: The solid residue derived from incineration processes. Fly ash can be used as a substitute for some of the portland cement in concrete.

footcandle: A unit of illuminance equal to one lumen of light falling on an area of one square foot from a one candela light source at a distance of one foot. Abbreviated fc.

formaldehyde: A naturally occurring VOC found in small amounts in animals and plants. Formaldehyde is carcinogenic and an irritant to most people when present in high concentrations—causing headaches, dizziness, mental impairment, and other symptoms. When present in the air at levels above 0.1 parts per million, it can cause watery eyes; burning sensations in the eyes, nose, and throat; nausea; coughing; chest tightness; wheezing; skin rashes; and asthmatic and allergic reactions.

friable: Easily crumbled. Often used to describe asbestos that can be reduced to dust by hand pressure.

full disclosure: For products that are not formulated with listed suspect carcinogens, full disclosure is defined as (1) disclosure of all ingredients (both hazardous and nonhazardous) that make up one percent or more of undiluted product, and (2) use of concentration ranges for each of the disclosed ingredients. *Full disclosure* for products that are formulated with listed suspect carcinogens is defined as (1) disclosure of listed suspect carcinogens that make up 0.1% or more of the undiluted product, (2) disclosure of all remaining ingredients (both hazardous and nonhazardous) that make up one percent or more of the undiluted product, and (3) use of concentration ranges for each of the disclosed ingredients. Suspect carcinogens are those included in authoritative lists available for MSDS preparation: International Agency for Research on Cancer (IARC), U.S. National Toxicology Program (NTP), and California Proposition 65 lists. Concentration range definitions are available from OSHA, or in Canada, from WHMIS Standards.

full-cutoff luminaire: Luminaires that have no direct uplight (no light emitted above horizontal) and comply with the glare requirement limiting intensity of light from the luminaire in the region between 80 and 90 degrees.

full-time equivalent (FTE): The number of total hours worked divided by the maximum number of compensable hours in a work year.

full-time equivalent building occupant: A measurement of occupancy determined by taking the total number of hours that all building occupants spend in the building during the peak eight-hour occupancy period, and dividing by eight hours. For buildings used for multiple shifts each day, the shift with the greatest number of FTE building occupants determines the overall FTE building occupants for the building.

functional performance testing (FPT): The process of determining the ability of commissioned systems to perform in accordance with the owner's project requirements, basis of design, and construction documents.

G

glare: Any excessively bright source of light within the visual field that creates discomfort or decrease in visibility.

glazing factor: The ratio of interior illuminance at a given point on a given plane (usually the work plane) to the exterior illuminance under known overcast sky conditions. LEED uses a simplified approach for its credit compliance calculations. The variables used to determine the daylight factor include the floor area, window area, window geometry, visible transmittance (Tvis), and window height.

global warming potential (GWP): A measure of how much a given mass of greenhouse gas is estimated to contribute to global warming. It is a relative scale that compares the gas in question to that of the same mass of carbon dioxide (whose GWP is, by definition, 1).

grassed swale: Trenches or ditches covered with vegetation to encourage subsurface infiltration, similar to infiltration basins and trenches. They utilize vegetation to filter sediment and pollutants from stormwater.

graywater: Defined by the *Uniform Plumbing Code* (UPC) in App. G, "Graywater Systems for Single-Family Dwellings," as untreated household wastewater that has not come into contact with toilet waste. Graywater includes water from bathtubs, showers, bathroom wash basins, and water from clothes washer and laundry tubs, but not wastewater from kitchen sinks or dishwashers.

The *International Plumbing Code* (IPC) defines graywater in App. C, titled "Graywater Recycling Systems," as wastewater discharged from lavatories, bathtubs, showers, clothes washers, and laundry sinks.

Some states and local authorities allow kitchen sink wastewater to be included in graywater. Other variations from the UPC and IPC definitions are likely to be found in state and local codes. Project teams should comply with graywater definitions as established by the authority having jurisdiction in their areas.

green cleaning: The use of cleaning products and practices that have reduced environmental impacts in comparison with conventional products and practices.

greenfield: A site that has not been previously developed or graded and that remains in a natural state.

greenhouse gas: Gases such as carbon dioxide, methane, and CFCs that are relatively transparent to higher-energy sunlight, but which trap lower-energy infrared radiation.

green rater: In LEED for Homes, "an individual that performs field inspections and performance testing of LEED for Homes measures for the LEED for Homes Provider."

group multi-occupant space: Conference rooms, classrooms, and other indoor spaces used as places of congregation for presentations, training sessions, and so on. Individuals using these spaces share the lighting and temperature controls. Group multi-occupant spaces do not include open office plans that contain standard individual workstations.

H

halon: A substance used in fire suppression systems and fire extinguishers in buildings. Halons deplete the stratospheric ozone layer.

hard costs: In a building project, the costs of labor and materials. Compare with *soft costs*.

hardscape: Structures such as fountains, benches, and gazebos that are incorporated into a landscape design.

hazardous waste: Waste material that presents a risk to human or environmental health.

heat island effect: Urban air and surface temperatures that are higher than nearby rural areas. Principal contributing factors include greater numbers of dark, non-reflective surfaces such as roofs and parking lots, elimination of trees and vegetation, waste heat from vehicles, factories, and air conditioners, and reduced airflow near tall buildings and narrow streets.

high-efficiency particulate air (HEPA) filter: A filter designed to remove at least 99.97% of the airborne particles measuring 0.3 microns in diameter that pass through it. Particles of this size are the most difficult to filter; larger and smaller particles are filtered more efficiently.

high-efficiency toilet: Toilet that uses 1.3 gallons (4.9 L) per flush or less.

high-occupancy vehicle: A vehicle with more than one occupant.

high-volume copier: A machine used to copy many pages on a regular basis.

Home Energy Rating System (HERS): Part of the Energy Star program; evaluates residential building energy consumption relative to IECC requirements.

horizontal view at 42 inches: The approach used to confirm that the direct line of sight to perimeter vision glazing remains available from a seated position. Section drawings that include the installed furniture can be used to determine if a direct line of sight is present.

HVAC systems: Heating, ventilating, and air conditioning systems used to provide thermal comfort and ventilation for building interiors.

hybrid vehicle: A vehicle that uses a gasoline engine to drive an electric generator and uses the electric generator and/or storage batteries to power an electric motor that drives the wheels.

hydrochlorofluorocarbon (HCFC): A refrigerant used in building equipment that depletes the stratospheric ozone layer, but to a lesser extent than a CFC.

hydrofluorocarbon (HFC): A refrigerant that does not deplete the stratospheric ozone layer. However, some HFCs have high global warming potential and, thus, are not environmentally benign.

hydronic system: Heating/cooling system that uses water to transfer heat.

I

illuminance: The luminous flux per unit area at any given point of an intercepting surface.

impervious surface: A surface that promotes runoff of precipitation instead of infiltration into the subsurface. The imperviousness, or degree of runoff potential, can be estimated for different surface materials.

imperviousness: Resistance to penetration by a liquid, calculated as the percentage of area covered by a paving system that does not allow moisture to soak into the earth below the paving system.

indigenous plants: See *native plants*.

individual occupant workspaces: Workspaces in which individuals occupy standard workstations for the purpose of conducting individual tasks. These workstations can be located in private offices or multi-occupant spaces, such as open office areas.

indoor adhesive, sealant, and/or sealant primer product: Defined as an adhesive or sealant product applied on site, inside the building's weatherproofing system.

indoor air quality (IAQ): The nature of air inside the space that affects the health and well-being of building occupants.

indoor carpet system: Carpet, carpet adhesive, or carpet cushion product installed on site, inside the building's weatherproofing system.

indoor composite wood or agrifiber product: Composite wood or agrifiber product installed on site, inside the building's weatherproofing system.

indoor environmental quality (IEQ): A qualitative and quantitative evaluation of the air quality and other factors such as comfort, noise, lighting, ergonomic stressors (such as poorly designed workstations and tasks) and job-related psychosocial stressors.

indoor paint or coating product: A paint or coating product applied on site, inside the building's weatherproofing system.

infill development: Development of vacant or underused parcels within a developed urban area.

infiltrate: To permeate something by penetrating its pores or interstices; to pass into by filtering or permeating.

infiltration: Uncontrolled inward air leakage to conditioned spaces through unintentional openings in ceilings, floors, and walls from unconditioned spaces or the outdoors caused by the same pressure differences that induce exfiltration. (ASHRAE 62.1-2004.)

infiltration degree days: Sum of heating and cooling degree days.

infiltration basin and trench: Land forms used to encourage subsurface infiltration of runoff through temporary surface storage. Basins are ponds that can store large volumes of stormwater. They need to drain within 72 hours to maintain aerobic conditions and to be available for the next storm event. Trenches are similar to infiltration basins, but are shallower and function as subsurface reservoirs for stormwater volumes. Pretreatment of the water may be necessary in order to remove sediment and oil and to avoid clogging of infiltration devices. Infiltration trenches are more common in areas where infiltration basins are not possible.

infrared emissivity (or infrared emittance): Also known as *thermal emissivity* or *thermal emittance*. A parameter between 0 and 1, or 0% and 100%, that indicates the ability of a material to shed infrared radiation (heat). The wavelength range for this radiant energy is roughly 3 microns to 40 microns. Most building materials (including glass) are opaque in this part of the spectrum, and have an emissivity of roughly 0.9. Materials such as clean, bare metals are the most important exceptions to the 0.9 rule. Clean, untarnished galvanized steel has a low emissivity, and aluminum roof coatings have intermediate emissivity levels.

***in situ* remediation:** Remediation of a site that involves treatment of contaminants without leaving the site, using technologies such as injection wells and reactive trenches. These methods utilize the hydraulic gradient of groundwater and usually require only minimal disturbance of the site.

installation inspection: The process of inspecting components of the commissioned systems to determine if they are installed properly and ready for systems performance testing.

integrated part load value (IPLV): A measure of the efficiency of an air conditioner under a variety of conditions—that is, when the unit is operating at 25%, 50%, 75% and 100% of capacity and at different temperatures.

integrated pest management (IPM): The coordinated use of pest and environmental information and pest control methods to prevent unacceptable levels of pest damage by the most economical means, and with the least possible hazard to people, property, and the environment.

interior lighting power allowance: The maximum light power in watts allowed for the interior of a building.

interior nonstructural components reuse: Determined by dividing the area of retained components by the larger of the area of the prior condition or the area of the completed design.

International Building Code (IBC): A model building code published by the International Code Council (ICC) that provides complete regulations covering all major aspects of building design and construction relating to fire and life safety and structural safety.

invasive plants (or invasive species): Both indigenous and non-indigenous species and strains that are characteristically adaptable and aggressive, have a high reproductive capacity and tend to overrun the ecosystems they inhabit. Collectively, they are one of the great threats to biodiversity and ecosystem stability.

L

laminate adhesive: An adhesive used in wood and agrifiber products (veneered panels, composite wood products contained in engineered lumber, door assemblies, etc.)

landfill: A waste disposal site for the deposit of solid waste from human activities

landscape architecture: The analysis, planning, design, management, and stewardship of the natural and built environment.

landscape area: Planted area of a site; equal to the total site area less the building footprint, paved surfaces, water bodies, patios, and so on.

least-toxic pesticides: These include boric acid and disodium octoborate tetrahydrate; silica gels; diatomaceous earth; nonvolatile insect and rodent baits in tamper-resistant containers or for crack and crevice treatment only; microbe-based insecticides; pesticides made with essential oils (not including synthetic pyrethoids) without toxic synergists; and materials for which the inert ingredients are nontoxic and disclosed. A least-toxic pesticide is *not* a pesticide that (1) is determined by the U.S. Environmental Protection Agency to be a probable, likely, or known carcinogen or endocrine disruptor; (2) is a mutagen, reproductive toxin, developmental neurotoxin, or immune system toxin; (3) is classified by the U.S. Environmental Protection Agency as a toxicity I or II pesticide; (4) is in the organphosphate or carbamate chemical family; or (5) contains inert ingredients categorized as "List 1: Inerts of Toxicological Concern." Least-toxic pesticides do not include any application of pesticides using a broadcast spray, dust, tenting, fogging, or baseboard spray application.

life-cycle analysis (LCA): A holistic evaluation of the environmental effects of a product or activity, which analyzes the entire life cycle of a particular material, process, product, technology, service, or activity.

life-cycle cost (LCC) analysis: A method of measuring the total cost of a system, device, building, or other investment over its expected useful life by summing the costs of the initial investment, replacements, operations, maintenance, and repair of an investment, and subtracting the resale value.

life-cycle inventory (LCI): An accounting of the energy and waste associated with the creation of a new product through use and disposal.

light pollution: Waste light from building sites that produces glare, compromises astronomical research, and adversely affects the environment. Waste light is light that does not increase nighttime safety, utility, or security and needlessly consumes energy and natural resources.

lighting power density (LPD): The installed lighting power per unit area.

local heat island effect: Higher air and surface temperatures in an area caused by absorption of solar energy by surrounding structures or surface materials

local zoning requirements: Local government regulations imposed to promote orderly development of private lands and to prevent land use conflicts.

low-impact development: Defined by the U.S. EPA as an approach to land development that attempts to manage stormwater as close to the source as possible

low-slope roof: A roof slope with an incline of less than 2 inches per foot (9.5 degrees).

lot: Parcel of land on which a project is built. Lot boundaries are defined in the property owner's deed.

lumen: A unit of luminous flux equal to the light emitted in a unit solid angle by a uniform point source of one candle intensity.

M

makeup air: Any combination of outdoor and transfer air intended to replace exhaust air and exfiltration. (ASHRAE 62.1-2004.)

mass transit: Transportation facilities designed to transport large groups of persons together in vehicles such as buses or trains.

mass transit vehicle: A vehicle typically capable of serving 10 or more occupants, such as a bus, trolley, light rail, and so forth.

mechanical ventilation: Ventilation provided by mechanical powered equipment, such as motor-driven fans and blowers, but not by devices such as wind-driven turbine ventilators and mechanically operated windows. (ASHRAE 62.1-2004.)

MERV: Stands for *minimum efficiency reporting value*. A measure of filter efficiency based on a test method established by the American Society of Heating, Refrigerating and Air-Conditioning Engineers (ASHRAE 52.2-1999, *Method of Testing General Ventilation Air Cleaning Devices for Removal Efficiency by Particle Size*). Values range from 1 (very low efficiency) to 16 (very high efficiency).

metering controls: Manual-on/automatic-off controls that are used to limit the flow time of water. These are most commonly installed on lavatory faucets and showers.

methylmercury: Any of a variety of toxic compounds of mercury containing the complex CH_3Hg—that often occur as pollutants and that bioaccumulate in living organisms, especially in the higher levels of a food chain.

microirrigation: Irrigation systems with small sprinklers and microjets or drippers designed to apply small volumes of water. The sprinklers and microjets are installed within 2 inches to 4 inches (50 mm to 100 mm) of the ground, while drippers are laid on or below grade.

mitigated stormwater: Precipitation falling on a site that does not become runoff. Runoff is defined as stormwater leaving the site by means of uncontrolled surface streams, rivers, drains, or sewers. Factors affecting stormwater mitigation include site perviousness, stormwater management practices (structural and nonstructural), and on-site capture and reuse of rainwater.

mixed-mode ventilation: A ventilation strategy that combines natural ventilation with mechanical ventilation, allowing a building to be ventilated either mechanically, naturally, or, at times, using mechanical and natural ventilation simultaneously.

monitoring points: Locations where measurement sensors are installed.

N

native/adapted vegetation: Plants indigenous to a locality or cultivars of native plants that are adapted to the local climate and are not considered invasive species or noxious weeds, and that require only limited irrigation following establishment, do not require active maintenance such as mowing, and provide habitat value and promote biodiversity through avoidance of monoculture plantings.

native plants: Also called *indigenous plants*. Plants that have been adapted to a given area during a defined time period and are not invasive. In North America, the term often refers to plants growing in a region prior to the time of settlement by people of European descent.

natural area: Areas covered with native or adapted vegetation or other ecologically appropriate features.

natural ventilation: Ventilation provided by thermal, wind, or diffusion effects through doors, windows, and other intentional openings in the building.

net metering: A system of metering and billing that allows on-site generators to send excess electricity flows to the regional power grid. These electricity flows offset a portion of the electricity flows drawn from the grid. For more information on net metering in individual states, visit the DOE's Green Power Network website at www.eere.energy.gov.

no-disturbance zone: Area undisturbed during construction.

non-flat coating: A coating that registers a gloss of 5 or greater on a 60-degree meter and a gloss of 15 or greater on a 85-degree meter.

non-friable: Too hard to be reduced to dust by hand (often used to describe asbestos).

non-occupied space: Space used by maintenance personnel that is not open for use by occupants. Janitorial, storage, and equipment rooms are examples of non-occupied spaces.

nonporous sealant: A substance used as a sealant on nonporous materials, such as plastic or metal. Nonporous materials do not have openings in which fluids may be absorbed or discharged.

nonpotable water: Water that is not suitable for human consumption without treatment. The treatment method must meet or exceed EPA drinking water standards.

non-regularly occupied space: Corridors, hallways, lobbies, break rooms, copy rooms, storage rooms, kitchens, restrooms, stairwells, and so forth.

non-roof impervious surface: Any surface on a site with a perviousness of less than 50%, not including the roof of the building. Typical examples of impervious surfaces include parking lots, roads, sidewalks, and plazas.

non-water using urinal: Also called *waterless urinal*. A urinal that uses no water, but instead replaces the water flush with a specially designed trap that contains a layer of buoyant liquid that floats above the urine layer, blocking sewer gas and urine odors from the room.

O

occupied zone: The region normally occupied by people within a space. Per ASHRAE 55-2004, it is defined to generally consist of the space between the floor and 6 feet (1.8 m) above the floor, more than 3.3 feet (1.0 m) from outside walls/windows or fixed heating, ventilating, or air conditioning equipment, and more than 1 foot (0.3 m) from internal walls.

offgassing: The emission of volatile organic compounds from synthetic and natural products.

on-site wastewater treatment: Localized treatment systems designed to transport, store, treat, and dispose of waste-water volumes generated on the project site.

open site area: The total site area less the footprint of the building.

open space area: Defined by local zoning requirements; consult the authority having jurisdiction. If local zoning requirements do not clearly define open space, it is defined for the purposes of LEED calculations as the property area minus the development footprint. Areas defined as "open space" must be vegetated and pervious, with exceptions only as noted in the credit requirements section. For projects located in urban areas, open space can also include non-vehicular, pedestrian-oriented hardscape spaces.

open grid pavement: Defined for LEED purposes as pavement that is less than 50% impervious and contains vegetation in the open cells.

operation and maintenance staff: Staff or contractors involved in operating, maintaining, and cleaning the building and site.

outdoor air: The ambient air that enters a building through the ventilation system, through intentional openings for natural ventilation, or by infiltration. (ASHRAE 62.1-2004.)

outdoor lighting zone definitions: Developed by IDA for the Model Lighting Ordinance, these definitions provide a general description of the site environment/context and basic lighting criteria.

owner's project requirements (OPR): An explanation of the ideas, concepts, and criteria that the owner regards as important to the success of the project. (Previously called the *design intent*.)

P

paints and coatings: Defined by the Green Seal Standard GS-11 as "liquid, liquefiable, or mastic composition that is converted to a solid, protective, decorative, or functional adherent film after application as a thin layer. These coatings are intended for on-site application to interior surfaces of residential, commercial, institutional or industrial buildings." Standard GS-11 excludes stains, clear finishes, and paints sold in aerosol cans from this category.

parking subsidy: The cost of providing occupant parking that is not recovered through parking fees.

pedestrian access: A route by which pedestrians can walk to community services without being blocked by walls, freeways, or other barriers.

percentage improvement: The percentage of energy cost savings for the proposed building performance versus the baseline building performance.

permeable surfaces: Materials used as a substitute for impermeable surfaces which allow runoff to infiltrate into the subsurface. These surfaces are typically maintained with a vacuuming regimen to avoid potential clogging and failure problems. Porous pavement is one type of permeable surface.

personal environmental controls (PEC): Means by which individuals in a workspace can control heating, ventilation, and lighting (as opposed to being controlled by timers and sensors).

perviousness: The percentage of the surface area of a paving material that is open and allows moisture to pass through the material and soak into the earth below the paving system.

phenol-formaldehyde: A type of formaldehyde that is offgassed only at high temperatures. It can be used in either indoor or outdoor products.

photovoltaic energy: Electricity produced by photovoltaic cells, which convert the energy in sunlight into electricity.

picogram: One trillionth of a gram.

picograms per lumen hour: A measure of the amount of mercury in a lightbulb per unit of light delivered over its useful life.

point source: A discrete conveyance of a pollutant, such as a pipe or human-made ditch. As stated in the NPDES Permit Program Basics: Frequently Asked Questions, a point source is "any discernable, confined and discrete conveyance, such as a pipe, ditch, channel, tunnel, conduit, discrete fissure, or container."

pollutant: Defined by NPDES in the Clean Water Act as "any type of industrial, municipal, and agricultural waste discharged into water." Those regulated in the NPDES program include conventional pollutants (such as BOD5, total suspended solids, pH, fecal coliform, and oil and grease), toxic pollutants (such as metals and manufactured compounds), and nonconventional pollutants (such as ammonia, nitrogen, and phosphorus).

polychlorinated biphenyl (PCB): Any of a number of potentially toxic and environmentally persistent mixtures of synthetic organic chemicals that have similar chemical structures and physical properties, ranging from oily liquids to waxy solids. The manufacture, processing, and distribution of PCBs is legislated by Congress through the Toxic Substances Control Act (TSCA).

porous sealant: A substance used as a sealant on porous materials, such as wood, fabric, paper, corrugated paperboard, or plastic foam. Porous materials have tiny openings, often microscopic, through which fluids may be absorbed or discharged.

post-consumer recycled content: The percentage of material in a product that is recycled from consumer waste.

post-consumer waste: Waste material generated by households or by commercial, industrial, and institutional facilities in their role as end users of the product, which can no longer be used for its intended purpose. According to ISO 14021, this includes returns of materials from the distribution chain. Examples of this category include construction and demolition debris, materials collected through curbside and drop-off recycling programs, broken pallets (if from a pallet refurbishing company, not a pallet-making company), discarded products (e.g., furniture, cabinetry, and decking) and urban maintenance waste (e.g., leaves, grass clippings, and tree trimmings).

post-consumer waste recycling: The recycling of materials collected from consumer waste following consumer use of the products containing these materials.

post-industrial recycled content: The percentage of material in a product that is recycled from manufacturing waste.

post-industrial waste recycling: The recycling of materials collected from industrial processes. This includes collection and recycling of waste from industrial processes within the same manufacturing plant or from another manufacturing plant.

potable water: Water suitable for drinking which is supplied from wells or municipal water systems.

pre-consumer content: As defined in ISO 14021, material diverted from the waste stream during the manufacturing process. Materials such as rework, regrind, and scrap that could be reclaimed within the same manufacturing process that generated them are excluded. Examples in this category include planer shavings, plytrim, sawdust, chips, bagasse, sunflower seed hulls, walnut shells, culls, trimmed materials, print overruns, over-issue publications, and obsolete inventories. (Previously referred to in the LEED rating systems as *postindustrial content*.)

preferred parking: Parking spots that are preferentially available to particular users, usually closer to the main entrance of the project, exclusive of spaces designated for handicapped.

previously developed site: In LEED for Homes, "a lot consisting of at least 75% previously developed land."

primer: A material applied to a substrate to improve the adhesion of a subsequently applied finish material or adhesive.

prime farmland: Defined in U.S. CFR, Title 7, Part 657.5 as "land that has the best combination of physical and chemical characteristics for producing food, feed, forage, fiber, and oilseed crops, and is also available for these uses."

prior condition area: The total area of finished ceilings, finished floors, full height walls, and demountable partitions, interior doors, and built-in case goods that existed when the project area was selected. Exterior windows and exterior doors are not considered part of the prior condition area.

process water: Water used for industrial processes and building systems such as cooling towers, boilers, and chillers.

productivity: The quantity and quality of employee output per unit time.

property area: The total area within the legal property boundaries of a site, which encompasses all areas of the site, both constructed and non-constructed.

proposed building performance: The annual energy cost calculated for a proposed design, as defined in ANSI/ASHRAE/IESNA Standard 90.1-2004, Informative App. G.

provider: In LEED for Homes, "an organization that recruits, trains and coordinates LEED for Homes Green Raters to serve as third-party verifiers of LEED homes. Providers are the official certifiers of LEED for Homes on behalf of USGBC."

public transportation: Bus, rail, or other transportation service for the general public, which operates on a regular, continual basis, and which may be publicly or privately owned.

R

radon: Radioactive gas that vents from the ground. Known to be carcinogenic.

rapidly renewable material: An agricultural product, either fiber or animal, that takes 10 years or less to grow or raise and then harvest in an ongoing and sustainable fashion.

rated power: The nameplate power on a piece of equipment. It represents the capacity of the unit and is the maximum a unit will draw.

receptacle load: The electrical load due to all equipment plugged into the electrical system, from office equipment to refrigerators.

recirculated air: The air removed from a space and reused as supply air.

reclaimed material: Salvaged or reused material integrated into a new project in its original state.

recycled content: Calculated by dividing the weight of recycled material by the total weight of an assembly.

recycling: The collection, reprocessing, marketing, and use of materials that were diverted or recovered from the solid waste stream.

refrigerants: The working fluids of refrigeration cycles. Refrigerants absorb heat from a reservoir at low temperatures and reject heat at higher temperatures.

regionally extracted materials: Materials generated from a raw material located within a 500-mile (805 km) radius of the project site.

regionally manufactured materials: Materials which are assembled as finished products within a 500-mile (805 km) radius of the project site. Assembly, as used for this LEED definition, does not include on-site assembly, erection, or installation of finished components, as in structural steel, miscellaneous iron, or systems furniture.

regularly occupied space: Areas where workers are seated or standing as they work inside a building; in residential applications, this refers to living and family rooms.

relative humidity: The ratio of partial density of water vapor in the air to the saturation density of water vapor at the same temperature and total pressure.

remediation: The process of cleaning up a contaminated site by physical, chemical, or biological means. Remediation processes are typically applied to contaminated soil and groundwater.

renewable energy: Energy from sources that are renewed on an ongoing basis, such as sun, wind, and small hydro-power. The sun's energy can be captured through photovoltaic or thermal solar energy systems. It can also be captured through bioenergy (energy generated from a crop, such as ethanol from corn); however, the amount of bioenergy captured must be weighed against the amount of fossil fuel energy consumed to produce it.

renewable energy certificate (REC): A representation of the environmental attributes of green power, sold separately from the electrons that make up the electricity. RECs allow the purchase of green power even when the electrons are not purchased.

Resource Conservation and Recovery Act (RCRA): RCRA focuses on active and future facilities. Enacted in 1976, it gives the EPA authority to control hazardous wastes from cradle to grave, including generation, transportation, treatment, storage, and disposal. Some non-hazardous wastes are also covered under RCRA.

retained components: The portions of the finished ceilings, finished floors, full height walls and demountable partitions, interior doors, and built-in case goods that existed in the prior condition and remain in the completed design.

return air: Air removed from conditioned spaces that is either recirculated through the building or exhausted to the outside.

reuse: A strategy to return materials to active use in the same or a related capacity.

risk assessment: A methodology used to analyze potential health effects caused by contaminants in the environment. Information from the risk assessment is used to determine cleanup levels.

R-value: Measure of thermal resistance.

S

salvaged materials: Construction materials recovered from existing buildings or construction sites and reused in other buildings. Common salvaged materials include structural beams and posts, flooring, doors, cabinetry, brick, and decorative items.

salvaged material (off site): Building materials recovered from an off-site source that are reused in a different building.

salvaged material (on site): Building materials recovered from and reused at the same building site.

sealant: Any material with adhesive properties that is formulated primarily to fill, seal, or waterproof gaps or joints between two surfaces. Sealants include sealant primers and caulks.

seasonal affective disorder (SAD): A form of depression triggered by a decrease in exposure to sunlight.

sedimentation: The addition of soils to bodies of water by natural and human-related activities. Sedimentation decreases water quality and accelerates the aging process of lakes, rivers, and streams.

setpoint: A normal range outside which an automatic control system will take action.

shared (group) multi-occupant space: Includes conference rooms, classrooms, and other indoor spaces used as places of congregation for presentations, trainings, and so forth. Individuals who use these spaces share the lighting and temperature controls. These spaces should have, at a minimum, a separate zone with accessible thermostat and air-flow control.

sick building syndrome (SBS): A situation in which the occupants of a building experience acute discomfort and poor health effects after time spent in the building, often with symptoms disappearing soon after leaving the building, but without any specific identifiable cause.

site assessment: An evaluation of aboveground (including facilities) and subsurface characteristics of a site, including its geology and hydrology, to determine whether a release of some type of pollutant has occurred, as well as its extent and concentration. Information generated during a site assessment is used to support remedial action decisions.

soft costs: Soft costs in a building project include design fees, taxes, permit fees, office and project management expenses directly related to the project, insurance, legal fees, closing costs and finance charges, and contingency monies. (Compare with *hard costs*.)

soil waste: Unneeded or unusable soil from construction, demolition, or renovation projects.

solar heat gain coefficient (SHGC): Measure of a window's effectiveness in blocking heat.

solar reflectance: A measure of the ability of a surface material to reflect visible, infrared, and ultraviolet light, measured on a scale of 0 to 1. By definition, white paint (titanium dioxide) has a solar reflectance of 1, while black paint has a solar reflectance of 0. Solar reflectance is also called *albedo*.

solar reflectance index (SRI): A measure of a material's ability to reject solar heat, as shown by a small temperature rise. By definition, a standard black (reflectance 0.05, emittance 0.90) is 0 and a standard white (reflectance 0.80, emittance 0.90) is 100. For example, a standard black surface has a temperature rise of 90°F (50°C) in full sun, and a standard white surface has a temperature rise of 14.6°F (8.1°C) Once the maximum temperature rise of a given material has been computed, the SRI can be computed by interpolating between the values for white and black.

Materials with the highest SRI values are the coolest (lowest-albedo) choices for paving. Due to the way SRI is defined, particularly hot materials can take slightly negative values, and particularly cool materials can even exceed 100 (source: Lawrence Berkeley Natural Laboratory Cool Roofing Materials Database).

source reduction: Reducing waste by reducing the amount of unnecessary material brought into a building. Purchasing products with less packaging is an example of source reduction.

space occupied for critical visual tasks: Rooms used for tasks like reading and computer monitor use.

square footage of a building: The total area in square feet of all rooms of a building, including corridors, elevators, stairwells and shaft spaces.

steep-slope roof: A roof slope with an incline equal to or greater than 2 inches per foot (9.5 degrees).

stormwater runoff: Water volumes created during precipitation events which flow over surfaces into sewer systems or receiving waters. All water from precipitation that leaves the project site boundaries on the surface is considered to be stormwater runoff volumes.

submetering: Metering added by a building's owner and managers to track water and energy use and where it is occurring. Submetering is in addition to meters installed by utility companies for billing purposes; it can be used to bill utility use to building tenants.

supply air: The air delivered by mechanical or natural ventilation to a space, composed of any combination of outdoor air, recirculated air, and transfer air.

sustainable forestry: The practice of managing forest resources in a manner that meets the long-term forest product needs of humans while maintaining the biodiversity of forested landscapes.

sustainable purchasing policy: The preferential purchasing of products that meet sustainability standards.

sustainable purchasing program: Includes the development, adoption, and implementation of an organizational policy that outlines the types of materials that should be purchased to meet specified sustainability criteria. This can include office paper, office equipment, furniture, furnishings, and other types of building materials for use in the building and on the site.

swale: A low-lying and often wet stretch of land. Artificially-constructed swales are often used to control water run-off.

system lifetime: The length of time from installation to until a system needs to be replaced.

system operator: A facility management staff person who is responsible for the operation of the building and for receiving and responding to HVAC system out-of-range performance alarms.

system performance testing: The process of determining the ability of a commissioned system to perform in accordance with the owner's project requirements, basis of design, and construction documents.

T

tertiary treatment: The highest form of wastewater treatment, which includes the removal of nutrients, and organic and solid material, along with biological or chemical polishing (generally to effluent limits of 10 mg/L BOD_5 and 10 mg/L TSS).

thermal bridge: An area within the building envelope where heat transfers from inside to outside or vice versa.

thermal comfort: A condition of mind experienced by building occupants expressing satisfaction with the thermal environment.

thermal emissivity (or thermal emittance): The ratio of the radiant heat flux emitted by a sample to that emitted by a blackbody radiator at the same temperature. (See also *infrared emissivity*.)

thermal envelope: Building exterior and insulation.

threatened species: An animal or plant species that is likely to become endangered within the foreseeable future.

tipping fees: Fees charged by a landfill for disposal of waste. The fee is typically quoted per ton of waste.

total phosphorus (TP): organically bound phosphates, polyphosphates and orthophosphates in stormwater, most of which originate with fertilizer application. Chemical precipitation is the typical removal mechanism for phosphorus.

total suspended solids (TSS): Particles or flocs that are too small or light to be removed from stormwater by settling. Suspended solid concentrations are typically removed by filtration.

tuck-under parking: A ground-level parking area established within the building footprint.

turbidity: Stirred-up or suspended sediment in water. Turbidity in lakes and estuaries affects water clarity, light penetration, and suitability as a habitat for aquatic plants and animals.

U

underground parking: A tuck-under or stacked parking structure that minimizes the exposed parking surface area.

ureaformaldehyde: A combination of urea and formaldehyde used in some glues; it may emit formaldehyde at room temperature.

utility metering: The use of meters by utilities to measure consumption.

U-value: Measure of thermal conductivity. The inverse of *R*-value.

V

variable air volume (VAV): A type of HVAC system that varies the volume of conditioned air delivered to rooms.

vegetated (green) roof: A roof of a building that is partially or completely covered with vegetation and soil or another growing medium planted over a waterproofing membrane.

vegetated filter strip: Strips of vegetation designed to filter sediment and pollutants from stormwater. Strips are appropriate for treating low-velocity surface sheet flows in areas where runoff is not concentrated. They are often used as pretreatment for other stormwater measures, such as infiltration basins and trenches.

vegetated roof: Roof partially or fully covered by vegetation, which can minimize runoff and moderate interior temperatures.

ventilation: The process of supplying air to and removing air from interior spaces by natural or mechanical means for the purpose of controlling air contaminant levels, humidity, or temperature within the space.

verification: The full range of checks and tests carried out to determine if all components, subsystems, systems, and interfaces between systems operate in accordance with the contract documents. In this context, "operate" includes all modes and sequences of control operation, interlocks and conditional control responses, and specified responses to abnormal or emergency conditions.

visible transmittance (Tvis): The fraction of visible light that passes through a glazing surface. A higher Tvis value indicates that a greater amount of visible spectrum incident light is passing through the glazing.

vision glazing: Glazing that provides views of outdoor landscapes to building occupants for vertical windows between 2.5 feet (0.76 m) and 7.5 feet (2.3 m) above the floor. Windows above and below this range (including daylight glazing, skylights, and roof monitors) do not count as vision glazing for LEED credits.

volatile organic compound (VOC): Organic compounds that vaporize (become a gas) at normal room temperatures. The specific organic compounds addressed by the referenced Green Seal Standard GS-11 are identified in U.S. EPA Reference Test Method 24 "Determination of Volatile Matter Content, Water Content, Density, Volume Solids, and Weight Solids of Surface Coatings," Code of Federal Regulations, Title 40, Part 60, App. A.

W

walk-off mats: Mats placed inside or outside building entrances to remove dirt from people's feet and equipment entering the building.

waste disposal: The process of eliminating waste by means of burial in a landfill, combustion in an incinerator, dumping at sea, or some other way that is not recycling or reuse.

waste diversion: Waste management activities that divert waste from disposal through incineration or landfilling. Typical waste diversion methods are reuse and recycling.

waste reduction: Source reduction and diversion of waste by means of reuse or recycling.

waste reduction policy: A policy that includes (1) a statement describing the organization's commitment to minimizing waste disposal by using source reduction, reuse, and recycling, (2) assignment of responsibility within the organization for implementation of waste reduction program, (3) a list of the general actions that will be implemented in the waste reduction program to reduce waste, and (4) a description of the tracking and review component in the waste reduction program to monitor waste reduction success and improve waste reduction performance over time.

watershed: A drainage basin. The extent of land where water from rain or snow melt drains downhill into a body of water, such as a river, lake, dam, estuary, wetland, sea, or ocean. The drainage basin includes the streams and rivers that convey the water, as well as the land surfaces from which water drains into those channels, separated from adjacent basins by a drainage divide.

weathered radiative property: The solar reflectance and thermal emissivity of a roofing product after three years of exposure to the weather.

wetland: Defined by U.S. CFR 40, Parts 230–233 and Part 22.

wetland vegetation: Plants that require saturated soils to survive and certain tree and other plant species that can tolerate prolonged wet soil conditions.

wind energy: Electricity generated by wind machines.

wood waste: Unneeded or unusable wood from construction, demolition, or renovation projects.

Workplace Hazardous Materials Information System (WHMIS): The Canadian standard of hazard communication, which incorporates cautionary labeling of containers of controlled products, the use of material safety data sheets (MSDS), and worker education and training programs.

X

xeriscaping: Landscaping that does not require supplemental irrigation, using plants whose need for water is matched to the local climate, and preparing the soil to reduce water loss to evaporation and runoff.

Z

zero emissions vehicle (ZEV): A vehicle that produces no emissions or pollution when stationary or operating.

Resources

Online Resources

PPI maintains a list of current links to online resources for LEED, including recommended references for study, referenced standards, and many others, at **www.ppi2pass.com/ LEEDreferences**. The PPI website, **www.ppi2pass.com**, also provides LEED exam study materials, classes, online review, and a LEED exam forum.

A candidate for the Green Associate exam should be familiar with the following references, which are listed in the Candidate Handbook. All are available online; see **www.ppi2pass.com/ LEEDreferences** also for current links.

Primary References

- *Cost of Green Revisited: Reexamining the Feasibility and Cost Impact of Sustainable Design in the Light of Increased Market Adoption* by Davis Langdon (2007)
- *Guidance on Innovation & Design (ID) Credits* (U.S. Green Building Council, 2004)
- *Guidelines for CIR Customers* (U.S. Green Building Council, 2007)
- *LEED for Homes Rating System* (U.S. Green Building Council, 2008)
- *LEED for Operations & Maintenance Reference Guide:* Introduction and Glossary (U.S. Green Building Council, 2008)
- *Sustainable Building Technical Manual: Part II* by Anthony Bernheim and William Reed (Public Technology, Inc. & U.S. Green Building Council, 1996).
- *The Treatment by LEED of the Environmental Impact of HVAC Refrigerants* (U.S. Green Building Council, LEED Technical and Scientific Advisory Committee, 2004)

Ancillary References

- *AIA Integrated Project Delivery: A Guide* (American Institute of Architects Documents Committee & AIA California Council, 2007)
- *Americans with Disabilities Act (ADA): Standards for Accessible Design* (Department of Justice, 1994)

- *Best Practices of ISO 14021: Self-Declared Environmental Claims* by Kun-Mo Lee and Haruo Uehara (Asia-Pacific Economic Cooperation, Ministry of Commerce, Industry and Energy, Republic of Korea, 2003)
- Bureau of Labor Statistics website: Construction and Building Inspectors
- *Energy Performance of LEED for New Construction Buildings: Final Report* by Cathy Turner and Mark Frankel (New Buildings Institute, 2008)
- *Foundations of the Leadership in Energy and Environmental Design Environmental Rating System: A Tool for Market Transformation* (U.S. Green Building Council, LEED Steering Committee, 2006)
- *GSA 2003 Facilities Standards* (General Services Administration, 2003)
- *Guide to Purchasing Green Power: Renewable Electricity, Renewable Energy Certificates and On-Site Renewable Generation* (U.S. Department of Energy, U.S. Environmental Protection Agency, World Resources Institute, and Center for Resource Solutions, 2004)
- International Code Council website: Codes and Standards
- *Review of ANSI/ASHRAE Standard 62.1–2004: Ventilation for Acceptable Indoor Air Quality* by Brian Kareis (Workplace Group).

The USGBC website, www.usgbc.org, provides a number of helpful LEED exam preparation resources and links to additional information. Of particular interest are the following items. Because direct links to these items change frequently, search for them by name.

LEED rating systems (for all areas of specialization currently available)

LEED Online sample credit templates

credit interpretation rulings (must be a USGBC member and signed in on the site)

green building research and statistics

associations and nonprofit organizations

building codes and standards

building materials, guides, and certification

case studies

commissioning and post-occupancy evaluation

design and simulation tools

design resources

economics

energy

funding

government initiatives and guidelines

life-cycle analysis and costing

media

rating systems

research centers

sustainability

The website of the Green Building Certification Institute, www.gbci.org, provides a downloadable copy of the *LEED Green Associate Candidate Handbook* and registration for and announcements regarding updates to the LEED credentials exams.

The U.S. Department of Energy's Building Technologies Program website includes a section on information resources and a building toolbox with valuable information. The program is part of the DOE's Office of Energy Efficiency and Renewable Energy. A current link to the website can be found at **www.ppi2pass.com/LEEDreferences**.

Review Questions

The number in parentheses indicates the page on which a question is answered.

Introduction

1. What are the three tiers of LEED AP designation? (5)
2. What are the five AP specialty designations? (6)
3. Describe the responsibilities of GBCI and USGBC with respect to LEED. (2-4)
4. How many hours of continuing education must a LEED Green Associate complete biennially? (5-6)
5. What does *opt in* mean in regard to LEED credentials? (7)

An Overview of LEED

6. What are the LEED rating systems and how should they be applied to projects? (15-17)
7. List four things that are new to the LEED 2009 rating systems. (19)
8. What are the seven credit categories of the LEED rating systems? (25)
9. What does *balloting* mean in regard to the LEED rating systems? (19)
10. Which credit category offers the most points in the LEED rating systems? (21)
11. How many points must a commercial project achieve to become Certified? Silver? Gold? Platinum? (37)
12. What is LEED Online? (33)
13. What is the role of the decision maker for a particular credit? (33-34)
14. In the LEED EBO&M rating system, if data can not be obtained from all tenants in a multitenant building, up to _____ % of the gross floor space may be excluded. (31)
15. How many points can a project earn for Innovation in Design? (25)
16. Who determines applicable Regional Priority credits for a project? (22)
17. What are Minimum Program Requirements? (23)
18. Briefly describe how LEED credits are weighted. (20)
19. Which LEED rating system includes a minimum occupancy requirement? Why? (28)
20. The gross area of the project building may not be less than _____ % of the LEED project site area. (24)
21. LEED NC projects must have a minimum of _____ square feet of indoor, enclosed building area. (24)
22. List two reasons that ID credits may be awarded. (25)
23. In which rating system may a project use a streamlined path for credits already earned under another rating system? (29)
24. Which LEED rating system requires a minimum level of acoustical performance? (31)
25. Three LEED Accredited Professionals are working on a project. How many ID credits will be awarded for their participation? (25)
26. An owner will occupy one-third of a new office building. Which LEED rating system should be used for certification? (27)
27. How often must LEED EBO&M buildings submit for recertification? (31)

28. Describe the performance period. (*30*)

29. USGBC will refund the application fee if a project achieves _____ certification. (*32*)

30. After a project team has submitted application materials and payment, what will it receive *first* from USGBC? (*32*)

31. The person who coordinates a LEED project in LEED Online is called the _____. (*32*)

32. When can a project submit a CIR? Briefly describe the submission process. (*34*)

33. The primary tool used in LEED Online to track progress on a project is _____. (*33*)

34. What is a TAG, and what is its role in the CIR process? (*35*)

35. What are the advantages of a split review? (*33*)

36. How many times can a LEED credit decision be appealed? (*37*)

37. What is a *provider*? A *green rater*? (*38*)

LEED in Practice: Credit Synergies and the Cost of Building Green

38. What are synergies and trade-offs? Give specific examples of each. (*44*)

39. List three types of cost analysis methods and briefly describe each. (*46*)

40. A LEED-certified building typically costs ____% more than a non-certified, similar building designed in a conventional way. (*43*)

LEED Project and Team Coordination: Pre-Design

41. What are the key objectives of green building? (*52*)

42. What are some advantages of a design-build approach over design-bid-build? (*53*)

43. What is characteristic of the design team when the whole-building design approach is being used? (*59*)

44. Describe integrated project delivery and how it differs from design-bid-build and design-build project delivery methods. (*53-56*)

45. List three ways of structuring IPD agreements. (*58*)

46. Building operations in the United States account for _____% of total U.S. energy use. (*51*)

47. List at least five things that should be accomplished during the pre-design phase. (*60*)

48. Who is responsible for determining the project budget? (*61*)

49. Define *LEED project boundary* and *property boundary*. (*61*)

50. In a multi-prime delivery model, coordination of the work is the responsibilty of the _____. (*59*)

51. True or False? The Americans with Disabilities Act is a building code. (*62*)

52. What are the two methods of complying with ASHRAE Standard 90.1? (*62-63*)

53. Who may NOT be a building commissioner on a LEED NC project of more than 50,000 square feet? (*63*)

54. When should the commissioning process begin? (*63*)

55. What five things must the commissioning team do to earn credit for enhanced commissioning? (*64*)

56. Which LEED rating system requires a durability management plan? (*65*)

Green Building Basics

57. A project can recieve LEED points for being located within _____ mile(s) of commuter rail, light rail, or subway stations, or within _____ mile(s) of bus stops served by two or more routes. (*68*)

58. For optimal daylighting opportunities, the long axis of a building should be oriented _____. (*71*)

59. What factors are important when considering the placement of a building on a site? (*71-72*)

60. What is the heat island effect, and what are some strategies for reducing it? (*73*)

61. Does a white sidewalk have a higher or lower albedo than an asphalt parking lot? (*73*)

62. What is the main goal of sustainable stormwater management? (*74*)

63. What are the two basic challenges of stormwater management? (*74*)

64. Define *graywater*. How is it collected and how can it be used? (*75*)

65. What is *xeriscaping*? (*75*)

66. What are some strategies for water efficient landscaping? (*75*)

67. What does *full-time equivalent occupancy* mean? (*76*)

68. A LEED 2009-certified building must use at least ____% less water indoors than a baseline water use calculated for the building. (*76*)

69. What kind of materials should be used for the envelope of a building in a hot/dry climate? (*79*)

70. List two ways insulation could be added to an existing building. (*80*)

71. What is *thermal bridging*? (*80*)

72. What are the main advantages and disadvantages of using steel in building construction? (*84*)

73. What is a *Trombe wall*? (*84*)

74. How do roof designs and materials typically differ for commercial and residential buildings? (*86*)

75. A vapor barrier should be placed on the _____ side of a wall. (*88*)

76. Describe three ways to purchase green power. (*89*)

77. What is distributed generation, and what are its advantages? (*90*)

78. Name five cooling strategies. Under what conditions is each strategy most appropriate? (*93-94*)

79. What are the three components of the daylight that hits a work surface, and how can the balance of these components be enhanced? (*98*)

80. Skylights and clerestory windows are examples of _____ strategies. (*99*)

81. What are the characteristics of sustainable building materials? (*102*)

82. What is the difference between post-consumer and pre-consumer recycled content? Give examples of each. (*103*)

83. A regionally manufactured material is produced within _____ miles of the project site. (*103*)

84. A plant must be harvested on a cycle of _____ years or less to be considered rapidly renewable. List five examples of rapidly renewable materials. (*103*)

Putting It All Together: Construction, Operations, and Maintenance

85. Name two hazardous building materials that may be present in existing buildings built in the 1970s or earlier. (*109*)

86. Who is responsible for developing a waste management plan? (*108*)

87. The primary waste product in building construction is _____. (*109*)

88. Which components in a building's mechanical system should have a Minimum Efficiency Reporting Value (MERV) of 13? (*109*)

89. Name the seven elements that should be addressed in a building's O&M plan. (*111*)

Referenced Standards

90. What purpose do referenced standards serve relative to LEED credit requirements? (*115*)

91. The Montreal Protocol is an international agreement to phase out substances connected to _____. (*129*)

92. What two procedures can be used to demonstrate compliance with ANSI/ASHRAE 62.1, *Ventilation for Acceptable Indoor Air Quality*? (*117*)

93. Which credit category references definitions from the U.S. Code of Federal Regulations for wetlands and prime farmlands? (*121*)

94. Which credit category references the Energy Policy Act of 1992? (*122-123*)

95. Which organization certifies responsible forest management and operations? (*128*)

96. Projects in _____ can substitute compliance with local energy codes for compliance with ASHRAE Standard 90.1. (*118*)

97. What does the *fan pressurization method* test? Which prerequisite references this test? (*119*)

98. What is the *Energy Star Portfolio Manager* used for? (*124*)

99. Which LEED rating system references standards for cleaning products? (*124, 126*)

100. A building receives a score of 1 on an assessment based on APPA's *Custodial Staffing Guidelines*. Does this score represent a good or a bad result? (*126*)

Index

173